The
CHARM
– of –
OLD ROSES

The
CHARM
– of –
OLD ROSES

Nancy Steen

MILLDALE PRESS

First published 1966
This edition published 1987

MILLDALE PRESS, INC.
1718 Connecticut Ave., #300
Washington, D.C. 20009

Library of Congress Catalog Card Number 86-63811

ISBN 0-941569-00-4

Printed by Kyodo-Shing Loong Printing Ind. Pte Ltd., Singapore

Preface to the Second Edition

IN LATER YEARS Nancy used to ponder on and wonder how she wrote this book. I think now that it was the urge she had to record her intensive love of roses — in particular those of an older era — and of the pleasures we had in searching for them and the experience we had in so doing.

Finding Mme Caroline Testout growing on the site of an abandoned old timber mill in a remote and very isolated spot caught her imagination and she thought of the woman who had lived there and, temporary though it was, had taken and planted this rose. A cutting from it now grows in our garden.

An enormous froth of white on a steep hillside in the Coromandel Range once caught our eye — an amazing sight of a mass of musk roses spreading up the hill, so unusual as to prompt prolonged enquiries to discover its origin. Then there were our visits to the Bay of Islands and our search for the oldest rose garden, the old houses and the roses that grew there.

While moving around the country in Akaroa on Banks Peninsula in the South Island and in the Collingwood District around Nelson we have looked for and discovered old roses there, too.

I now realise that Nancy wrote this book simply because of the charm of old roses.

DAVID STEEN
Auckland

November 1986.

To my husband, without whose help and encouragement this book would not have been written

ACKNOWLEDGMENTS

THE CHARM OF OLD ROSES IS AS MUCH MY HUSBAND'S book as it is my own. We have shared a love of roses for many years, have travelled to many countries in search of old roses and for information about them, and our New Zealand garden contains as many roses – old and new – as we can happily accommodate.

In lectures Mr Steen has been my invariable partner, in charge of the projector; in photography and writing he has been an invaluable critic and helper. This book could not have been written without him, both in the knowledge of old roses we have gathered together and in the pleasurable task of passing some of that knowledge on in the pages that follow.

My thanks are also due to the many kind and generous rose lovers, who have not only sent me cuttings and plants, but have been able to produce a great deal of valuable information about the old roses and old days in their districts. This assistance has been very much appreciated.

Mr G. S. Thomas, F. L. S., Gardens Adviser to the National Trust and an authority on old roses, has studied colour slides we have sent him to help in the identification of roses. During our visit to England we were able to discuss some of our problems with him; and for this privilege we were grateful. Dr Gordon Rowley, of Reading University, was previously Keeper of the National Rose Species Collection at the John Innes Horticultural Institute at Bayfordbury, in Hertfordshire. During my visit to this establishment he kindly pointed out and discussed a number of roses of particular interest which we had not seen previously. Mr Wilson Lynes, of Taberg, New York – an expert on the wild roses of North America – kindly identified, from slides and pressed specimens, two roses over which there was some confusion. Mrs M. E. Coon, until recently Managing Editor of the *American Rose Annual*, has given me much valuable help and encouragement. We are indebted to Monsieur Robelin, Director of the Seine Parks, for information regarding Roseraie de l' Hay and the garden of the Chateau of Malmaison. Dr A. S. Thomas, O. B. E., of Melbourne, Australia, generously gave me technical assistance and information.

We acknowledge, gratefully, the interest and help of Mr A. F. Hurlstone, M. B. E., and Mr D. N. Davies, both of England, through whose good offices we were sent valuable information concerning the perfume roses grown in Morocco.   The authoritative article, most generously sent to us, was prepared by members of the Etablissements Antoine Chiris and the Société Aromag, two of the large perfume concerns operating in that part of North Africa and in Grasse at the present time.

For the help given by Mr and Mrs J. W. Matthews, editors of *The New Zealand Gardener*, and Mr G. A. R. Phillips, editor of *New Zealand Plants and Gardens*, – the Journal of the Royal New Zealand Institute of Horticulture – we are greatly indebted; and also for their permission to make use of material in articles of mine they have published. My thanks are due, also, to Mr Mervyn Evans, editor of the *New Zealand Rose Annual*. Dr R. Cooper, head of the Botany Department of the Auckland War Memorial Museum and Miss Joan Dingley, of the Department of Scientific and Industrial Research at Mt Albert, have helped in the identification of some of the rose species found in this country, particularly a number of forms of *R. rubiginosa* and *R. moschata*. Mr J. A. Hunter, also of the Department of Scientific and Industrial Research, has rooted difficult cuttings for me; and Miss P. Mason, of Manurewa, has budded roses collected during mid-summer, when they would not have rooted easily from cuttings. For all this valuable help I am very grateful.

Rose catalogues and copies of old gardening magazines have been of tremendous assistance. Some we were able to refer to at the Auckland War Memorial Museum; and copies of others were sent to us by the late

Mr Michael Standish of National Archives, Wellington, and by the Alexander Turnbull Library, Wellington. Three early rose catalogues Mr Standish sent us proved the existence in New Zealand of many old roses. One was published by William Hale of Nelson, in 1860, and two were from Dunedin – Robert Thomson's catalogue of 1876-7, and Thomas Allen's general catalogue of 1878-9. Mrs Nelson Mitchell, whose grandfather, Dr D. Hay, started the Mt Pellier Nursery in Auckland a hundred years ago, lent us a number of late nineteenth and early twentieth century catalogues which lined up well with the earlier ones.

Grateful acknowledgment is due to the following authors and publishers for permission to include copyright material in my book: – *The Old Shrub Roses* and *Shrub Roses of Today*, by G. S. Thomas (Phoenix House), who gave permission also, to refer to Dr C. C. Hurst's *Notes on the Origins and Evolution of our Garden Roses; History of the Rose*, by Roy E. Shepherd (The Macmillan Co., New York); *The Genus Rosa*, by Ellen Willmott (John Murray Limited) – here, permission was granted by the author's nephew, Mr R. G. Berkeley, Berkeley Castle, Gloucestershire; *A Naturalist's Voyage around the World*, by Charles Darwin, M. A., F. R. S., (John Murray Limited); *How we got our Flowers*, by A. W. Anderson (Ernest Benn Limited); *Old Garden Roses*, by Edward Bunyard (Country Life Limited); *Roses for English Gardens*, by Gertrude Jekyll and Edward Mawley (Country Life Limited); *Old Fashioned Flowers*, by Sacheverell Sitwell (Country Life Limited); *Old Garden Roses*, by Sacheverell Sitwell and James Russell (George Rainbird, Limited); *Summer and Autumn Flowers*, by Constance Spry (J. M. Dent and Sons Limited); *Even More for Your Garden*, by Victoria Sackville-West (Michael Joseph Limited); *The Rainbow Bridge*, by Reginald Farrer (Edward Arnold Limited); *A Book about Roses*, by S. Reynolds Hole (Edward Arnold Limited); *In a Gloucestershire Garden*, by Henry N. Ellacombe (Edward Arnold Limited); *Journeys and Plant Introductions*, by George Forrest (The Royal Horticultural Society); an article on Ancestral China Roses, by Dr Gordon Rowley, (The Royal Horticultural Society); *Roses, Their History, Development and Cultivation*, by J. H. Pemberton (Longmans, Green & Co. Limited); *The Amateur Gardener's Rose Book*, by Dr Julius Hoffmann (Longmans, Green & Co. Limited); *The Scented Garden*, by Eleanour Sinclair Rohde (The Medici Society Limited); *The Rose*, by A. B. Ellwanger (Dodd, Mead & Co.); *The Book of the Rose*, by A. Foster-Melliar (Macmillan & Co. Limited); *Better Roses*, by A. S. Thomas,

O. B. E., (Angus and Robertson); *The Diary of a Scotch Gardener at the French Court*, by Thomas Blaikie (Routledge and Kegan Paul, Limited); *Roses and Rose Growing*, by Rose E. Kingsley (The Macmillan Co., New York, and Whitaker & Sons Limited).

For information regarding the copyright of older books we are indebted to the Publishers' Association, and to Mrs Esther Faigan of Minerva Bookshop, Auckland.

Our grateful thanks are due to Miss Margaret Whittaker, Honorary Secretary of the Auckland Rose Society, who typed the whole of this manuscript and coped splendidly with the mass of technical, botanical and place names.

INTRODUCTION

MY FIRST INTRODUCTION TO an old rose was in my parents' Southland garden – it was a very small one – but I can return to it at will by inhaling the rich and intoxicating perfume of the grand old cherry-red Bourbon, Madame Isaac Pereire, a rose which grew so well there. Paeonies, lilacs and roses were the other flowers I remember most vividly – possibly because of their size, but more probably because of their lovely scent. All throve well in that cool, southern part of New Zealand. All had been planted by settlers from the United Kingdom and Europe during the early 19th century.

New Zealand was discovered by the Dutch navigator, Abel Tasman, in 1642. It was forgotten thereafter, until 1769. Then, the country was revisited by a European – this time, Captain James Cook, who greatly extended the exploratory work of Tasman. In the early 1800s the sea coast was visited by occasional whalers; and gradually the white man or Pakeha, came to settle. By 1840, though white people were here in very small numbers, mission settlements were well established, milling had started, and the country formally taken over as a Colony of Great Britain. So civilisation came to New Zealand – and with it the roses.

The rose is not indigenous to the Southern Hemisphere, so it was quite amazing to find that such a number were well established in the Colony's first twenty years. Though so far away from their native haunts all the roses brought out to New Zealand settled well in our temperate climate; and many, growing in early mission stations, and, later, in milling and mining settlements, successfuly survived years of neglect. There are few rose groups not represented in the country; but my husband and I, in many miles of journeying have been unable to find out just who introduced many of them to these shores. How they travelled out is another matter. The Sweet Brier and the Dog Rose were grown from seed: we read of sweet brier hedges being well established round homes in Paihia when Charles Darwin called there, in H. M. S. *Beagle*, in 1835. The little Red and Pink China Roses, probably the first arrivals in the country, grew so readily from cuttings that small potted plants were safely brought over the long and slow sea route, charcoal helping to keep the soil pure. Cuttings of certain rare and tender French Roses, and of some species, were packed in dry moss and hermetically sealed in long, metal surveyors' tubes; thus, they travelled well. Plants were introduced, also in Wardian cases – these were first used by plant collectors and sea-faring men when bringing roses and other shrubs from the Far East to Europe, in the days when the British East India fleet operated between China and England.

We have a reasonably comprehensive reference library at our command – a library that is still being enlarged – and those books that were beyond our means, we studied at the Royal Horticultural Society's Library, in Vincent Square, London – obtaining the most precious volumes from the Lindley collection. For the help given, and the interest shown, by the Librarians of the Society, we are very grateful. As well, we have built up a collection of coloured slides. These show clearly the details of each rose, and are invaluable aids when roses are sent to us for identification, and are useful, also, for sending to England and the United States of America when we require further information about roses that are unknown to us. This photographic record was added to, extensively, in many of the countries we visited.

I always liked gardening: and when I married and settled in Auckland my husband and I began to be particularly interested in roses. We collected books on their history, and these old treasures stimulated our interest. From then on, as we travelled round New Zealand, particularly in the north, we made a point of visiting early mission, milling and mining settlements, and old cemeteries; and we were surprised at the diverse types of roses that the missionaries and settlers had brought with them into the country. When other rose lovers and interested people became aware of our search for the old plants, they generously sent us others from their gardens, or told us where stands of old roses were to be found in out-of-the-way spots. We began, also, to receive letters asking us to visit old gardens and help to identify roses: and this we did whenever possible. It was a rewarding experience to meet elderly people and chat about roses and the early days. Later, we decided to import a number of roses: and were also able to buy some in New Zealand. So, now, practically all rose families are represented in our garden.

Each year, more and more old roses disappear: so we hope this record will serve to remind us of some of the beauties that, of necessity, have had to be swept away – beauties that must have brought a breath of their homeland to lonely pioneers, and particularly to their wives. The more we delve into the history of these fascinating plants, the more our interest in these garden treasures is stimulated; but, in spite of their great beauty, fragrance, and undeniable hardiness, many of these old and, in some cases, ancient roses flower only for a few weeks in early summer. For this reason, we do not advise young people, who are starting their first garden, to plant summer-blooming roses. Instead, we suggest to them that they buy the best of the modern varieties, and then, if they wish to include a few older roses in their gardens, we give them a short list of perpetual-flowering varieties, such as the Chinas, Portlands, Bourbons, Hybrid Musks and Rugosas. While we ourselves are prepared to wait from season to season to enjoy the sumptuous beauty and generous flowering of Gallicas, Damasks, Albas and Centifolias, we do not wish others to be disappointed at the shorter blooming season of some of our real favourites. It was this that led us to plant other free and perpetual-flowering species with the old roses and add, where feasible, a number of modern roses suitable to the general colour scheme, and the perimeter planting needed to give small gardens a feeling of space and restfulness. Areas of pleasantly shaped unbroken lawn give this effect, as does the soft colouring of the complementary plants. Here, fuchsias, clematis, perennials and foliage plants, as well as larger shrubs, are invaluable.

Though many of the roses we grow were collected in New Zealand, quite a number are new to the country. Most types of roses are represented, if not by actual type, then by a close relation. The roses thus planted have their origins in Asia – from as far east as Japan, the Middle East, Europe, and North America. Some grow fairly close to the Equator; while others come from within the Arctic Circle. With such a climatic range, it is no wonder that roses vary in size from the low-growing, small-flowered, prickly R. *spinosissima* – which grows in Iceland and Northern Europe – and its North American relatives, to R. *gigantea* from Burma, which has a spread of over sixty feet and flowers measuring six inches in diameter. Some have tiny, firm leaves that make them able to stand extreme cold, while others have long, soft leaves that fit them for life in hot climates; the heps of some are small and multitudinous, while the heps of others are as large as apples, or as prickly as some gooseberries, or as dark and shiny as currants. Some roses trail naturally over the ground; others throw firm, strong shoots boldly upwards and need no support. Some are completely unarmed; while others have such wicked thorns that they can be a menace to the unwary gardener.

It has often been remarked that old roses are healthy and need no special care. Alas, we have not found this to be the case. Though many keep quite free of all disease, others need to be carefully watched if the garden is to be kept healthy and clean. The rose breeders of today are well aware of such failings, and are endeavouring to see that all new introductions are as disease-free as possible. This will be to the ultimate advantage of all rose growers. We, ourselves, try to include only the healthiest varieties when we purchase modern roses; but with a mixture of old and new in one garden, we do adopt, in our humid and continual growth-producing climate, a regular spraying programme.

As it is with pictures, furniture and silver, so it is with roses. All that is old is not necessarily good. Neither, for that matter, is everything new. So we concede that among our best roses may be counted some that are very old, some that are reasonably old, and some that are quite new. In our search for, and cultivation of, old roses, we have grown them in a propagating garden for purposes of record. This having been done, we have applied the maxim quoted above. The best we have kept, some we have just had to let go, and others we have parted with willingly.

But still our garden is full of roses, and it is a garden to which rose lovers come in larger and larger numbers. For more and more people in New Zealand are becoming interested in the old roses that our ancestors in Europe grew; some visitors come from great distances to see them, when they are in full bloom, and must go away charmed with their beauty, as we continue to be.

N. S.

Remuera, Auckland.
May 1965

CONTENTS

COLOUR PLATES

The following are reproductions of colour transparencies from the author's collection.

BLACK AND WHITE PLATES

The above plates are from photographs taken by Sparrow Pictures, Auckland.

GARDEN PLANS

BIBLIOGRAPHY

All the books listed below are in the author's library except the three titles marked with an asterisk.

Anderson, A. W. – *How we got our Flowers*. 1950

*Andrews, H. C. – *Roses*. 1805–28

Blaikie, T. – *Diary of a Scotch Gardener at the French Court at the End of the Eighteenth Century*. 1951

Blunt, W. and Russell, J. – *Old Garden Roses*. Part 2. 1957

Bunyard, E. A. – *Old Garden Roses*. 1936

Cartwright, Julia – *Italian Gardens of the Renaissance*. 1914

Cobban, A. – *A History of Modern France (1779–1945)*. 1961

Curtis, H. – *Beauties of the Rose*. 1850–53

Darwin, C. – *A Naturalist's Voyage round the World*. 1845

Denham, H. – *The Skeptical Gardener*. 1949

D'Ombrain, H. H. – *Rosarian's Year Book* (6 Vols. 1877–1898)

Du Cane, Florence – *The Flowers and Gardens of Madeira*. 1909

Earle, Alice Morse – *Sundials and Roses of Yesterday*. 1902

Earle, Mrs C. W. – *Pot-Pourri from a Surrey Garden*. 1900

Earle, Mrs C. W. – *More Pot-Pourri from a Surrey Garden*. 1901

Earle, C. W. and Case, E. – *Pot-Pourrie Mixed by Two*. 1914

Ellacombe, H. N. – *In a Gloucestershire Garden*. 1895

Ellwanger, H. B. – *The Rose*. 1914

Farrer, R. – *The Rainbow Bridge*. 1918

Fearon, Ethelind – *The Reluctant Gardener*. 1952

Forest, G. – *Journeys and Plant Introductions*. 1952

Fortune, R. – *A Residence amongst the Chinese*. 1857

Foster-Melliar, A. – *The Book of the Rose*. 1919

Hadfield, M. – *Gardening in Britain*. 1960

Harvey, N. P. – *The Rose in Britain*. 1951

Hellyer, A. G. L. – *Roses*. 1954

Henfrey, A., Moore, T., Ayres, F. – *The Garden Companion*. 1852

Hibberd, Shirley – *The Amateur's Rose Book*. 1894

Hoffman, J. – *The Amateur Gardener's Rose Book*. 1905

Hole, S. R. – *A Book about Roses*. 1874

Jekyll, Gertrude – *Wood and Garden.* 1899
Jekyll, Gertrude – *Home and Garden.* 1901
Jekyll, G. and Mawley, E. – *Roses for English Gardens.* 1902
Jekyll, G. – *Colour Schemes for the Flower Garden.* 7th Edition
Johnson, A. T. – *The Mill Garden.* 1949
Keays, Francis – *Old Roses.* 1935
Kingsley, Rose – *Roses and Rose Growing.* 1908
*Lawrance, Mary – *A Collection of Roses from Nature.* 1799
Lester, F. M. – *My Friend the Rose.* 1942
Lough, J. – *An Introduction to Eighteenth Century France.* 1960
Mansfield, T. C. – *Of Cabbages and Kings.* 1945
National Rose Society Year-Books (Great Britain) 1910–1914
Park, B. – *Collins' Guide to Roses* 1956
Paul W. – *The Rose Garden.* 1848, 1888 and 1903
Pemberton, J. H. – *Roses.* 1920
Poulson, S. – *Poulsen on the Rose.* 1941
*Redouté, P. J. and Thory, C. A. – *Les Roses.* 1835
Rohde, Eleanour S. – *The Scented Garden* 1948
Rivers, T. – *The Rose Amateur's Guide.* 1837–1877
Robinson, W. – *The English Flower Garden.* 1900
Ross-Craig, Stella – *Drawings of British Plants.* Part IX, *Rosaceae.* 1956
Rowley, G. – Ancestral China Roses. *Journal of the Royal Horticultural Society.* 1959
Sackville-West, V. – *In Your Garden.* 1951
Sackville-West, V. – *In Your Garden Again.* 1953
Sackville-West, V. – *Even More for your Garden.* 1958
Salisbury, Sir E. – *The Living Garden.* 1949
Shepherd, R. E. – *History of the Rose.* 1954
Sitwell, S. – *Old Fashioned Flowers.* 1948
Sitwell, S. and Russell, J. – *Old Garden Roses.* Part 1. 1955
Stevens, G. A. – *Climbing Roses.* 1933
Société Nationale d'Horticulture de France. *Les Plus Belles Roses.* 1886
Spry, Constance – *Summer and Autumn Flowers.* 1951
Spry, Constance – *Favourite Flowers.* 1959
Studio Gardening Annual. *Gardens and Gardening.* 1950
Studio Gardening Annual. *Labour-saving Planning and Planting.* 1954
Synge, P. A. – *Diversity of Plants.* 1953
Taylor, G. – *The Book of the Rose.* 1949
Thomas, A. S. – *Better Roses.* 1950
Thomas, G. C. Jnr. – *The Practical Book of Outdoor Rose Growing.* 1914
Thomas, G. S. *The Old Shrub Roses.* 1955
Thomas, G. S. – *Shrub Roses of Today.* 1962
Thomson, R. and Wilson Helen V. P. – *Roses for Pleasure.* 1957
Thomson, R. – *Old Roses for Modern Gardens.* 1959
Tillotson, W. – *Roses of Yesterday and Today* (catalogue). 1958
Wheatcroft, H. – *My Life with Roses.* 1959
Willmott, Ellen – *The Genus Rosa.* 1910–14
Wright, W. P. – *Roses and Rose Gardens.* 1914
Wylie, A. P. in *Journals of the Royal Horticultural Society.* 1954

GALLICA ROSES

To loiter mid the lovely, old-time flowers,
To breathe the scent of lavender and rose . . .

                    John Russell Hayes

ONE OF THE MOST PROLIFIC OF THE OLD ROSES GROW-
ing semi-wild in New Zealand, and one that has been out here since
the earliest days of the colony, is a rosy-purple Gallica, Anaïs Ségales.
This was the first rose introduced into our garden from a roadside planting.
For many years we had passed up and down the main south road through
the Rangiriri district without noticing a certain large stand of old roses.
Then returning home one summer evening we saw, in the warm glow from
the setting sun, an unusual flash of colour by the roadside. This turned
out to be the blooms of a low-growing rose that had struggled up through
a tangle of bracken and bramble. Although we have since found many
other old roses growing semi-wild throughout the country, we shall never
forget the excitement of this first discovery. We identified it as Anaïs
Ségales; and this we confirmed, later, when we saw it growing in private
and botanical gardens overseas. The Rangiriri district was the scene of one
of the early battles during the Maori Wars. It was here that General Cam-
eron's forces attacked a strongly fortified settlement on a hillside above
the Waikato River.

Obviously, the many roses found by New Zealand roadsides have
either escaped from gardens, or are growing on garden sites that have been
cut through by modern roading systems. Sometimes hoary fruit trees and

fallen masonry are the only tokens left of an old homestead. Unless you knew where this stand of Gallica Roses is, it would be quite possible to pass them by unnoticed. Even in the autumn, when the dark leaves turn russet-red, they blend so perfectly with the tints of blackberry bushes, that no one would be aware of the early summer beauty created in this spot. The flowers are typical of those of most of the large family of Gallica or French Roses, as they are frequently called – being full, flat, perfectly round with small, incurving central petals surrounding a green button eye; and a delicious fragrance. When the blooms first open, the colour is a rich rosy-mauve – even purple on some soils – which quickly fades to rosy-lilac, and then to lilac with a hint of blue and grey in certain lights. This last, faded stage, is so fascinating that the rose is sometimes called the "blue" rose. For this reason it is so often confused out here with a Centifolia, The Bishop, which acquires similar shades in its petals as it ages. In point of fact in 1848 Anaïs Ségales was listed by William Paul as a Crimson Centifolia. Its thorny stems certainly suggest a hybrid origin, but it is far more of a Gallica than a Centifolia; and the term crimson does not adequately describe its subtle colouring.

In old gardens, early milling and mining settlements, and cemeteries, as well as in the vicinity of the first mission stations in this country, Anaïs Ségales abounds, some of the stands being enormous. In most instances, this Gallica has survived over a hundred years of neglect, and still produces an abundance of bloom each season. Its hardiness is indisputable; the plants renew their vigour by suckering freely in all directions. Lately, some of the roadside stands have disappeared when roads have been widened and the grassy verges swept away. But, in the heart of Auckland the old Grafton cemetery is an attractive sight in early summer when the rosy-mauve blooms of Anaïs Ségales appear. This rose of 1837 covers many a grave and many a grassy pathway, the blooms looking well alongside the heavily lichened tombstones. Many of these tombstones show rose designs in bas-relief; others, cut from one of our finest New Zealand trees, the kauri, are now heavily encrusted with a vivid reddish-brown growth, the rosy-mauve of the roses, and the striking shade of the lichen, making a pleasing discord of colour.

High above the Firth of Thames, on a well wooded hillside, is the old secluded Tararu graveyard, where many miners and early settlers were buried; while at the base of the long, narrow Coromandel Peninsula is another hillside cemetery behind the gold-mining town of Thames. Many of the graves in these early burial grounds are covered with old roses, the most rampant being Anaïs Ségales. It was to this district that people flocked in their thousands when rich deposits of gold were found a hundred years ago, bringing with them many plants, some of which are still there. Timber was being felled at an even earlier date across the peninsula at Whangapoua; and, in the little cemetery in this bay—once so busy and boisterous, but now peaceful – there are more suckering bushes of the low-growing Gallica Rose. Near the site of another early mill, we were shown a hedge of Anaïs Ségales which had been planted by a Maori woman at the rear of one of the oldest homes in that district.

The Church Missionary Society, the Wesleyan Missionary Society, and the Roman Catholics all established mission stations in the far north of New Zealand before 1845. The countryside round these historic spots is rich with old roses. On one hilltop above Kaeo, near the site of the first Wesleyan Mission, Anaïs Ségales was rampaging across cleared land where heavy timber-milling was carried out in the past. Here, in poor soil, amongst old, lichened, weather-beaten stumps, the little French rose was suckering over quite an area. Though the plants were small, compared with the cultivated ones in our garden, they were tremendously free-flowering; and looked charming, backed as they were by the grey stumps, and huge clumps of semi-wild mauve-coloured watsonias. Further west, round the shores of the Hokianga Harbour where missionaries and early traders settled, and southward, at Te Kopuru on the long northern arm of the huge Kaipara Harbour, the rosy-purple Gallica grows in colourful patches, the colour varying a little according to whether the soil is heavy clay, poor gumland – buried forests dug over for fossil kauri gum – or light and sandy. Some of the blooms of this rose that we saw in England seemed almost pure rose in tone, though, in other respects they were identical with those on our New Zealand bushes; so we were very interested, on our return, to find that certain bushes of Anaïs Ségales in the Grafton cemetery had produced paler blooms than usual.

Though we have not much personal knowledge of this Gallica in the South Island, apart from those in old cemeteries in Marlborough, Nelson, and in historic Akaroa, where many French families settled, friends and old-rose lovers have told us of various stands which exist in the mining districts of the West Coast; and also of plants to be seen near Lake Ohau on the route from Canterbury to Otago, as well as in Otago itself, where more mining settlements were invaded by this rosy-purple Gallica. There is scarcely a district thoughout the country that cannot produce plants of this hardy and long-lived rose – the easy propagation by rooted suckers being responsible for its wide distribution.

Until we introduced Anaïs Ségales into our garden—where it is one of the earliest old roses to bloom, the flowers being profuse and of fine size and colour under better conditions—the only Gallica Roses we possessed were two that, many years ago, we were able to purchase in New Zealand, Rosa Mundi and Charles de Mills. As these roses gave us a great deal of pleasure, and as our interest in their history increased with the years, we decided to import more from England. These plants have all done splendidly in our sometimes very wet, but often warm and humid, climate.

In the dawn of recorded history, the wild prototype from which all Gallica Roses were derived came from countries at the eastern end of the Mediterranean, where it was known as the Red Rose, R. *rubra*. One ancient writer described it as a rose with a vivid red flower, semi-double in form, though a dwarf variety—illustrated by Redouté as R. *gallica pumila*, and described by Mr Graham Thomas in *The Old Shrub Roses*—apparently had single pink flowers. According to M. Jules Gravereaux, who created the internationally famous Roseraie de l'Hay, near Paris, this was the rose of the Persian Magi and Median fire worshippers in the twelfth century B.C.; and was used in their religious ceremonies. Monsieur Gravereaux brought back this information in documents he acquired on a rose collecting trip to Serbia, Bulgaria, Turkey and Asia Minor in 1901. The precious information is now housed in the rustic building, situated in the heart of the rose garden, which is known as the Museum. The collections there are divided into four sections, one being for Roses in Science, one for Roses in Literature, another for Roses in the Fine Arts, and still another for Roses in the Decorative Arts.

The rich colouring of this low-growing, suckering rose, its fragrance, medicinal properties, and general hardiness, made it a treasured plant, not only in its native haunts, but also in most countries bordering the Mediterranean. As so many roses of that period were pale in tone, the rich, fiery flowers of R. *rubra* were highly esteemed and there were extensive plantings of it in ancient gardens. Arab physicians made use of the dried petals of the

Red Rose for their astringent and invigorating properties, since these petals held their scent to an amazing degree. At the same time, the fresh blooms were steeped in oil for the preparation of attar of roses. Greece and Italy knew it well, the flowers being used by the ancients at festive times.

The form most generally grown was the one we now know as R. *gallica officinalis*. This was considered to have been the Red Rose of Lancaster. In an early book on Provins, the following incident is described: "Somewhere about the year 1277, a son of the King of England, Count Egmond, who had taken the title of Comte de Champagne, was sent by the King of France to Provins with troops to avenge the murder of the mayor of the city, who had been assassinated in some tumult. He remained at Provins for a considerable period; and, on his return to England, he took for his device the Red Rose of Provins which Thibaut had brought from Syria."

R. *gallica* is mentioned in early English herbals—Gerard listing it, in 1596 as R. *rubra*. He grew it in his Holborn garden, and it was also cultivated in the environs of many an English monastery. Even before the Great Fire, conserves were being made in London from its red petals; and in the south of England large plantings were made of this Apothecary's Rose for medicinal purposes.

By 1670, self-pollinated seed of R. *gallica* was being planted extensively in Holland—artificial pollination being practised very rarely at that time —and many varieties, of dubious parentage, were being sold. In the early part of the nineteenth century, a thousand named varieties of the French Rose were available. Many had no real merit and were of inferior quality, the growers of those days marketing indiscriminately all the plants they raised; but a great impetus was given to the culture of roses when the Empress Josephine established her rose garden round the Château of Malmaison. In all, over 200 varieties were planted here between 1804 and 1814; and, of these, 107 were forms of R. *gallica* or the Rose of Provins, thirty-two were Centifolias, eight were Damasks, seven were Albas, twenty were Chinas, the remaining number comprising one or more plants of the following species—*lutea, arvensis, setigera, pimpinellifolia, sempervirens, cinnamomea, alpina, ferruginea, moschata, banksiae, carolina, laevigata, rugosa* and *clinophylla*. On reading through this list—kindly sent to us by Monsieur Robelin, Director of the Seine Parks, in which is now incorporated Roseraie de l'Hay—we were amazed to find that we had in our garden specimens of all these species with the exception of three—*arvensis*, *cinnamomea* and *clinophylla*: though we do grow first generation hybrids of *arvensis* and *cinnamomea*, the rampant Dundee Rambler and R. *francofurtana*. Later, unfortunately, through war and neglect, this famous rose garden, where Redouté painted so many of his wonderful rose studies, was destroyed; but in 1912, through the interest and inspiring help of a few French rose lovers, Monsieur Gravereaux was able to replant the Empress's rose borders with nearly 200 of the original varieties. When doing this fine work, he made use of the garden plans designed for her by a French architect.

At the same time as the collection at Malmaison was being re-established, Monsieur Gravereaux was making a similar planting in his own rose garden in the village of l'Hay-les-Roses; and we were priviledged to see the two small gardens planted with the roses of Malmaison—one section being devoted entirely to Gallica Roses. These intimate gardens were decorated with tall vases and a well of amusing design, the whole area being surrounded by supports carrying garlands of roses. On the other hand, we were disappointed to find, when we visited Malmaison in 1961, that, for a second time, the roses of the Empress Josephine had disappeared from the garden, the beds that had held them being now grassed over. This was verified by old plans of the château grounds we had carried with us from New Zealand. The fact that so many of her roses were Gallicas, and bloomed for only a few short weeks each year, may have accounted for their removal. Many possessed not only charming and unforgettable names, but also full flowers of rich and subtle colouring, their petals frequently being adorned with stripes, spots and marbling—a characteristic more often seen amongst the hybrids of the ancient R. *rubra* than in any other rose family.

Nowadays, many roses grow at Malmaison, both up the broad carriageway and in the long garden in front of the royal stables; but the nearest approach we could see to a rose of that period was in a circular bed, set into the long lawn, in front of the stable buildings. This bed was planted with a number of bushes of the lovely, low-growing, blush-pink Bourbon, Souvenir de la Malmaison, a rose that came into existence long after the days of the Empress Josephine. However, since our return to this country, we hear that the collection at Malmaison is once more to be restored—the great majority of the roses for this scheme being available in the Gallica Rose garden within Roseraie de l'Hay.

Though the French Roses bloom for a comparatively short period, their foliage is luxuriant right through the season, the smallish, rough-textured, dark green leaves, paler on the undersides, persisting right into the winter. The stems are clothed with bristles and fine prickles; and the buds, unlike the elegant ones of their descendents, the Damask Roses, are, in the typical forms, rather fat and blunt, with short calyx lobes. Gallicas will thrive in poorer soil than most other roses, as well as being resistant to heavy frost; but, like all plants, they do relish being well fed and cared for, producing better and larger blooms in consequence. The true Gallicas are all low in stature; and, holding their fine flowers erect, make very attractive and appealing garden plants. This is particularly so in the case of R. *gallica officinalis*, the Red Rose of Lancaster, and its striped sport, Rosa Mundi. We noticed that both on the Continent and in the British Isles these two bushes were generally grown close to one another, the bushes and blooms being particularly fine in England. They were remarkable at Newby Hall in Yorkshire, where they were grown near the front of tremendous mixed borders; at Nymans, in Sussex, where a special bed was devoted to them, and where they carpeted the ground round the base of a specimen tree; at Highdown, also in Sussex, where they grew splendidly in an old chalk pit in front of tall, wild, Asiatic species; and in an old rose garden at Woking in Surrey.

Rosa Mundi, well striped with carmine on a blush-pink ground, and one of the best of all striped roses, is fully described in a later chapter. The ancient semi-double rose, from which it sported and to which it occasionally reverts, R. *gallica officinalis*, has luminous flowers of a glowing carmine which fade softly, the slightly waved petals standing out well around a ring of fine stamens. These blooms are large for the size of the plant and, being held erect, are very showy in the garden. This rose is to be found suckering over graves and pathways in the Roman Catholic section of the Grafton cemetery – at one spot even forcing its way up through a large, prostrate bush of the *sempervirens* hybrid, Adelaide d'Orléans, a rose that was bred in the garden of Louis Philippe, who later became King of France. *Gallica officinalis* grows, also, in the early section of the extensive Whakapuaka cemetery, which is situated on a steep hillside overlooking Nelson, commanding a magnificent view across Tasman Bay. Very few roses were in flower when we visited this historic spot, but a keen old-rose enthusiast who lives in Nelson was able to give us a list of varieties of roses that grow on and around the oldest graves. These are Sweet Briers, Dog Roses, French Roses, Damasks, Mosses, Chinas, Teas, Bourbons, Noisettes, and Hybrid Perpetuals, as well as *sempervirens* and *wichuriana* hybrids. So far, we have not found the striped sport of R. *gallica officinalis*, Rosa Mundi, growing semi-wild in this country, though it may be established in some areas.

One of the really old Gallicas, which does splendidly on a raised bank in this garden, is Tuscany, the Old Velvet Rose. The thick petals of the glowing maroon-crimson flowers certainly do suggest the rich texture of this sumptuous material: a deep purple tint spreads over the blooms as they develop. Our bush of Tuscany came to us from England as a budded plant; but, in spite of this, it suckers freely and there is always a succession of new plants available for passing on to friends who love the old roses. We grow the Old Velvet Rose alongside Prince Camille de Rohan, with flowers of similar colouring, and richly hued fuchsias. Recently, Tuscany Superb has been planted nearby; and already it is doing splendidly. The fuller, larger blooms of this Gallica rather hide the lovely stamens which are such a feature in Tuscany; but, for all that, it is a striking and very handsome rose in the garden, and is going to prove a real acquisition.

Conditorum, in type between R. *gallica officinalis* and Tuscany, a rose that was probably used in the making of conserves; Violacea, or La Belle Sultane, with almost single blooms of violet-purple showing rich yellow stamens against a paler centre; Alain Blanchard, with cupped blooms of rich maroon-crimson, and yellow stamens, the petals later turning purple and showing pink spots; and Sissinghurst Castle, which we have now acquired, were all very old Gallica Roses which we admired in gardens overseas. The last of these was discovered by the late Miss Sackville-West, growing amongst a tangle of weeds and bramble, when she began to reconstruct the garden at Sissinghurst. It has a charming, semi-double flower of rosy-purple and paler shades. Actually, the day was overcast when we saw this rose—which was planted in a long narrow border in front of a high, dark hedge—so the deep toned blooms did not show up as advantageously as they did in full sun in other gardens.

Though the original R. *rubra* was a clear red in colour, many of the hybrids of this rose have deep, rich and most unusual shading in their petals, blue, purple and slate tones predominating in some. These lines of Francis Thompson's could vividly describe the beauty of some of the sumptuous

French Roses which were hybrids of *R. rubra*.

> " . . . the splendid rose
> Saturate with purple glows;
> Cupped to the marge with beauty; a perfume press
> Whence the wind vintages
> Gushes of warmed fragrance, richer far
> Than all the flaverous ooze of Cyprus' vats."

Belle de Crécy—a rose that was supposed to have been found in the garden of Madame la Pompadour, at Crécy—is one of these. The flat flowers, with small incurving centre petals surrounding a button eye, open carmine shaded with mauve; but this colouring quickly changes until slaty, blue-purple tones appear, which give the rose an unusual and most distinctive appearance. The bush is upright, with thin flexilbe stems—almost too light for the weight of flowers which smother it in early summer.

Charles de Mills is another fine Gallica Rose with extra large, very flat flowers which look as though they had been sliced level with a knife. Though we are now used to the pointed, high centre of so many modern roses, there is a tendency amongst present day breeders to produce roses with this same flat look—roses such as Rosemary Rose and Magenta. The short-petalled, packed blooms of so many of the Hybrid Gallicas—and other old roses as well—were bred in the fashionable shape favoured in an earlier century—one which was considered essential, at that time, if their rich, heady perfumes were to be fully savoured and appreciated. And certainly their scents are marvellous and a great asset when the flowers are used in lavish old-rose arrangements indoors. In colour, Charles de Mills is at first a rich rosy-purple; but this soon changes; blue, purple, and slate tones subtly change and darken the appearance of the flower. This moderately-sized bush, with very dark, rough leaves, is smothered with blooms at the height of the season and presents a rich tapestry of unusual shades, each flower, instead of a button eye, having a green hollow in the centre. This Gallica Rose also grows on an early grave in the Grafton cemetery and, like other roses of this family nearby, has spread considerably. An old-rose enthusiast of Akaroa told us of large stands of Charles de Mills which were growing, not only in the Akaroa district, but in Marlborough and Nelson as well. On a recent trip to the South Island, we visited several old cemeteries where this hardy Gallica grew wild. At Tua Marina, the scene of a tragic massacre of British settlers and troops in 1843, it abounds all over the steep hillside cemetery, spilling out beyond the graves and cascading down the hillside. We purchased our plant, in New Zealand, many years ago, as Cardinal Richelieu; but soon realised it must be mis-named, so we imported the true Cardinal Richelieu from England—a rose that has since given us endless pleasure in the garden.

This fine Gallica Hybrid was called after the eminent ecclesiastic and statesman who was Louis XIII's Minister for years—in fact, he practi-cally ruled France during that period. The rose Cardinal Richelieu was actually bred in Holland but was sent, unnamed, to the famous French rose breeder Laffay who decided, on seeing the unusual shade of the flowers, that it must have an ecclesiastical name. In colour it is a rich burgundy-red, with a bloom on it like that of a luscious dark grape. The fat buds open in an unforgettable manner, rather reminiscent of those of the old-fashioned, pink camellia, Lady St Clair. The outer petals—which have a touch of white at the base and are a rosy-buff on the reverse—turn back, leaving a tight, balled bunch of rosy-purple petals in the centre. By the next day, these central petals, also have turned back, the whole ball-like bloom showing a subtle, burgundy-brown colour before assuming the slaty, metallic hue so striking in the mature flower. When the French author Honoré de Balzac dined with Georges Sand in 1840 and saw a bloom of Cardinal Richelieu, he thought he had discovered the blue rose, so sought after in those days, for the creation of which English and Belgian horticulturalists were offering a prize of 500,000 francs! Now, in our gar-den, we do not find Cardinal Richelieu nearly as blue in tone as roses such as Charles de Mills, Hippolyte, Belle de Crécy, Anaïs Ségales or the early hybrid perpetual, Reine des Violettes. In *The Rose Amateur's Book* by Shirley Hibberd, in a chapter on rose curiosities, the author refers to an "Essay on Roses" by the Marquis D'Orbessan, who stated that blue roses could be produced at will, by watering the plants with a solution of indigo—a method, he claimed, that the Moors used with those grown in the gardens of the Alhambra. This simple treatment was too good to be true; for, though present-day breeders have introduced some delightful roses in subtle tones of lavender-blue, none of them have the rich purple-blue of the Gallica Roses of a hundred years ago, and none at all are the true blue of delphiniums. As an experiment, we placed the flowers of some of our bluest old roses alongside delphiniums and photographed them. The peren-nials came out true to colour, the roses nearby appearing almost red.

The rosy-purple and blue-purple shades in the old roses are enhanced and set off to perfection when grey-foliaged plants are grown around them. This is certainly the case with Hippolyte, one of the most free-flowering of all the Gallica Roses in our garden, and one which cascades down from a raised bank over the silvery Ghost Bush, Cotton Lavender, *Convolulus cneorum*, and grey-leaved perpetual carnations. The purples and greys are charming together, and though it seems wrong to mix old roses with new, we have planted next to Hippolyte, bushes of Magenta, which look equally well near the grey-toned plants, and which continue in bloom right through the season. The full, medium-sized blooms of Hippolyte make a spectacular display, as there must be thousands in bud, or fully out, on the bush at the same time, the mass of flowers bending down the flexible stems. So their raised position is a very valuable aid in showing them off.

Some years ago, when we visited the interesting old mission house at Tauranga, the present owner, Mr D. H. Maxwell—a descendant of the Venerable Archdeacon A. N. Brown, who arrived in New Zealand in 1829, and established the first mission station in the Bay of Plenty in 1838— showed us many of the fine old roses growing in the spacious garden, amongst them bushes of Anaïs Ségales, and another rosy-purple Gallica very similar to, but less thorny than, the former. This French Rose closely resembled one we photographed overseas called Nanette—a rose that was described by William Paul in the first edition of *The Rose Garden*—and was struggling and suckering up through the driveway alongside punga ferns. The first mission house, later destroyed by fire, was erected on this spot. When the wife of Judge Martin—afterwards Sir William Martin—visited Archdeacon Brown, she became ill and was nursed to health by a kindly Maori woman. Mr Maxwell told us that a rose grew outside her window, one branch of which had found its way through the raupo and reed walls of the early home. This hanging down from the low ceiling, had given the invalid much pleasure. The only rose growing on the exact spot today is this rosy-purple Gallica—a piece of which is planted in our garden. Though Gallica Roses are low-growing, given some support, they do increase in height; but it is hardly conceivable that a Gallica could have reached even a low ceiling, so it is almost certain that other roses must have grown beside this raupo house.

Other Gallicas, in colour between the pale pinks and those of sultry, dark, metallic shades, are Jenny Duval, Président de Sèze, and Du Maître d'École. The first of these, Jenny Duval, grows in a part of our garden devoted to old roses and fuchsias. With us, it is not a tall plant; but the flowers are exquisite, though less flat and quartered than those of some varieties, and show a number of subtle shades on the one bloom. After opening a lilac shade, the petals quickly assume tints of magenta, purple, rose and buff. When the sun comes out after a shower of rain and the petals are freshly washed, these colours are itensified and are quite unlike those of any other Gallica in the garden. Du Maître d'École has quite a large flower in comparison with the bloom of Jenny Duval, and is much coarser in appearance. For the size of the bush, which is only moderate, the flowers are rather heavy and inclined to hang down on the end of the branches. To see them properly it is necessary to lift the branches up, which is why we now grow the rose on a raised bank. In colour these flowers are at first a subtle, uniform shade of old rose; but, like all the Gallica family, the blooms quickly acquire other tones, in this case lilac and mauve tints which appear when the flower is exposed to the sun. Président de Sèze, with fuller, less flat blooms, but still the same delicious scent, is an unusual rose, as the deep magenta-crimson of the centre of the flower is not repeated on the outer edges of the rolled-back petals. These are quite pale in colour, and give the bloom its unusual and arresting appearance.

As well as Rosa Mundi, we grow several other striped Gallicas which we imported from England and which are fully described in a later chapter, all roses of great charm, both in the house and in the garden. These are the outstanding Camaieux, one of our favourite striped roses, Tricolore de Flandre, which sports freely in this garden; and Perle des Panachées, which grew so beautifully in Rome. All are delightful and decorative plants and add distinction to that corner of the garden where they thrive amongst low-growing fuchsias and dwarf perennials.

Though in general these French Roses are rich and sumptuous in colour, there are, amongst their number, some with exquisite, pale-toned flowers. One of the loveliest of these, the Duchesse d'Angoulême, is often referred to as the Wax Rose, because of its shell-like, transparent petals. It was named after the wife of a Bourbon prince in Napoleon's day—a son of the famous Comte d'Artois. Both the Duke and his wife were interested in gardens, and were even more so, after they became acquainted with Thomas Blaikie—the man who wrote the fascinating book, *A Scotch Gardener at the French Court*. It was Blaikie who designed a garden in the

English tradition for the Duke's father, and who also helped to lay out the Bagatelle Gardens in Paris. The Duchesse d'Angoulême is not a pure Gallica, the leaves and stems being pale in colour and unexpectedly smooth. As the flower heads are inclined to nod, we grow this rose on a raised site between the pale pink Damask, Gloire de Guilan, and Raubritter, an unusual rose with shell-like very cupped pink flowers.

Some of these Gallicas have been imported from England over a period of many years but the delicate-toned Duchesse de Montebello was sent to us from Hawke's Bay. The smallish flowers, which look as though they have been created artificially by placing fold upon fold of beautifully moulded and swathed blush-pink chiffon round a pale green button eye, are a sheer delight and are always admired, both on the tall bush in the garden and in old-rose arrangements. It was grown from a cutting, so suckers freely; but, because of its rare beauty, it is allowed a good deal of latitude in the garden. At the beginning of the last century, many roses were named after the famous men of the day, or their relatives, in the hope that, by so honouring them, favours could be gained. It is not surprising therefore that one should have been called after the charming and beautiful wife of Maréchal Lannes, a soldier Napoleon honoured by creating him Duc de Montebello. His huge castle near Milan—where Napoleon once spent a summer—gave the name to his title. The rose Duchesse de Montebello, thrives happily in semi-shade beneath a pale pink flowering cherry, the flowers retaining their delicate colour better in this position than when we grew it in full sun. Another pale toned Gallica, Antonia d'Ormois, grows nearby. We found this low-growing rose, and also R. *centifolia variegata*, by the roadside in the centre of the North Island not far from Mangaweka, and were able to confirm its name on the Continent. Antonia d'Ormois grows also in two old cemeteries—one near Nelson and the other on Banks Peninsula. It possesses the unusual characteristic of producing fresh green shoots and flowers at the same time. Though the blooms are a soft blush pink, the fat buds are surprisingly red in colour. The freshly opened flower is slightly cupped; but the petals quickly reflex back and pale at the edges. There is an excellent description of this rose in *The Old Shrub Roses*, where it is likened to the bloom of the lovely Alba Rose, Maiden's Blush.

Only one of the Gallicas has flowers with a faint tone of salmon-pink in the petals. This is Belle Isis, a charming little rose sent to us from Waitara. Because of its hybrid origin it has more decorative and larger sepals than those of the pure Gallicas. An Alba Rose growing nearby has the same warm tone in its pink petals. This is the lovely Belle Amour—a rose that blends well with the low-growing Belle Isis at its feet. Gloire de France is beautiful and rather different—its double flat blooms of deep lilac-rose pale to off-white at the outer edges of the petals. This low-growing rose, seldom seen in New Zealand, graces the garden of a rose loving friend who lived nearby—the late Mr Frank Penn, a past President Emeritus of the New Zealand Rose Society. It was he who gave me my treasured copy of Edward Bunyard's book, *Old Garden Roses*. Apparently, he collected this choice Gallica, Gloire de France—which has now been added to our collection—many years ago in the Otaki district, and also its garden companion, the delicious Alba, Celestial. Recently cuttings of two further Gallica Roses were sent to us—a purple-crimson one from Nelson, and a pale pink one from Taranaki. These will be grown on, and later studied in the hope that they can be named.

In the very small garden, it is advisable to grow Gallica Roses that have been budded on a non-suckering stock; but where space permits they can be allowed to develop into spreading thickets, an underplanting of old-fashioned flowers such as forget-me-nots, primulas, primroses, campanulas and dwarf aquilegias doing the roses no harm, and adding greatly to the attractiveness of such a spot. A little shade does not hinder the production of excellent blooms; so these low-growing, hardy roses can be planted with safety underneath taller deciduous shrubs—in fact, they look well grouped in this manner. Though they can be left unpruned —as they are when found neglected in old settlements—far larger and better blooms result when spindly shoots and old tired wood are removed after flowering, and the stronger, newer stems shortened a little. This should be done at the same time as modern roses are pruned.

Like all other shrubs, roses are better and more vigorous when well looked after. We find that the Gallicas respond well to a heavy spring dressing of animal manure and consistent watering during our dry summer. The Gallica Roses are prone to mildew, in the late summer, under hot, dry conditions. Apart from that, they cause little trouble and do not appear to be affected by either rust or black spot. Consequently spraying is not necessary until after flowering is over—a great boon, as the flowers are unblemished. However, any work required to keep them in good heart is well repaid by the generous mass of blooms they produce annually.

Though these old French Roses, all of them hybrids of the ancient R. *rubra*, are not now listed in their hundreds, as they were in the middle of the last century, those that are available still in old gardens, settlements, and overseas nurseries, are of considerable interest and great decorative value. Their ancient historical background, their aristocratic names, their unusual colouring, their fascinating stripes, spots, and marbling, and their heavenly scent combine to give us roses that recapture the grace and charm of an era now gone.

Upon her head a crimson coronet,
With damask rose and daffodillies set.

Spenser

THE HISTORY OF THE DAMASK ROSE READS LIKE A TALE
from the *Arabian Nights*. For centuries poets, writers, and artists
have sung its praises and extolled its beauty and its fragrance. Four thousand years ago, a Minoan artist on the island of Crete painted a clearly
defined picture of a single rose on one of the frescoes, and also on a vase,
that decorated the ancient palace of Cnossos. Excavations, successfully
carried out in 1926, revealed these treasures; and the painted rose, after
being examined by experts, was definitely identified as a form of the
Damask. Friends who frequently visit this Mediterranean island tell us
that there has been a great deal of controversy about the restoration work
carried out on many of these excavated treasures; but the fragment showing
the single pink rose is the original plaster and has not been touched since
it was first painted.

This historical and famous Summer Damask, which originated as a
natural hybrid between R. *phoenicia*—a form of the white Musk Rose—
and R. *rubra*—a single, red form of R. *gallica*—was common in ancient
times to several countries at the eastern end of the Mediterranean, as well
as to Crete. From Phoenicia—the modern Syria—it was carried to Abys-
sinia by the Phoenician saint who established Christianity in that country.
The Holy Rose or R. *sancta*, as it became known, is still to be found

growing in Abyssinian churchyards. Dried garlands of roses discovered in Egyptian tombs near the Pyramids have proved its early existence in that country, where it was called the Rose of the Tombs. Though the Cretan artist probably drew a single rose as being more suitable to his design, it is quite likely that double forms also existed on the island at that time, as many-petalled Damasks grew wild, not only in Asia Minor, but as far north as the regions of Persia bordering the Caspian Sea, and in the wild, mountainous country of Kurdistan. Though we grow no true single Damask Rose in our garden, we did see this ancient rose overseas.

R. *damascena* was spread far and wide by successive waves of early traders and slow-moving invaders, who travelled northwards and east-wards over the mountains of Persia and on into Turkestan, following the old caravan routes that led to Kashmir, Afghanistan, and India. In India the red form was highly prized, as so many roses native to that country were pale in colour. In Bengal as well as in other parts of the country a from of R. *damascena* was established as a perfume rose—great fields being planted to provide blooms for the making of attar of roses and rose-water.

In Asia Minor, after the expulsion of the Crusaders from Jerusalem in 1187, the Sultan Saladin used 500 camel loads of rose-water, procured from Damask Roses, in order to purify the Temple of Omar, which, for a time, had been used as a Christian church. This episode shows the great use made of these ancient roses; but their petals also were in constant demand, being strewn on roadways before important personages, and used to carpet and sweeten the floors of banqueting halls. The blooms them-selves were often made into garlands for personal adornment.

The Damask Rose was carried westward, also, at a very early date, to Greece and Italy, where it was cultivated largely so that masses of the blooms could be used for festive occasions and where, even now, it is grown extensively. In Greece, the Damask Rose and R. *gallica* grow side by side in peasant cottage gardens bordering the roadsides along the route down the Peleponnese peninsula; in Italy we saw it frequently in quiet walled gardens, near running water and sparkling fountains. From Asia Minor, Greece, and Egypt, Phoenician and Greek traders carried this rose with them to Tunisia, Algeria, and Morocco, where it throve so well that the foundation was laid for the great perfume industries that flourish there today. From North Africa the Moors took it with them to Spain, where it is now to be found growing wild on the hills of Andalusia; and much later, when the Spaniards invaded the New World, the Damask Rose went with them.

France and England appear to have acquired it somewhat later, about the middle of the sixteenth century. A Dr Linaker, physician to Henry VII and Henry VIII, is credited with having brought the Damask Rose to England on his return from a trip to Italy; and Monsieur Dupont, of the Luxembourg gardens, carried plants of this rose back to France, after a visit to Florence. By 1785, four varieties of the Damask Rose were procurable in France, and it was not long before French rose breeders were raising other interesting Damasks from these early introductions.

With all their romantic and historic associations, the Damask Roses in our garden are a constant source of joy to us. We treasure them, not only for their beauty—and in some cases their rarity—but also for their endearing habit of flowering freely and for their luxuriant, healthy foliage. Most of these ancient roses bloom only once in the season; but this is compensated for by the veritable shower of blossom they produce during several weeks in early summer. On the other hand, our perpetual-flowering Damasks, the Pink and Red Four Seasons Roses, though less tall and less showy than their summer-flowering relatives, are even more famous; they were the first native roses of the Western world to flower again in the autumn. Later, when they were crossed with the ever-blooming China Roses from the Far East, the first step was taken in the development of the modern perpetual-flowering rose.

The most significant of the perfume roses is our tallest-growing Summer Damask, R. *damascena trigintipetala*—a rose which was planted extensively in India, Persia, Turkey, Bulgaria, and in several parts of North Africa, particularly in Morocco for the distillation of attar of roses and the making of various forms of rose-water. Our plant of this ancient and delightfully free-flowering rose was grown from cuttings sent to us from Hawke's Bay. These struck very freely and within a few years grew into eight-foot shrubs. At first we managed this rose very badly, as we pruned it in late winter when we trimmed back the Gallica Roses. As Summer Damasks only flower well on mature wood, this meant that there was very little bloom the following season: only the twiggy growths, left uncut, produced a few poor flowers to our disappointment. Now we remove old wood immediately the flowering is past, and fine new growth appears very soon. From these fresh, strong stems, a magnificent display of bloom is produced in early summer. Our bush of R. *damascena trigintipetala* grows on top of a high wall at one corner of the pink garden. It is supported by, and completely covers, a tall wire-netting fence through which the clusters of semi-double rosy flowers spray out, making a charming picture as they hang down gracefully from this height. Viewed from below, with a background of clear blue sky and golden kowhai blooms, the rosy *trigintipetala* is very decorative.

A typical and historically famous Summer Damask, R. *damascena versicolor*, is thought to have originated as a sport from the perfume rose, R. *damascena trigintipetala* and certainly there is a strong resemblance between these two tall members of the Damask family, as we realised this season when the flowers on some branches of the striped *versicolor* reverted to the rosy, self-coloured blooms of *trigintipetala*. This striped rose is more commonly referred to as York and Lancaster or the Rose of the Wars. It was round a bush of *versicolor*, growing in the Temple Gardens, that the Lancastrians and the Yorkists had the brawl which is supposed to have precipitated the Wars of the Roses. Shakespeare immortalised this incident in Henry VI:

> And here I prophesy. This brawl today,
> Grown to this faction, in the Temple Garden,
> Shall send between the red rose and the white,
> A thousand souls to death and deadly night.

On a recent visit to this old London garden in the heart of the Law Courts, we searched in vain for a bush of York and Lancaster, thinking that one might have been preserved there because of its historical association. Shakespeare must have been thinking of this same rose when he spoke of "roses damasked red and white"; for the loosely double flowers are variable in colour, some being white, others a pale carmine-pink – some having just one or two entirely reddish petals, and some being splashed and unevenly striped with the rosy shade. Redouté, known as the Raphael of the Flowers, was the official painter for the Empress Josephine; much of his finest work was executed in her garden at Malmaison, and York and Lancaster was one of the roses he painted there.

In Auckland it is one of the earliest of this group to come into flower, the medium-sized blooms being produced in abundance on rather thorny stems. At first we were a little disappointed in this famous rose but, within a few years of its arrival from England, it has become well established in the garden. From time to time it rejuvenates itself by producing fresh

suckering shoots round the base and it is on this new growth that we get
the best quality blooms. A drastic trimming after flowering is most beneficial; if it is allowed to run wild, this Damask soon becomes straggly and
poor, the tired-looking wood then providing only inferior flowers. *R. damascena versicolor* is often confused with the lowly striped Gallica, Rosa
Mundi, though the two are quite distinct in every way. We grow York and
Lancaster near another historic rose, the tall, grey-leaved *R. alba semi-
plena*, or the White Rose of York; and there is no doubt that plants of such
historic interest and charm do add character to a garden. We were told
that this old striped Damask Rose survives in an early churchyard at Te
Uku, on the southern side of Raglan harbour. When the original church
was pulled down, most of the old roses were cleared away—the only one
remaining being a bush of York and Lancaster.

A name that conjures up pictures of Persian bazaars, camel caravans,
and all the mysteries of that ancient land is that of Omar Khayyám, the
poet who sang of roses and nightingales and on whose grave at Naishapur,
in Northern Persia, a Damask Rose was planted so that:

> When Omar died the Rose did weep
> Its petals on his tomb,
> He would be laid where north winds keep
> The rose in freshest bloom.

Centuries after the death of the Persian poet, the English poet Edward
Fitzgerald translated Omar Khayyám's verse. On his death, seed was collected from the rose on the grave at Naishapur and sent to England; and
later, bushes of this Persian Damask were planted on Edward Fitzgerald's
grave in Suffolk. Later still, plants were propagated from this cemetery
rose; and it was from here that we acquired our plant. Vistors are always
interested in the Damask, Omar Khayyám, with its downy, grey-green
leaves and quartered rosy flowers—the calyx and long sepals being covered
with fine bristles. This Summer Damask grows to only half the height of
its neighbour, *R. damascena trigintipetala*, and has a very different appearance,
the greyish foliage being small in size compared with the clear lettuce-
green leaves of the taller variety.

A paragon amongst Damask Roses is Ispahan, Rose d'Isfahan or
Pompom des Princes—a rose that grows wild on the hills of Persia and is
particularly beautiful between Shiraz and the old caravan trading centre
of Ispahan. Friends who have lived in that country tell us of the glories

of this and other pink Damask Roses, and of the wild pink Persian lilac —which blooms at the same time as the roses—as they cascade over the hillsides. Residents of Shiraz grow the rose Ispahan in their quiet walled gardens, where ample water is led in to irrigate the trees and plants and also to create a cool and restful atmosphere in that hot dry land. An early 19th century writer considered that "no country in the world grew roses to such perfection as Persia, where they were well cultivated and prized by the inhabitants. Their gardens and courts were crowded with roses, their rooms ornamented with vases filled with gathered bunches, and every bath strewn with full-blown flowers". Many Persian roses only bloom in early summer after heavy spring rains which produce flowers in rich abundance.

Our tremendous plant of Ispahan is growing in a pink border along one side of a sunken garden. When this Damask Rose is in full bloom, literally thousands of perfect flowers weigh down the long arching branches until the bush looks like a fountain or shower of several shades of pink. The buds, which come in sprays, are really exquisite, as they open to show a deeper tone in the centre—the many-petalled flowers being a soft, uniform pink when fully out. On a grassy terrace above this Damask Rose is a narrow border alongside the house in which are planted pink fuchsias, and roses; one rose, the lovely Tausendschön, reaches to the eaves of the house before weeping down in a pink cascade above the Persian Damask.

An illustration of this corner of the garden gives some idea of the tree-flowering nature of some of these old roses, for Ispahan is a riot of bloom for over two months. It gives us endless pleasure and very little work; all we do is cut back the wood that has bloomed as soon as the first sign of fresh growth appears. The strong new shoots, covered with wonderfully healthy foliage, then develop rapidly and soon attain a height of over eight feet. These branches ripen well during the late summer and autumn; and are then in readiness to carry next season's heavy load of flower. Some of the longest branches can be shortened a little in the winter; and, if a number of stems are hooked over with strong wires, far more bloom will be produced.

Celsiana, one of the really old Damasks, and a rose most beautifully portrayed by Van Huysum and later by Redouté, never fails to thrill us when its glorious flowers first appear each year. This rose was grown extensively in Holland and was later introduced into France by the French breeder, Cels, from whom it acquired its name. The blooms on this rose are larger and, we feel, even lovelier than those of other members of this ancient family. The warm pink colour of the slightly fluted and rolled petals pales a little in the sun, but is still exquisite, as a translucent light filters through them. The first open flower in each spray rests in a nest of deep reddish buds which are encased in foliated sepals; and it is always a surprise when such a pale-coloured bloom emerges from such a dark bud. Soft yellow stamens and greyish-green leaves add to the beauty of this fine, upright shrub.

We did not see many plants of Celsiana when we were overseas; but at Lyegrove, a famous Gloucestershire garden, there was a perfect specimen in full bloom in one of the lovely mixed borders. Celsiana was growing there alongside tall blue delphiniums, lower-growing blue and white campanulas, and grey foliage plants. We were particularly interested in this garden as the colours blended beautifully in all the borders, and the old roses, instead of being massed together in one large bed, as we sometimes saw them, were interplanted with interesting foliage plants and fine perennials – these helping to set off, to full advantage, their beauty and colour.

A Damask Rose which was raised in 1813 in the garden of the Château of Malmaison was later called Marie Louise after the second wife of Napoleon Bonaparte. This rose has scented flowers of a clear, uniform, lilac-pink, the petals reflexing back from the button eye as they age. Marie Louise has been established for a very long time in the Grafton cemetery and has spread over a number of graves, coming up through concrete and out across the grassy pathways. This hardy Damask has survived years of neglect and still manages to produce fine flowers each year; grasses and tall daisies provide a natural mulch which keeps the roots cool and moist in summer. Gallicas, Caninas, Noisettes, Mosses, Sempervirens, Hybrid Perpetuals and many other old roses grow on the nearby graves, as well as a Hybrid Damask, La Ville de Bruxelles, which shows a little of the influence of R. *centifolia* in its longer, down-drooping leaves and heavier stems. The tightly packed, rosy petals, pale on the outer edges of the large, but rather flat flowers – the blooms being almost smothered at times by the handsome, luxuriant foliage. We find that these roses vastly increase in size and quality of flowers when cared for in the garden but, all the same, it is quite remarkable that they do so well under the very trying conditions they have to cope with in the old cemetery. This says a great deal for the hardiness and long life of many of these old roses. The fact that they are growing on their own roots, and sucker freely, accounts for this perennial rejuvenation.

Monsieur Hardy, who was superintendent of the Luxembourg Gardens in Paris at the beginning of the nineteenth century, created one marvellous rose which made his name popular, and which he called Madame Hardy in honour of his wife. This is a Hybrid Damask, R. *centifolia* having contributed somewhat to its vigour and beauty. It is considered to be one of the loveliest of all white roses. The plant he sent us from England has taken time to settle down in this garden; but last year, planted in a fresh position, it delighted us by developing splendidly and producing many fine blooms.

The buds are encased in long, attractive sepals and the foliage is a clear, fresh green – both attractive characteristics – but it is the fully open flower which has called forth such glowing praise. The blooms open flat and quartered round a clear green eye, the beautifully swatched petals reflexing a little at the edges, leaving the centre faintly cupped. A hint of blush-pink appears as the flower first unfolds, but this soft tone quickly fades out to a pure white.

In New Zealand, Madame Hardy has often been confused with another lovely white rose which has a lot of Damask in its parentage—the Noisette, Madame Plantier. Both these roses have a green eye in the centre of a full quartered flower, long attractive sepals, and the pure scent of a Damask; but there the resemblance ends. In Madame Hardy the upright stems are clothed with thorns and large leaves, whilst in the Noisette the arching, thin stems are practically thornless; and the leaves, pale green and very disease-resistant, are much smaller. In Italy we saw this white Damask Rose, Madame Hardy, growing to perfection, and we were able to photograph some really lovely blooms—the best we had been privileged to see anywhere—so it was a great thrill to return home and find our own bush doing so well.

Before this, we had begun to think that Madame Hardy had a serious rival in the pure white Damask, Botzaris. In fact we still consider this a very beautiful rose, as well as an easy and very floriferous one. The flat, quartered blooms, with a green eye, are not unlike those of Madame Hardy, though no hint of pink appears in the petals, neither are their centres concave. Botzaris, with its upright growth of medium height, is a valuable plant in our white and yellow border, and never fails to produce an abundance of perfect, richly scented, white flowers. It is also completely healthy and trouble-free, and strikes readily from cuttings, Madame Hardy failing badly in this respect.

Miss Nancy Lindsay, an enthusiastic plant explorer, has in fairly recent years collected some very fine Damask Roses from the Caspian district in northern Persia. One of these, Gloire de Guilan, a rose used in Persia for the distillation of rose-water, is a great treasure in this garden. It grows vigorously on top of a raised bank in company with many other old roses. The strong, prickly stems are well clothed with fresh green foliage: and the whole bush is covered with sprays of clear pink, fragrant flowers in early summer, the weight of these blooms arching over the branches in a graceful manner and the raised position showing them off to greater advantage. Instead of having a button eye these sweet blooms, though double, show a cluster of yellow stamens, the soft petals enclosing them most attractively. The flowers of Damask Roses show a great deal of variety in their shape and size, those of Gloire de Guilan being unlike any others of this charming family. While in England, we admired and photographed the unusual blooms of two other Damask Roses. These were Leda (the Painted Damask) and Hebe's Lip, a Damask-Brier Hybrid. Both these interesting roses have creamy flowers, edged with crimson, though in size and shape they are quite dissimilar.

Recently we obtained, in New Zealand, a rose that is sometimes referred to as Blush Gallica and sometimes as Blush Damask. The latter appears to be the correct name and the one commonly used in England, where this rose is very popular in old-rose gardens. In *Roses for English Gardens* Gertrude Jekyll describes the Blush Damask as a good rose for all gardens, and one that grows into a strong bush. It will put up with any treatment, thriving even on a dry bank. That is its position in our garden, though it could do with more shelter from cold winds, as its nodding, very double, lilac-pink flowers, deeper in tone in the centre, are often damaged in stormy weather. Because of its flexible growth it looks well growing on a raised position, as the flowers appear all along the arching stems weighing them down gracefully. Though the Blush Damask is a hardy rose, we did notice that the blooms were very lovely in a sheltered part of the famous English garden, Hidcote; so we are now going to plant another bush in a warm, sheltered corner, and compare its performance in

1. R. *gallica officinalis*

2. Charles de Mills

▲ 3. Anais Ségales

▼ 4. Hippolyte

this favourable position in our New Zealand conditions.

We have no true single Damask Rose in the garden, the nearest approach to a simple form being Mrs O. G. Orpen, a rose that was bred in England at the beginning of this century, and one which we purchased in New Zealand many years ago. The large rosy-pink flat blooms have five deeply notched and lightly veined petals. As well as these, there are a number of shell-like petaloids which surround a glorious ring of rich fat yellow stamens which embellish the centre of the rose. This Damask flowers late in the season, at the same time as its neighbour, the lovely Celsiana. The blooms of York and Lancaster, which grows nearby, are well past their best when these fine shrub roses come into flower. It is rather pleasant to have the season of the Damask Roses extended in this manner, as it means that we can gather blooms of one variety or another for up to three months. Miss Rose Kingsley, in her book *Roses and Rose Growing*, has included an excellent coloured illustration of Mrs O. G. Orpen, which gives a good idea of this modern Damask.

St Nicholas, a very beautiful rose, was discovered in 1950, at Richmond, Yorks, in the garden whose name it bears. We imported this valuable shrub rose from England, and it has never failed to charm and delight us with its profusion of rosy-pink, semi-double flowers, which come in sprays and last well on the plant. These are followed by handsome heps, and foliage that colours well in the autumn. Being of sturdy, vigorous growth, the flowers are held erect for all to see and admire. St Nicholas grows in full sun beneath a grey stone wall, next to Red Damask, a fine double, cultivated form of our native manuka.

One of the most ancient roses in the garden, and also a very historic one, is R. *damascena bifera* or the Pink Four Seasons Rose—an autumn Damask which, for centuries, was held in very high esteem. Even before the Christian era Phoenician traders had carried it, from its home in Asia Minor to far away Southern Europe, and the Atlantic coast of North Africa. In the days of Greek and Roman splendour, vast quantities of roses were used for festive and state occasions, both for personal adornment and the decoration and sweetening of banqueting halls and streets; so this Pink Four Seasons Rose was cultivated extensively in Greece, Italy, and Egypt. In Egypt, where it was called the Alexandrian Rose, large plantings were made so that the flowers could be sold in Rome. Until we read Edward Bunyard's book *Old Roses*, it puzzled us to know how, before the days of cool storage, these blooms could have been transported across the Mediterranean in slow sailing vessels. Apparently, huge earthen crocks were used for the purpose, and the half-open flowers placed between layers of bay salt and sprinkled with wine. When they were opened up in Rome the roses were put into faintly warm ovens or tepid water until they started to open out. Then, with the aid of a feather, attar of roses was brushed into the heart of each bloom to restore its perfume, wine being brushed on to the leaves to give them a gloss. At the same time, many of these Damask Roses were being grown in the environs of Rome; and they must have been familiar to the inhabitants of Pompeii, also, as paintings of them have been found on excavated frescoes.

In order to provide the enormous quantity of rose blooms used for Bacchanalian feasts during the days of the great Roman Emperors—Nero is credited with having spent £30,000 on roses for one evening's festivities, as it was believed in those days, that roses offset the intoxicating effects of wine—Greek gardeners settled in Italy and planted large fields of Damask Roses round Paestum, in the Gulf of Salerno, not far from where our troops landed in World War II. Paestum, which had been settled by the Sybarites 500 years before the Christian era, became famous for its beautiful roses; and it is interesting and enlightening to read Martial's epigram "To Domitian on His Winter Roses":

> Some winter roses, Caesar, rarest flowers,
> The Nile had sent you, thankful for your care
> But when the Egyptian sailor saw your bowers,
> He could but scorn the present which he bare.
> So rich the fragrance your own Paestum showers,
> So bright Italia's spring – her blooms so fair.
> Fresh wreaths of roses from Rome's gardens torn
> Where'er the sailor turned his steps, he knew.
> Bright with the blooms Italia's soil had borne,
> Where'er he turned his eyes, plants prosp'ring grew.
> "I see" – he cried – "we may send you our corn,
> But winter roses we must get from you."

In Pliny's *Natural History*, written towards the end of the first century A.D., he mentioned a number of roses, one of which was the Pink Autumn Damask, which he called the Trachyean Rose. Apart from its botanical names, we find the Pink Four Seasons Rose being called the Rose of

Paestum and the Rose of Pompeii, other names being added later.

One of the highlights of our brief visit to Italy was to have been a trip to Paestum. But, to our great disappointment, a sudden indisposition put an end to these cherished plans; so we did not see the roses, some of which still grow amidst the grandeur of the Greek ruins. However, in Rome and Florence we saw plants of the Pink Autumn Damask, the finest bushes of all in the formal garden of the Villa de Castello near Florence. This once belonged to a member of the Medici family, and the garden has been changed very little since that time. Other flourishing plants of this same rose were growing beneath a large statute of Jove in the Boboli Gardens in Florence.

After Phoenician traders had successfully introduced this Damask Rose into the western extremity of North Africa it became known, in that part of the world, as the Rose of Carthage. Later, the Moors took it with them to Spain; and, later still, the Spaniards introduced it into the New World as the Rose of Castile. But even this imposing list does not complete the full number of names by which this modest-looking rose became known. When it was established in France, it was sometimes referred to, affectionately, as the Ready-made Bouquet—Bouquet Tout Fait—as the flowers in each spray often opened simultaneously, creating the effect of a tight posy. In the stirring days of the First Empire, the Pink Four Seasons Rose was cultivated on Mount Valérien, then on the outskirts of Paris—the local name for it being Rose of Puteaux. This spot was opposite the Bagatelle Rose Gardens, though the celebrated rosary had not by then been established.

Our bush of the Pink Four Seasons Rose was given to us by the owner of one of Auckland's finest gardens, and it was she who told us the story of its arrival in New Zealand. Apparently it was introduced by missionaries —as were so many of our old roses—and planted at a mission station which was established not far from Lake Rotoiti at Te Ngae. As is usual with these Damask Roses, it suckered freely; and an old Maori woman, who loved flowers, collected pieces from the original bushes, and planted them as a hedge round her garden. It was she who gave our Auckland friend the plant which we now treasure. A Tongan gardener, knowing our interest in this rose, told us that it was introduced into Tonga, also, by missionaries; and that it flourished there, in Queen Salote's garden, in spite of the tropical heat and rains.

On the other hand, we heard of a small potted plant of the hardy Pink Four Seasons Rose flowering, at mid-winter, in a tiny sod hut at Queenstown. This was a hundred years ago, when the fabulous gold discoveries in Otago attracted thousands of people—the swift streams pouring into Lake Wakatipu giving up incredible quantities of gold. As is usual in gold rushes, many of the seekers were inexperienced, as well as unsuitably clothed and housed. The changes in temperature in Central Otago from extreme heat to fierce snowstorms caught hundreds unprepared, and many died in such conditions of hardship. But the little pink rose—a native of Asia Minor—survived the rigorous climate of this southern part of New Zealand, as it has survived the heat of Tonga.

For a long time, the origin of Blanc Mousseux—a white, perpetual-flowering Damask Moss—was not known but, in 1950, it sported back to the Pink Four Seasons Rose in two gardens—one in the United States and one in England. Mr G. S. Thomas, the English expert on old roses, said that until this sporting occurred nothing definite was known about the history of this rose, the botanical names of which are R. *quatre saisons blanc mousseux* or R. *damascena bifera alba muscosa*. In France it was called Rosier de Thionville. Though our plant came from England many years ago, we have since found bushes of this rose in early gardens and old cemeteries; and we were able to tell Mr Thomas that we had discovered a plant in the Grafton cemetery, sporting back in a similar manner. Several branches were producing the non-mossy blooms of the Pink Four Seasons Rose, while others carried the brown-mossed, rather muddled blooms of the white rose, Blanc Mousseux. The buds of this rose are really beautiful, though the open flowers, faintly flushed with pink, are rather disappointing.

From an Akaroa correspondent we heard of a plant of the White Perpetual Moss growing in an early cemetery; this plant also had sported back to the Pink Damask parent. Our friend mentioned also that her mother, who lived on Banks Peninsula, was quite disappointed one year to find that her White Moss Rose had reverted to the old original, Pink Damask which grew in that district; she did not realise that the pink form was of such historic interest. In an Auckland garden, it was the Pink Four Seasons Rose itself which produced white blooms. To our knowledge, this is the only bush of the Pink Damask which has done this in our district. It is generally the white sport which reverts to the original form. It is rare finds, such as this, that keep our interest in rose collecting alive.

The tall bush of Blanc Mousseux in our garden, being budded on *canina* stock, has not, so far, shown the slightest tendency to sport, though a number of other roses have done so.

As well as the Pink Four Seasons Rose, a red form of the Autumn Damask was grown in Asia Minor and Persia, and was probably the highly fragrant, many-petalled red rose that flourished in Macedonia in the garden of King Midas. These pink and red roses were earlier thought to be the ones referred to in ancient writings as forms of R. *centifolia* or the Cabbage Rose. This has now been disproved: and it is considered that the old, very full roses, referred to by early writers, must have been forms of these Autumn Damasks. The particular variety of the Scarlet Four Seasons Rose in this garden was introduced from Persia, comparatively recently, by Miss Nancy Lindsay, and named Rose de Resht. Forming a sturdy upright bush of moderate height, and having fine, abundant foliage, this Damask Rose is a decided acquisition. The flowers, of pompom shape, are cerise-crimson in colour, the tightly packed petals reflexing back from a button eye. There is scarcely a day throughout the year when this rose is without flower; and at present, in the depth of winter, the bush is gay with bloom, and the foliage still lush and healthy. With us, it is even more perpetual-flowering than the Pink Four Seasons Rose. The paler rose has longer, more elegant buds than the red form, and larger sprays of bloom; while the leaves of the pink variety are paler in colour and softer in texture than those of its scarlet relative. Both possess the marvellous scent of the Damask family that has made them famous as perfume roses.

By 1785, the flowers of four varieties of the Four Seasons Rose were being sold in France—these being the scarlet, the pink, a near-white, and a dwarf form. So it is not surprising that, at the beginning of the nineteenth century, breeders were using them to create new varieties. An early cross between the Scarlet Four Seasons Rose, the Crimson China and the red R. *gallica officinalis*, produced the first Portland Rose, so called in honour of an enthusiastic rose lover of that period, the Duchess of Portland. Only eight of the sturdy Portland Roses are available today; but those we grow —two of which were imported from England, the other having been found in an old Auckland garden—are all perpetual-flowering and valuable roses, that appear to revel in Auckland's hot summer and tolerate the wet months of winter. The Comte de Chambord has rosy flowers with delightfully crimped and waved petals; Jacques Cartier has full pink blooms with a button eye; and Blanc de Vibert has very pale green leaves and many-petalled white flowers—the last two bearing a strong resemblance to the Autumn Damasks. In turn, these Portland Roses became the parents of the first Hybrid Perpetuals; and their damask ancestry shows up very plainly in some of the earliest members of this large and vigorous family—particularly so in the variety Baronne Prévost. And so, from one group to another, the story builds up until we arrive at the beautiful roses of the twentieth century. Whenever we hear people exclaim over a new rose and praise its rich damask perfume, we wander back, in thought, through the centuries, recalling the history of the ancient roses that made such a scent possible.

3   THE WHITE ROSE OF YORK AND OTHER MEMBERS OF THE ALBA FAMILY

White as the native rose....

Spenser

JUST AS FRANCE TOOK THE RED R. *GALLICA*—THE ROSE of Provins—to her heart and made it her own, so did England adopt the White Rose, R. *alba*. It was thought to have been brought to her shores by the earliest Roman traders, though the actual date of its introduction is not known. However Pliny, writing on gardening at the end of the first century A.D., describes R. *alba* as the Thorn Rose, and puts it first in his list of roses. In ancient times England was known as the Isle of Albion; and in 77 A.D. Pliny stated that it might have been so called because of the white roses with which it abounds. R. *spinosissima* and R. *arvensis* were already there before the Roman invasion; but this rather suggests that R. *alba* could have been well established at the time mentioned by this early writer.

Old English botanical and horticultural writings refer to R. *alba* as being one of the earliest known roses to be cultivated in England. It grew in the London garden of the Bishop of Ely, whom Queen Elizabeth I dispossessed in favour of Sir Christopher Hatton, though the bishop was afterwards allowed to walk through his beloved garden and to gather roses from it. Gerard not only mentioned R. *alba* first in his list of roses – as did Parkinson – but grew it in his Long Acre garden; and from then on it has been cultivated extensively both in England and Scotland, where it flourishes by the roadside and in old cottage gardens. R. *alba* is thought to have originated in the Crimea – Kurdistan area as a natural hybrid between R. *damascena* and a thornless, pure white form of R. *canina*. This Dog Rose is similar, except in colour, to *canina coriifolia*, or the Leatherleaf Rose which, was introduced into New Zealand over a hundred years ago, and which has the same tall upright growth as the Alba Roses. The oldest types of Albas were the five-petalled single, the semi-double, and the double. All these had white flowers; but, centuries later, many exquisite hybrid forms began to appear with very full flowers and soft pink colouring; and still with the same delicious scent. At the height of their popularity, over a hundred different varieties were listed; but today, less than twenty are available, which is strange, when R. *alba* held so honoured a place in English history and heraldry for 500 years.

R. *alba* was established in Kew Gardens by 1797; and later at Malmaison in France where Redouté painted the Alba, Great Maiden's Blush, and also *alba semi-plena*, for the Empress Josephine. Later still, Dean Hole mentions seeing these White Roses growing by old farmhouses and in cottage gardens—huge bushes of them covered with snowy flowers; and Gertrude Jekyll, in *Wood and Garden*, commends the taste of the cottage gardeners who cultivated this ancient rose. So it seems difficult to understand why so many Albas have been lost, when their unusual foliage alone would merit their inclusion in any garden scheme—to say nothing of the rare beauty of their flowers and their intoxicating perfume. They are often referred to as Tree Roses because of their tall, upright growth, which in some cases, exceeds eight feet, and so makes them useful for background plantings and informal hedges. They have the distinction of a foliage of very unusual colour, as have two other roses—R. *villosa* or the Apple Rose, which has very grey leaves, and R. *rubrifolia*, whose foliage is of a subtle shade of metallic grey tinged with plum colour.

R. *alba* was used as a stock rose in the seventeenth century; and a useful one it must have been, as it does not sucker nearly as freely as some other roses used for this purpose. It requires to be pruned lightly, or not at all, if it is to develop its full beauty; but for a smaller garden it can be cut back a certain amount to induce more compact growth. The flower display will not be as generous as on a plant that is allowed to develop naturally, but the individual blooms will be better. In England, R. *alba* is now generally budded on to *canina* stock, as we have found to our cost.

This stock suckers on our imported plants and we have to waste time we can ill afford, removing the *canina* shoots which sap the growth of the main plant. Increased by cuttings, and allowed to develop on their own roots, these Alba Roses will grow vigorously and live to a great age.

Though we have never found them by our own roadsides, and very seldom indeed in early gardens, Alba Roses are seen all over the British Isles by roadsides, in cottage gardens, and in parks. They appear to thrive in sun or shade – even amongst the roots of other shrubs; and they are not fussy as to soil though, like most plants, they do appreciate good feeding and will produce finer blooms in consequence. Their leaves, particularly those of the three original white types, appear to keep quite free from the mildew which attacks the Gallicas and Bourbons in hot, dry weather. This is indeed an asset in Auckland. The clusters of flowers open slowly, and last well on the plant, so lengthening and enhancing the floral display. As for their perfume, it is wonderful. It has been likened to the scent of white hyacinths, of spicy apples, and of honey; but, whichever it is, this fragrance is delicious in the garden, particularly towards evening or after rain. Albas are summer-flowering only, and possibly it is this that makes the bushes so sturdy; so much strength goes into the making of the coarse, grey-green leaves, instead of into extra blooms.

In the fifteenth century, Botticelli painted his Birth of Venus, and in this picture can be seen flattish white flowers which have been identified as the blooms of Alba Roses. Other artists of the Renaissance, Giotto, Ghirlandaio—who taught Michaelangelo for a time—and Crivelli, all included these ancient roses in their paintings; and, in *Italian Gardens of the Renaissance* Julia Cartwright quotes Boccaccio describing gardens near his home at Settignano, on the outskirts of Florence. He speaks of "the beauties of these gardens, of the broad alleys shaded by pergolas laden with purple grapes, and bordered with red and white roses and jessamine". These red roses would have been Gallicas, the white ones Albas. As we had recently visited many of the old Florentine gardens, and seen for ourselves similar plantings, we found Boccaccio's description intensely interesting.

For a long time, it was thought that the Great Double White was the rose adopted, during the Wars of the Roses, as the emblem of the House of York; but now it is considered that R. *alba semi-plena* or *suaveolens* was the chosen one. Recently Mr Graham Thomas noticed, both in his

own garden and at the Sunningdale Nursery, bushes of R. *alba maxima* which
were sporting back to the semi-double form. Until then the origin of the
double form had been unknown. As the two plants are identical except
for the fullness of the flowers, they may have accounted for the confusion
as to which one was the true Yorkist Rose.

We find the fragrant, semi-double, white R. *alba semi-plena* one of the
tallest-growing and hardiest of our shrub roses. The lovely flowers, with
their bright yellow stamens, have been perfectly portrayed by Alfred
Parsons R.A. in *The Genus Rosa*. In this fine book there is an excellent
likeness of the white-flowered form of R. *canina coriifolia* – one of the parents
of this Alba Rose, and one that, in its pink form, grows in a hedge at the
bottom of our garden. From this wild rose, R. *alba* has inherited its beautiful buds, with their long, leafy sepals and the wide and decorative bracts.
Gay orange-red heps are a feature of this tall shrub in the autumn and
make a fine display in the garden; they look charming against the background of large, grey-green leaves. A bush of white broom grows beside
the rose, and we generally have a planting of pure white foxgloves nearby,
which bloom at the same time as the rose and the Mediterranean Lily,
Pancratium illyricum. For centuries, hedges of R. *alba semi-plena* have been
planted round the fields of pink Damask Roses at Kazanlik, in Bulgaria,
where the blooms of these perfume roses are still used in the distilling of
attar of roses. An Englishman writing from Sofia in 1888 said that "Prince
Ferdinand has gone to visit Kazanlik, the Valley of Roses. The valley is,
at this season, full of bloom, and, with its countless thousands of rose
bushes, it constitutes a lovely scene."

Apart from forms of the Dog Rose and the Sweet Brier, the Great
Double White or Cheshire Rose, R. *alba maxima* was seen more frequently
in the hedgerows and cottage gardens throughout the British Isles than
any other semi-wild rose; and a very lovely sight it was too, with its large,
flat flowers, and luxuriant, greyish foliage, as it hung over stone walls
and hedges. Though our own Alba Roses have done magnificently in
Auckland, it was a great thrill to see these ancient roses growing on sites
where they had been established for a very long time. Of all the lovely
bushes of R. *alba maxima* we saw in the British Isles, one of the finest was
growing partly over an old, lichened, grey stone wall, and partly over a
slate-roofed outbuilding adjoining a charming, white-washed, stone cottage. The owner saw us photographing the roses and kindly came across

the roadway to invite us in to see her garden. Other Alba Roses grew near the house, and this Welsh gardener was delighted when we told her we were going to show slides of her rose in New Zealand, as it was the finest bush of its kind we had seen. This cottage was situated in the valley of the River Conway, in Northern Wales not far from Bodnant, Lord Aberconway's famous garden, which we had just been visiting, and from which one gets extensive views across this lovely river valley to Snowdonia. Several cottages attached to this property had Alba Roses growing against their walls and we were to see many more on our trip back across the Vale of Clued to Cheshire. This was not surprising as this Alba is called, also, the Great Cheshire Rose.

On our way south we travelled through the lovely country of Gloucestershire to visit Hidcote, the late Major Lawrence Johnston's famous garden. In the charming village of Chipping Camden – a village in which all the houses were built of warm-coloured Cotswold stone, and perfectly thatched – we saw more Alba Roses growing over cottage walls in company with other old roses, clematis, valerian, and our own grey-leaved *Senecio greyii*. In the peaceful valley of the Windrush we came across the tiny village of Lower Slaughter, near which were fine Alba Roses.

In Scotland this Double White Rose is known as the Jacobite Rose because of its association with Bonnie Prince Charlie. The legend goes that Flora Macdonald gave him the flowers of this lovely old rose to wear in his bonnet; and judging by the number of bushes of R. *alba maxima* we saw in our travels round Scotland in the summer, she should not have had much difficulty in securing these blooms. It was connected with royalty in England, also, as well as on the Continent. King George IV incorporated this Alba Rose in the floral decoration of his royal signature; and later, in 1846, the Prince Consort used it in a similar manner. King Christian IV of Denmark, who was enchanted with the Cheshire Rose, had plants imported from Holland—where it was grown commercially—and planted as a hedge in the Rosenberg gardens in Copenhagen. We saw immense bushes of both R. *alba semi-plena* and R. *alba maxima* in full and magnificent flower at the Roseta Communale in Rome. This lovely garden is situated on the Aventine, the Hill of Romulus, and faces out towards the Palatine, the Hill of Remus. Strangely enough one legend gives this spot as the burial place of Aventinus – a King of Alba: so we were charmed to see these Alba Roses flourishing on that warm and sunny hillside.

The French saint and martyr, Jeanne d'Arc, had an Alba Rose named in her honour in 1818. We grow other white-flowered members of this family in our garden—this time in the yellow and white border, where between the double Persian Yellow and Blanc Mousseux, Lamarque is trained on supports at its rear. The blooms of Jeanne d'Arc and those of R. *alba maxima*, when separated from their bushes, are not unalike; though those of Jeanne d'Arc are sometimes faintly tinged with blush in the centre as they first open, this shade quickly fading out to a smooth ivory. The foliage is not as large and coarse as that of the Great Double White, and is a little darker in tone: neither does the bush grow as tall, which makes it a useful rose for the smaller garden.

Maiden's Blush, a very lovely form of R. *alba*, was obviously grown in Italian Renaissance gardens, as it was depicted in famous paintings of that era. It was also described in *Parkinson's Herbal* as the Incarnation Rose —a rose "in most things like unto the White Rose, both for the growing of the stock, and the bigness of the flower; but that is more spaced abroad than the white is when it is blown, and is of a pale blush colour all the flower throughout." This is the Great Maiden's Blush, a particularly strong grower with greyish foliage and full, flat, warm blush-pink blooms which fade to cream at the edges and have a delicious scent. This is considered to be one of the loveliest of all the old roses. Actually, the plant we grow in our pink border is the one known as the Small Maiden's Blush, which, except that it is more compact in form, is similar to the vigorous and larger-flowered variety. All Alba Roses have lovely and distinctive buds, those of Maiden's Blush looking as if the tip had been cut off with a knife, leaving a blunt end. Whilst this may sound grotesque, the combination of leafy calyx and the greenish-blush undersides to the blunt petals gives a delightful and unique effect. When fully open, there is something very appealing about this sweet, fresh, young-looking rose, and we are charmed anew each spring when it first appears. Maiden's Blush was listed in a New Zealand catalogue in 1860; but, so far, we have not seen it in the very early gardens in the north, though it is an easy and a long-lived plant.

The Alba Celestial, has less full bloom than those of Maiden's Blush and the loveliest buds – buds which are exquisitely scrolled and only slightly blunted on the tip. The flowers are a warm soft pink in tone, the inner petals curving in round the yellow stamens. The leaves differ from those of the Albas generally, in that they are rounder and deeply cup-shaped, and quite pink-toned in the young stages. This, together with the mature grey-green foliage, gives the plant a distinctive appearance which, once seen, can never be mistaken. The colouring of both leaf and flower makes it an admirable rose for planting in a pink border or garden. Celestial was created in Holland towards the close of the eighteenth century and became known, later, as the Minden Rose. A legend connected with this name is rather interesting. When the men of the Suffolk Regiment were passing through a garden after this battle, they gathered roses and wore them in their head-dress. These roses were probably gathered from bushes of the Alba Rose, Celestial—the rose later being adopted by the regiment. However, a friend who recently visited the headquarters of the Suffolk Regiment told us that it is not this particular rose which is now worn by the men on state occasions, such as a monarch's birthday, but red and yellow roses showing the regimental colours. Apparently several other regiments that played their part in the Battle of Minden—the Lancashire Fusiliers, the King's Own Yorkshire Light Infantry, the Royal Welch Fusiliers, and the Border Regiment—all wear a rose on Minden Day, though it appears that they wear a white rose, possibly a form of R. *alba*.

All our Alba Roses have come to us from England; and we find they are not only valuable, but most accommodating plants, which thrive equally well in sun or shade. Our lovely bush of Félicité Parmentier is growing on the south side of the house with Madame Legras de Saint Germain and Koenigin von Danemarck—these Alba Roses being interspersed with fuchsias, and bordered, in spring, with pink and blue polyanthus. Félicité Parmentier has grown into an arching shrub—not an upright one; and the blooms, which come in tight clusters, are not as large as those of most of the other varieties. The pale pink flowers are tightly packed with deliciously scented petals which pale to cream at the edges, and later reflex back. The blooms open rather slowly and last well on the bush, giving a good display over a fairly long period. This year there were still flowers opening out on Félicité Parmentier when all other Albas were over for the season—an endearing trait, especially as the flower sprays last well in water and look charming in mixed bowls.

Madame Legras de Saint Germain is a beautiful Hybrid Alba with smaller, green leaves and almost thornless, whippy stems, somewhat resembling those of Madame Plantier, to which it may be distantly related.

It has the typical flat flowers of the Alba Roses, very full, with an entrancing hint of lemon-yellow at the base of the petals—an unusual colour
combination in this group. The buds, as in all this family, are lovely, surrounded by long and leafy calyx lobes. For one Christmas decoration we
were able to arrange a low bowl of Madame Legras in which leaves, buds
and fully open blooms were used to surround a tall red candle. As the
stems of this rose are rather flexible, it was necessary to wire a few of the
flowers—a practise we do not indulge in as a general rule. In a shady bed
at the rear of the house Madame Legras de Saint Germain has grown into
a tremendous bush which is always well covered with blooms in the
season. Behind it we have trained the lovely modern fuchsia, Whitemost,
up a wide brick chimney to a height of over ten feet. These two plants,
the rose and the fuchsia, make a grand display when in flower at the same
time. This year many of our Albas—including Madame Legras de Saint
Germain – and other summer-flowering roses, bloomed again in the
autumn, an unheard-of occurrence. Because of an exceptionally windy
and stormy season our old roses were cut back much earlier and much
harder than usual after flowering. Whether this was the cause of the second
burst of bloom, or whether it was just a freakish season, we shall not discover until we experiment next year; but, whatever the reason, it was
exciting and delightful to find such lovely roses producing a second crop
of flowers.

Belle Amour, with its semi-double, cupped flowers of salmon-pink,
though a very attractive rose, has not done as well in this garden as its
reputation warrants: so, this coming winter, we plan to move it out of
full sun, into a semi-shaded position, in the hope that it will grow more
vigorously. It was found originally in the garden of an old convent at
Elboeuf and appears to be of hybrid origin with some of the characteristics
of R. *damascena* in its ancestry. And last, but not least of our lovely Alba
Roses, comes Koenigin von Danemarck or Queen of Denmark. Anyone
who has read that delightful book *The Old Shrub Roses* will be familiar with
the lovely picture of this rose on the cover jacket. Its blooms a·e deeper
in colour than those of the other Albas we grow, being a vivid carmine-
rose at the base of the beautifully moulded and swathed petals, and paling
at the edge of the flowers. This rose makes a strong growing shrub with
coarse but attractive grey-green leaves; and flowers well in a semi-shaded
spot, each slightly flattened bud opening slowly till it attains its full beauty.

Alba Roses, though they flower only in the summer, can be recommended to add fragrance, harmony, grace and lasting beauty to a garden. In addition, they are easy to grow, and require very little attention throughout the year.

4   *THE ROSE OF THE PAINTERS:*
R. CENTIFOLIA

Its beauties charm the gods above;
Its fragrance is the breath of love;
Its foliage wantons in the air;
Luxuriant, like the flowing hair.

Sappho

THE NEWLY AWAKENED INTEREST IN OLD-FASHIONED flowers, be they roses, primroses, fuchsias, or pinks, is probably a sign of the unsettled times, and shows a desire on the part of many gardeners to recapture the quietness and the graciousness of bygone days. As well, flower lovers are beginning to appreciate their highly decorative value, both in the house and in the garden.

Bunyard, who wrote that delightful book *Old Garden Roses*, refers to *R. centifolia* as being of ancient lineage, the rose of the Greeks and the Romans. It was thought to have been lost for centuries, reappearing again in Holland, but this theory was recently disproved. The late Dr C. C. Hurst, working at the Cambridge University Botanic Gardens, unfortunately died before he had completed his study of the origins of the Genus Rosa; but he lived long enough to determine the fact that *R. centifolia* was a plant of complex origin—*R. rubra*, *R. phoenicia*, *R. moschata*, and *R. canina* being the four wild species that had been crossed and re-crossed by painstaking enthusiasts until they achieved success. Generations of selected seedlings produced, in time, a full and fragrant rose that differed greatly from anything that had previously been cultivated. It was so lovely that all the great artists of those days included it in their flower studies particularly the form known as the Rose des Peintres. Before Dr Hurst's dis-

▲ 5. Duchesse de Montebello

▼ 6. Pink Four Seasons Rose

▲ 7. Celsiana

◄

8. York and
Lancaster and
R. *trigintipetala*

covery concerning its origin R. *centifolia* was thought to have been the double rose depicted in ancient paintings, but it is now considered more likely that they were forms of the Autumn Damask, a full rose of at least sixty petals.

For over 300 years, from the beginning of the sixteenth century, when the earliest rose-red forms of R. *centifolia* were produced, to the middle of the nineteeth century, when such lovely types as La Noblesse, Fantin Latour, Blanchefleur and Paul Ricault appeared, Dutch and French breeders worked carefully and patiently to perfect this new type of rose. The Great Red Rose or Rose of Provence, and the Great Holland Rose must have arrived in England sometime during the sixteenth century, for Gerard lists them in his Herbal, in 1596, and mentions that they grew in his garden. John Tradescant the Elder was sent abroad, in 1607, to collect new plants for Robert Cecil, First Earl of Salisbury. He returned to England with bushes of this Rose of Provence, amongst many other lovely things collected. When in England we paid a visit to Hatfield House, which was built by Robert Cecil, and there we saw, on one of the newels on the staircase, a carving in wood of a gardener with a rake and basket. This is supposed to represent the famous John Tradescant, gardener to James I and Robert Cecil. Many old roses, some of which he may have introduced, are cared for in a special garden. A wing of an earlier palace still survives in the grounds of Hatfield House; and, in this old brick building, Elizabeth I spent some of her childhood before she was called to the throne.

The first Centifolias, being completely double, set very little seed; but later, to the joy of the breeders, a semi-double form appeared, which was to become known as R. *centifolia provincialis*. This was the red rose that, much later, was found growing happily in Lincoln's Inn Fields. It set seed freely, and from then on new varieties appeared each year until in 1825, one French nurseryman listed over a hundred Centifolias. Today only twenty-two of these roses are available commercially; though many more still may be discovered growing in old gardens on the Continent, and in the Commonwealth countries.

R. *centifolia* became extremely popular in France, where it was grown extensively round Provence and Avignon. In these districts, it was given the local names of Rose of Province, Rose d'Avignon, and the Troubadour's Rose. One of the roses which has been cultivated in Morocco for the perfume industry is a Centifolia, Rose de Grasse, which was introduced from Provence. R. *centifolia* is frequently referred to as the Cabbage Rose, though this is a dreadful misnomer, the thin-petalled, sweetly-scented blooms in no way resembling that coarse vegetable—it is the thick-petalled, full-bodied Hybrid Perpetuals that possess the true cabbage shape.

Gallica stems are clothed with bristles and a few small thorns; Damask stems have larger curved prickles; Centifolia stems are armed with short and long straight thorns—a useful guide when trying to establish the identity of these plants, particularly those of pure types. While Gallica leaves are smallish, dull green, and coarse, and the Damask leaves are large, round and of a softer green, Centifolia leaves are large, rough, and often coarsely serrated, even puckered and wrinkled in some cases. They have a distinctive, thornless petiole which hangs down from the stem, giving the rose a lax look. The buds vary considerably, depending on whether they favour one side of the family or another. Some have calyx lobes which do not extend very far beyond the bud; while others have such heavily foliated sepals that the flower appears to be surrounded by a ruff of green. In colour, the buds are often red just before they open, even in the white variety we grow, while the fully open flowers range from white through shades of pink to rosy-red, and even rosy-purple. None have any hint of yellow in their colouring.

Like many other old roses, these Centifolias flower only in the summer; but their foliage is handsome for the greater part of the year and colours well in the autumn and early winter—bronze tones predominating as the leaves age. It is advisable to train the taller varieties up a wall or through shrubs which will give them some support, or else they can be arched over and pegged down—this method being very successful with the flexible stemmed Tour de Malakoff, as it then throws out flowering shoots along the whole length of the branch. The stems of La Noblesse are stiffer and do not respond so well to this treatment; it is better left to its own devices, and this applies to the smaller varieties. Some of our Centifolia Roses came from overseas, but a few can be found in early gardens and even by the roadsides—roses such as the Rose of Provence, the semi-double, red, R. *provincialis*, Blanchefleur, Duc de Fitzjames, Paul Ricault, and R. *centifolia variegata*. During their season these old roses are a sheer delight in the garden, for their lovely perfume as well as their glorious flowers.

In a warm corner in front of a tall, grey, totara fence, there is a narrow raised bed which is planted with three interesting members of this family; this year a fourth, the low-growing Spong, is to be added where the raised rock edging curves in towards the steps that run down to the tennis court. The true Rose of Provence, that sweet and highly scented rose, holds pride of place in this border—a deep rose hydrangea separating it from a wide stone seat, which is placed under a rose arbour at the focal point of a formal sunken garden, in the centre of which is a rectangular pool. In H. C. Andrews' *Roses*, written at the beginning of the last century, he describes the Provence Rose as "the most fragrant of all roses, and therefore particularly desirable for, although it cannot be ranked amongst the rare, it is nevertheless one of the most beautiful. Its sweetness, joined to the abundance of its blossom, has rendered it an object of culture for the purpose of distillation, as it yields a much greater quantity of scented water than any other rose." A slightly raised bed suits this Rose of the Painters, as the branches are pendulous and the nodding flower heads inclined to hang down. The large, thin, outer petals of the handsome, globular blooms are a little paler in tone than the deep rose of the small, tightly-packed, inner ones. The foliage also appears to droop as each leaf stalk hangs slightly downwards, the leaflets themselves being blunt on the tip, deeply serrated, broad and a little wrinkled.

Next to this Provence Rose is R. *centifolia cristata*, the Mossy Centifolia or Chapeau de Napoléon. This beautiful plant has a similar habit of growth; and both these roses can do with fairly hard pruning, rich soil, and a generous amount of water and liquid manure when they are coming into flower. The Chapeau de Napoléon acquired its romantic name because of its heavily fringed and lacinated sepals, which grow in such a way as to give the bud the appearance of a French tricorne. The rose-pink flowers pale on their circumference and later assume lilac tints; they look enchanting nestling into this ferny, green collar, while the scent is that of the true old roses. Apparently this cresting on the flower buds has extended occasionally on to the leaves. William Paul, in *The Rose Garden*, described its unusual growth but, so far, we have not noticed it on any New Zealand plants although it is a rose that is seen frequently in our old gardens. R. *centifolia cristata* was found in 1820 growing wild on a ruined tower in Switzerland, and is thought to have been very like R. *centifolia prolifera*, an old Centifolia which grew in that district, and which was noted for its heavily fringed sepals. Edward Bunyard in *Old Garden Roses* mentions that the unusual rose, *prolifera*, was illustrated by Redouté; so does Roy E. Shepherd in *The History of the Rose*. It is described as another sport from R. *centifolia*, rather similar to R. *centifolia cristata*, and having the same very enlarged and heavily foliated sepals. The best plant we have seen of Chapeau de Napoléon was growing in a back country garden in Poverty Bay – the flowers on this plant appearing to be stronger in the neck than usual. When well grown, and covered with perfect blooms, R. *centifolia cristata* is a beautiful sight in the garden.

Petite de Hollande comes next in this border of old roses and a very lovely thing it is – quite upright with rich green, coarse, and very deeply serrated foliage, and perfect small blooms, often in sprays of three, that are held erect. A useful plant, this, for a rock pocket; and one which is described more fully in a later chapter. This coming season we are adding Spong to this small border: it is a rose which comes midway between Petite de Hollande, and the tiny De Meaux in size, one which we admired tremendously in England and which is now procurable in New Zealand. As all these roses flower only in the summer, we have planted along the fence at their rear two climbing roses which bloom in the spring and occasionally later. These are R. *sinica anemone*, with exquisite pale pink single flowers with a silvery reverse, and its deeper coloured sport, Ramona. Barbara Dibley and Lawsoniana, two large-flowered mauve clematis, are trained up this same wall and, if not allowed to seed, bloom on and off all season. This means that, with the rosy hydrangea for autumn colour, and cyclamen along the front of the bed for winter effect, this corner of the garden is gay all year.

Monsieur Dupont, who was in charge of the gardens at Malmaison in the days of the Empress Josephine, was particularly interested in the foliage of roses, and he bred two astonishing varieties of Centifolias. These were the Lettuce-leaved Rose and the Celery-leaved Rose. The latter, with deeply cut and serrated leaves, has not survived the passage of time, though the former is still available. One of Redouté's finest paintings was of R. *centifolia bullata*, or the Lettuce-leaved Rose—the Rose à Feuilles de Laitue, which has extra large, puckered and wrinkled leaves. From my window I can see a tremendous bush of this fine Centifolia which grows near the white Blanchefleur on top of a three-foot-high walled border. From this slight eminence, the thorny, strong, yet arching stems hang down: the unusual leaves are very drooping, and the flowers, extra large and heavy, of typical Centifolia pink. The lovely tall fuchsia, Whitemost, is trained on the broad trellis behind this old rose—a rose which has been in cultivation for over 150 years. The foliage colours well in the autumn; and the fragrance of R. *centifolia bullata* is rich and spicy—all one would expect of one of these cherished Roses of Provence.

Only two white centifolias are sold today—Unique Blanche or the White Provence, the oldest white in this group, a rose that originated as a sport from R. *centifolia*; and Blanchefleur, not as typical in bloom as the former, though still a lovely rose, and one we grow on our bank along with R. *centifolia bullata* and many other old roses. The bush has dull, rather coarse, dark green leaves, which do not hang down limply as they do in most Centifolias; and there are small thorns on the back of the petioles, suggesting a hybrid origin. Even the flowers are different; the packed, milk-white petals, blush tinted towards the centre, quickly reflex back, instead of remaining globular. But it is the buds of this variety that are exciting. Frequently, particularly early in the season, three of the calyx-lobes are heavily foliated along the edges, and the large, leafy sepals extend well beyond the corolla. Judging from pictures, these buds, which have a ferny appearance, must resemble closely those of R. *centifolia prolifera*, a rose related to Chapeau de Napoléon. Blanchefleur is found in old New Zealand gardens; but so far we have not come across either Unique Blanche or the sport Striped Unique. Long spurred aquilegias and fine coloured freesias associate delightfully with old roses; so many of them are planted on this long raised border.

A rose that is possibly related to Blanchefleur, and one that was sent us from an old country garden, is Paul Ricault. Here we find the same characteristics of thorns on the backs of the petioles—these are not found in the pure, early types—and very dark green, coarse, stiff leaves. Because of its free-flowering and vigorous habit Paul Ricault makes a great splash of colour in the garden, and well earns its position in an old-rose border.

Striped varieties appear in so many rose families that it is not surprising to find one amongst the Centifolias—a rose which originated near Angers in France over a hundred years ago. R. *centifolia variegata*—its common name is Village Maid—is a thorny vigorous rose which is found growing semi-wild in various parts of New Zealand as well as in old gardens. It has been well establshed in the country for a very long time. One particular stand of it, which we found by the roadside between Taihape and Mangaweka, had been known in this district for over eighty years. The lusty plant in our garden came from this spot many years ago: and, when we first saw it suckering freely and spreading right down a steep bank, we were most impressed with its vigour and abundant bloom. Hoary, lichened fruit trees grew near the rose; and it appeared as though the road had, at some distant date, been cut through the site of an old garden. Not far away was a bush of that lovely white Noisette, Madame Plantier, the Bride's Rose; while tangled up with the striped Centifolia was a pale, pink-flowered Gallica which we found out later was the lovely Antonia d'Ormois. On either side of the roadway were two frothing, arching bushes of R. *india major* a famous stock rose which grew freely throughout that hilly country and made the prettiest pictures in the fields and on the grass verges. Tall grasses and bracken were shading the roots of all these plants and helping to conserve moisture during the summer months. Village Maid or La Rubanée—it has several other names as well —produces globular flowers in great numbers, generally in small clusters. The full flowers are creamy-blush with rosy-lilac stripes; though, on the semi-wild bushes, this colour was intensified, probably because they were out in the full sun. Our bushes grow in the shade of a flowering cherry and of the tall double form of the Apple Rose of England; but they still flower freely; and we are able to gather long sprays in the season to include in arrangements of old roses.

La Noblesse is one of the beauties of this race—the fragrant flowers being very large, globular, and of an exquisite shade of pink and deep rose. Although it was bred over two centuries later than the original R. *centifolia* it has all the characteristics of an early rose—the thorny stem, large, lax leaves, and the deeply cupped flowers. It does not come into bloom until many of the others have finished flowering—a point greatly in its favour. This, also, is planted on a slightly raised site with the double pink R. *spinosissima bicolor* rampaging round its rather bare base. The ferny foliage of the small Scotch Rose thus makes an attractive ground cover in front of the tall Centifolia. Pink dianthus hang over the rock edging; and spring colour is assured by groups of rose-coloured freesias and pink *Gladiolus colvellii* between the roses—a good pink form of *Lilium speciosum* showing up well in the late summer against the grey stone wall at the back of the border.

One of the lower-growing Centifolias, Robert le Diable, is not unlike the Gallicas in the smallness of its dark, coarse, stiff leaves. The buds of this rose are exquisite when they open well, as the outer petals curl over, leaving the centre ones still furled. In colour, this rose is a slaty-purple, richly veined with crimson and scarlet. As the flower fades, the outer petals change to a soft dove-grey, and make an unusual but most attractive colour combination. With cerise and purple-toned fuchsias behind, and silver foliaged plants in front, Robert le Diable adds character to a border. Another rose of similar colouring, Tour de Malakoff, has much larger but thinner petalled flowers. This is one of the tall Centifolias, so we have placed it against a grey wall where its remarkable blooms of rosy-magenta, heavily veined with blue-purple, show off their subtle colours to advantage. As they fade, these blooms resemble in colour those of some of the richly hued Gallicas. Tour de Malakoff was bred in France over a hundred years ago, and has the elusive colouring of some of the old French silks—its papery petals earning for it the name Taffeta Rose. Two low-growing, winter-flowering shrubs planted nearby are *Ruellia macrantha*, with rosy-magenta, trumpet-shaped flowers; and the purple-flowered heliotrope or cherry pie, the carpeters used being *Omphalodes verna*, *Orchis purpurea*, and lilac freesias. These same smoky tonings are found in The Bishop, an interesting Centifolia which is often confused, out here, with the Gallica, Anaïs Ségales, as it has blooms of somewhat similar colouring. We first saw The Bishop in an old-rose garden near Waitara. The full blooms are not very large; but make up in colouring what they lack in size. The flowers, tightly packed with petals, open a cerise-magenta which quickly turns to violet and slaty-grey. We were shown this rose in England, where it is considered to be the same as the old French Gallica, L'Evêque; this, in the evening, more clearly approaches blue than any other colour. Anaïs Ségales fades to a blue-mauve and has the same effect in the garden late in the day, but there the resemblance ends, as The Bishop has slender upright non-bristly stems clothed with polished, smooth leaves quite unlike those of this Gallica.

One of our Centifolias was called after the Duc de Fitzjames, a descendant of James I through his natural son, the famous Marshal Berwick. This French noble was an enthusiastic lover of gardens, and a great admirer of Blaikie, who wrote *The Diary of a Scotch Gardener at the French Court*. Thomas Blaikie was first in the service of the Comte de Lauraguais, then with the Comte d'Artois—the future Charles X—and finally with the Duc d'Orléans—Philippe Egalité. While he was with the Comte d'Artois, Blaikie assisted Bélanger, who designed the great Bagatelle Gardens. One day, while he was planting the herbaceous borders, the Duc de Chartres and the Duc de Fitzjames came to visit Bagatelle; they were exceedingly pleased with what had been done, and Blaikie considered they had more taste than many who visited him. When we were in Paris recently we visited the famous rose garden at Bagatelle but could not find a bush of the Duc de Fitzjames amongst that lovely collection. Our plants, which came to us from two country gardens, one in Taranaki and one in Poverty Bay, are tall-growing and very free-flowering, producing masses of full, circular, quartered blooms of lilac-pink. Though the blooms, which come in large clusters, are inclined to be heavy and coarse, the Duc de Fitzjames makes an effective shrub in the garden. Here we grow it in front of vigorous large-flowered fuchsias of similar colouring, a carpeting of catmint covering the ground beneath the rose. Sacheverell Sitwell and James Russell in *Old Garden Roses* name Fantin Latour and La Noblesse as two of the most glorious Centifolias. The former was called after the great French painter of flowers and is an exquisite rose that grows into a very large, very free-flowering shrub. Actually, in our garden, it has now travelled up through a tall *Rhus cotinoides*, the smoke bush; and the two shrubs look delightful together, as the rose festoons down through the branches and out over the tennis court. It is not a typical Centifolia, since the Damask influence is very strong, both in the soft, uniform pink of the quartered flat flowers, and the heady perfume. These blooms, often with a green eye in the centre of the incurving small petals, come in clusters, and keep opening out for quite a long time, making it a plant that pays big dividends in a shrub border. On either side of this rose we have planted bushes of the low-growing, blue flowered *Ceratastigma willmottiana*; and these are cut hard back in early spring at the time when varieties of narcissus come into bloom.

In Chapter Six (Small Roses for the Rock Garden) we have described the Dwarf Centifolias, R. *parviflora* and De Meaux, interesting and exquisite plants which would be lost in a large border and need careful placing so that they can be seen to advantage. The Centifolias range in height from eighteen inches to over six feet; and in colour from white through pink to rosy-purple: they all enrich our garden with their heavenly flowers and wonderful scent.

. . . o'er the Rose
A veil of moss the Spirit throws,
And robed in nature's simplest weed,
Could there a flower that Rose exceed?

Flora Domestica by *Henry Phillips*

WHAT COULD BE MORE APPEALING THAN A PINK MOSS Rose, gathered fresh, with the dew still on it—the fresh pink and the softness of the mossy green never failing to enchant those who see it? This is the sweetest colour combination in this lovely and lovable family of the rose. Others are more striking—rich and warm in colour, or pure and cold and white; but none delight the heart more than the old Common Moss, the first rose of this type to appear, and still the most beautiful.

It is thought that the first Moss Rose appeared in France, on a bush of the Rose of Provence—the original R. *centifolia* or Cabbage Rose—which flourished in this area. No definite date is given for when this mossiness was first noticed, though it was near the end of the seventeenth century. A change in form from a bud mutation had occurred—not a change in colour as in striped sports; this produced very enlarged glands on sepals, calyx, flower stem and sometimes even on leaflets. These gave the mossy look and rich aromatic fragrance, which were to make this plant the darling of the rose world.

Early in the next century plants of the Moss Rose were sent to Holland and Italy, where they created great interest, and a little later they were brought to England from Holland. Breeders quickly became interested but it was some time before any great number were produced, though a single variety, which appeared a hundred years later and set seed freely, helped to create fresh and interesting roses. Most of the early ones were pale in colour; but when these were crossed with Gallicas in rich, dark shades, the first Crimson Moss was produced. Since then many others of deeper colouring have appeared; and now there are even yellow Mosses, modern developments which do not appeal to us, as do the old varieties we treasure in our garden.

We saw these unusual Mosses in France and in England, the finest specimens being in the Bagatelle Rose Garden in Paris. This was most interesting as William Paul wrote in the first edition of *The Rose Garden* in 1848, that: "I have heard persons, unacquainted with floriculture, maintain that they have seen pure yellow Moss Roses. A deception probably practised on them by a charlatan or some witty friend."

Moss Roses should be planted in good rich soil, in a warm position, and kept well watered as a guard against mildew, one of their enemies—the enlarged glands on the bud and stem harbouring this disease unless the bushes are well cared for. Like their relatives, the Centifolias, these roses need heavy pruning to keep them from becoming straggly; as well as the thinning out of old, poor wood immediately after flowering. As we grow only twelve varieties, the little labour involved is well worth while in return for the great joy these beautiful Moss Roses give us each year. The opening bud is one of the loveliest sights in the rose world. Pierre Joseph Redouté's painting of R. *centifolia muscosa* is a sheer delight; and artists, everywhere, have immortalised this entrancing flower. Its virtues have been extolled in poetry and prose. Edward Bunyard, who wrote *Old Garden Roses*, gives a romantic legend of its birth, from an old story:

"One day the Angel, who each day brings the dew on her wings, feeling weary, asked the Rose for shelter for the night. On awakening, she asked how this hospitality might be repaid. The Rose answered, 'Make me even more beautiful!' 'But what grace,' replied the Angel, 'can I give to the most beautiful of all flowers?' Meditating on this request, she cast her eyes down to the mossy bed from which the Rose sprang, and, gathering some, placed it on the young buds. Thus was born the Moss Rose."

A charming legend; and how like the softest of soft green moss is the covering of the buds, especially on the earliest variety of R. *centifolia muscosa*, or the Common Moss, which is anything but common, being a gem of rare beauty. We grow it near its parent R. *centifolia* or the Rose of the Painters. The blooms of the Moss Rose resemble those of the mother plant, being full and globular and of a delightful shade of rose. Both have the same heavenly scent; both have unfortunately, the same habit of drooping their heavy heads. This is their only failing; and, in the larger growing Centifolias, we grow the plants on a high bank, where we can look up at the nodding blooms.

Sporting was frequently to be seen on old roses, particularly on Centifolias and Gallicas, though the same thing does occur on modern roses. In New Zealand, recently, Prima Ballerina produced a pale pink sport which has been named Rima; and other modern roses have done the same thing in many parts of the world. It is not surprising, then, that the first White Moss occurred as a sport on the Common Moss. There had been some confusion over the name of this plant, apart from its botanical one, R. *centifolia muscosa alba*. In some books it is called Shailer's White Rose, as it is thought to have occurred as a sport on a plant in Shailer's nursery about 1790. It was known also as White Bath or Clifton Moss, some authorities stating that it was found in an English garden near Bristol, at another date, 1817. Whatever its name, it had the honour of being painted by Redouté; and is still sold and grown today.

We obtained our plant in New Zealand, and grow it in our white garden. Though this mossing on the bud and stem is extra fine, and the buds are beautiful, we do not find the fully open flower compares with that of the rose pink parent. For one thing, the petals are often not pure white—since a flush of pink shows on some of them; but it is worth growing for the buds alone. We have seen this rose growing in very old gardens throughout the country. Plants we saw in Akaroa had survived years of neglect before being moved into an old garden in this historic township. They, and some red and pink Moss Roses, had grown up through bricks, blackberry and grass alongside a fallen chimney on the site of a burnt out cottage near German Bay, on Banks Peninsula. These Moss Roses had suckered freely; so it was easy to find fresh-rooted pieces for removal. We saw this White Moss, also, in early gardens at Kerikeri and Rawene, and in an old cemetery at Thames; and we were told it used to grow on Okiato Point, the site of Mrs Clendon's historic rose garden.

White Bath later produced a striped sport which we saw overseas.

This is called Oeillet Panachée; we got a good photograph of it at the Roseta Communale in Rome, the bush there being of finer quality than the one we saw in England, which had been badly damaged by a late frost. Oeillet Panachée and the Single Moss were recently sent to us from an old rose garden in Nelson. Few of our mosses were bred till fifty years after the White Bath had put in an appearance, though in old gardens and cemeteries we have found bushes of the Crimson Moss, the first deep coloured one, and a highly prized plant in its day. William Paul in 1845 mentions seeing this Crimson Moss being trained as a pillar rose; and goes on to say that "some of our readers may doubt whether Moss Roses are suitable for this purpose; and writers have too often spoken of them collectively as being of dwarf and delicate growth. What will such say to a pillar formed with the Old Red Moss reaching to a height of fifteen feet?" We find this interesting, as our William Lobb grows to this height, and would do more if space permitted. Paul goes on to mention that wallflowers and fuchsias were doing well in the same soil in which the Moss Rose flourished; and here in Auckland our old roses, wallflowers, and fuchsias grow very happily, side by side.

From 1850 to 1890 French growers produced well over a hundred magnificent Moss Roses, though only forty are listed today. We saw a number of interesting varieties, that had previously only been names to us, at Roseraie de l'Hay near Paris. By the beginning of this century, Gravereaux, who built up this historical rose garden, had collected 135 Moss Roses to plant in a special area devoted to them. By this time, many subtle shades were appearing on the blooms—rich plum, smoky lavenders, and cyclamen-pinks—an inheritance from the rich tones of the Gallica ancestors.

Nuits de Young, one of the earliest of this group we possess, was bred in 1851. The small blooms, rich plum-purple and burgundy, are enclosed in reddish-brown mossing. This effective combination makes a charming rose, and one that the late Miss Constance Spry was fond of including in an unusual flower arrangement together with Cardinal Richelieu and Hippolyte, two dark Gallicas. In the garden, it makes a small upright shrub with dark rough foliage and very thin, wiry stems. Nuits de Young is not nearly as mossy as R. *centifolia muscosa*, but is a delightful plant for all that. Maréchal Davoust, another Moss Rose with red-brown mossing and large cyclamen-pink flowers with a green eye, was called after one of Napoleon's generals. When Napoleon was planning his march to Moscow in that ill-fated winter campaign of 1812, he sent this general on ahead to strengthen his hold on the Baltic—and to punish the Swedish renegade, Bernadotte—who would not keep his ports closed to the Russians. This association of plants with historic personages adds to the joy of rose collecting, and to the special interest in certain plants in our garden. During Napoleon Bonaparte's reign a number of his generals were honoured by having roses named after them, to say nothing of his Empress—the lovely rose called the Empress Joséphine or R. *francofurtana* being one of our garden gems.

Baron de Wassanaer appeared shortly after Maréchal Davoust. We grew it for a number of years before discarding it in favour of finer varieties. It has light crimson flowers of poor form and little mossing, lacking the quality of the true mosses, since it is a hybrid. We did hear of it once, however, proving itself adaptable by growing, quite effectively, as a semi-climber through a shrub. The year following the production of this Moss Rose, William Lobb, or the Old Velvet Moss, appeared. This, the most vigorous of all the mosses, has been a great success in our garden when treated as a semi-climber. It is growing on its own roots, the cuttings having been given to us in Christchurch—the original plant having come from Ilam, a fine South Island garden. In early summer, when this vigorous Moss Rose is smothered with hundreds of sprays of large, unusual-coloured roses, it is a truly breathtaking sight. The heavily mossed buds open out into flowers of rich crimson-purple; but quickly change to a slaty-mauve, odd flickers of cerise and royal blue showing in some of the petals. Two young Cornish nurserymen, William and Thomas Lobb, were sent to collect plants in South America by an English firm. Among the many things they brought back with them were some of the fuchsia species we grow here in Auckland. The Velvet Moss was named after the elder of these young plantsmen. Plants of William Lobb grow on two early graves in our oldest cemetery. These have suckered over the graves and out on to the grassy paths. They are scythed back annually when the tall grasses are cut, but they still produce lovely blooms. The stems, however, that are over ten feet high in our garden, are no more than eighteen inches tall on these neglected bushes.

When we first saw the plants, before the blooms had opened out, we thought they might turn out to be the dwarf Little Gem: so we were greatly surprised later on to discover that they were none other than our old friend William Lobb. This is an example of what good cultivation, or the reverse, will do for a plant. On the other hand we did see one plant of William Lobb growing in the midst of a field where cattle grazed. This spot had been the site of an early home: and the Moss Rose and Cloth of Gold had climbed together through an old lichened apple tree, the slaty-purple and gold flowers looking charming side by side. This plant was as tall as the one in the cemetery was low; but in both cases William Lobb was flowering freely, though the blooms were not as large as they are when the rose is well cultivated.

Général Kléber, whom Napoleon left in charge of his army in Egypt, was a kind, humane man, much loved by his men. The soft, lovely Moss Rose called after him has flowers of an exquisite pale pink that open rather flat, with a button eye. Large soft green leaves and mossing add to its beauty. Unfortunately it flowers for only a few short weeks—a great pity, as it is such a charming rose. Cuttings of Henri Martin, the finest red variety sold today, were sent to us from Wanganui but failed to strike. The original plant came out from England and did splendidly in Wanganui. Moss Roses are to be found in many of our old gardens and cemeteries; and a popular one in the past was Laneii or Lane's Moss, which was bred by Monsieur Laffay of France, who also raised other roses that we have in our garden —Fabvier, La Reine and Great Western. This fine, globular, very double rose, with fragrant flowers of a rich rosy-crimson tinted with lavender, is remarkably vigorous and free flowering; and was at one time recommended as a bedding plant. The deep rosy-coloured Moss Rose, Mrs William Paul, was sold out here at an early date, and is still a very popular garden plant, the buds, well mossed with soft green, being particularly appealing. A friend arranged some of these and other Moss Roses under an old-fashioned glass dome, a relic of our grandmothers' day; and they looked superb. The satin-pink, mossy Zenobia was another of William Paul's roses popular in New Zealand.

There were two dwarf Moss Roses, Little Gem and the Minor Moss. The former is described in Chapter Six but the latter one we have never seen, nor have we heard of it in this country, though French florists regarded it highly and treated it as a pot-plant. It was eminently suited for this type of culture and sold very well in the markets, the French always having made a feature of potted roses of various types.

All these roses were bred from R. *centifolia* or its hybrids; but the

Moss Roses that appeared in the family of the Damask Roses were recurrent in bloom, a trait which added greatly to their value in the garden. This type of Moss Rose has firm, rather brownish mossing, quite hard to the touch, and not nearly as appealing as the soft green mossing on R. *centifolia muscosa*. A rose whose origin puzzled rosarians for very many years was the Perpetual White Moss or Rose de Thionville, which appeared at Thionville in 1835. This grows into a tall, upright shrub and produces large sprays of bloom abundantly early in the season, and intermittently for the rest of the year. Though the mossing is hard and brownish-green in colour, the buds are attractive, and the half open flower quite enchanting; but the fully open bloom is rather a disappointment, and damages very easily in rough weather. The large, soft, pale green leaves are typically damask in character, as are the muddled looking petals of the flower.

Mr Graham Thomas found that plants of this Perpetual Moss sported back, in 1950, to the un-mossy Pink Four Seasons Rose, or R. *damascena bifera*, the Autumn Damask. This was most interesting, as it proved its origin beyond all doubt, particularly as the same thing occurred in the United States in the same year. We were able to tell Mr Thomas that a plant of the Perpetual White Moss or R. *damascena blanc mousseux*, planted in 1881 on a grave in the Grafton cemetery, had also reverted to the Pink Four Seasons Rose; both coloured roses, the white and the pink, the mossy and the un-mossy, coming up through the dog-daisies and grasses on the same bush. At first, we thought there were two rose plants on this grave; but a close inspection revealed only one bush. Finds such as this make rose collecting very interesting. We managed to get some clear colour slides of this example of sporting to take with us to England. Since then, we have heard of this reversion from white to pink—and, more uncommonly, from pink to white—occurring in many parts of New Zealand. This is particularly interesting, because in the case of the Pink Four Seasons Rose it produced, at one and the same time, not only a sport—which denotes a change in colour—but a bud mutation, which means a change in form from a smooth to a mossy bud.

On one trip down Coromandel Peninsula we stopped at Tararu and climbed up a steep and rugged path to an old cemetery where many gold miners and their families were buried. It had not been used as a burial ground for a very long time, so was overgrown and neglected; we found there many old friends among old roses, as well as one or two new ones.

These included the tall, handsome form of R. *canina agrestis*, or the Grasslands Rose, and a red Damask Moss. This rose had lovely crimson buds encased in firm brown moss, the fully opened blooms having the muddled look of some of the Damask Roses, quite unlike the lovely, cup-shaped flowers of the Centifolia Mosses. We found out afterwards that this Crimson Damask Moss was the very old Tinwell Moss, which had originated in the garden of a clergyman at Tinwell, in Rutland. It was one of the first deep coloured Moss Roses; and was much esteemed in the early part of the last century, plants being sold at one guinea each. The French Crimson Moss mentioned previously was deeper in colour and more double, but not such a luxuriant grower. The plant at Tararu is the only one of this type we have found so far.

The spot where the famous Maori canoe *Tainui* rested was just below the site of the old hillside cemetery where we found the rare red Damask Moss. Here, also, the famous Maori chief Hongi returned from Totara Pa after the treacherous massacre of a rival tribe. But Tararu is now a peaceful spot where roses sucker out from the graves, invading the pathways and creating delightful pictures from every angle. The stories and history surrounding these spots are fascinating; and help to fix the location of such roses as the Tinwell Moss in our minds.

Our most perpetual flowering Moss Rose is Salet, a rose sent to us from England, and which Dean Hole grew in his garden at Rochester. One year we pegged down the long branches of this Damask Moss; and were treated to a generous display of bloom, flowering stems appearing along the arching stems. As we were out of the country last year the plant was left alone, so had fewer blooms on longer stalks; but blooms of rather better quality. Wichmoss, a rose we admired in Italy, was bred from R. *wichuriana* and Salet. The Rev. J. H. Pemberton, creator of the famous Hybrid Musk Roses, recommended growing Salet and other Moss Roses on standards. Apparently, this was once a very popular way of growing them in England.

Blanche Moreau, a tall-growing, pure white Damask Moss with distinctive brown mossing, had as its parents two distinguished roses: the lovely blush-white Contesse de Murinais and the Perpetual White Moss. It is supposed to flower again in the autumn but we get few, if any, late blooms. We were able to procure this rose in New Zealand, where it is quite well-known. In a dry hot summer it needs water and extra manuring,

▲ 9. R. *alba semi-plena*

▼ 10. Koenigen von Danemarck

▲ 11. Félicité Parmentier

▼ 12. R. *centifolia*

if it is to bloom well in the autumn. Mousseline or Alfred de Delmas, unlike the tall Blanche Moreau, has grown into a dwarfer, more compact bush, which really does flower fairly perpetually. The blooms come in tight clusters and are only lightly mossed; but are very charming for all that, the colour being a creamy pink. Our plant, which came from England, is the only one we have seen out here.

Deuil de Paul Fontaine is a low-growing Damask Moss with dark stems, mossing, leaves and flowers. The blooms are large for the size of the plant, very full, and of a most extraordinary combination of colours —red, brown and near-black being easily discernible on the one flower. Unfortunately it produces very few flowers for us and is not a strong grower; Sacheverel Sitwell, in *Old Garden Roses* mentions the same fact. We intend to move it into a rock pocket and hope it will do better for us in the future than it has in the past.

Though new Moss Roses have been produced in this century, we do not grow them here. The lovely Madame Louis Lévêque was bred nearly seventy years ago. This is the newest of our old Moss Roses. It has the larger flowers, firmer stems, and upright growth of the Hybrid Perpetual from which it was bred. William Paul, writing in 1845, said that "the Perpetual Moss would appear easiest obtainable by hybridising the Hybrid Perpetuals with varieties of Moss Roses or Perpetual Mosses", and this plan was carried out in the production of Madame Louis Lévêque. The colour of the extra large, full, cupped blooms is a heavenly shade of pink —in fact, a perfect flower is an entrancing sight, though the mossing is rather sparse. We have had this rose for only two or three years but already it has won a place in our hearts.

If only the true Moss Roses flowered for as long as the Damask Mosses, they would undoubtedly be more widely grown than they are. Their short season of blooming excludes them from many modern gardens. It was interesting to read in *The Garden Companion*, published in 1952, that early Moss Rose enthusiasts endeavoured to overcome the brevity of their flowering period by not allowing the blooms on some bushes to develop before July—this was in the northern hemisphere of course – and by feeding and watering them lavishly as this time approached. In this way, they enjoyed early blooms on some of their plants, and late ones on others. Few would go to this trouble today, but we hope these old roses will not be forgotten or entirely neglected. Their buds, alone, should earn them a place in the garden, to say nothing of their rich aromatic perfume. More of these old treasures may still re-appear to enrich gardens. In the meantime, let us enjoy those we have; they are reminders of a gracious and pleasant age that has passed.

6

SMALL ROSES FOR THE ROCK GARDEN

A miniature of loveliness, all grace
Summed up and closed in little

Anon

WHEN A GARDEN IS BUILT ON SLIGHTLY VARYING levels, and has individual gardens within it, a useful way in which to link up these areas is to build a series of small rock gardens with pockets of varying size. These, used in conjunction with plantings of shrubs alongside winding paths, help to create added interest and also to segregate the various colour schemes. Thus a garden unfolds in a series of surprises. This can be achieved, even in a limited area, if correct proportions are used. On no account must the rock garden dominate the scene. It must fit into it naturally and unobtrusively.

Another useful idea for dividing off two portions of a garden (we used this scheme to separate the drive and carport area from the fuchsia and old-rose garden) is to erect a curving rock wall four feet in height with another lower wall in front of it. This forms a deep trough which can be filled with a suitable soil mixture and then planted attractively. Our local volcanic rock is easy to handle and kind to plants, so it was used for the walls. Cotoneasters and fuchsias are trained on to the rock at the back. We had put in two climbing forms of miniature roses, but these grew so rampantly that they had to be removed to make room for small roses and dwarf fuchsias spaced at intervals along the trough. China Roses love this spot; and some of the low-growing Polyanthus of the Seven Dwarfs

series add variety. With well chosen material to clothe the edge of the
lower wall this scheme can be of interest throughout the year. An inter-
planting of small bulbs and wood anemones adds colour in the spring;
and, for the autumn, crocuses and tiny cyclamen take their place.

The Centifolia family provide us with the oldest of our tiny roses.
Early in the seventeenth century several roses appeared which have
charmed, and still charm, gardeners old and young. Their origin appears
to have been uncertain, though they were first noticed some time after the
earliest forms of R. *centifolia* had been produced by Dutch and French
breeders. These were miniature forms of the Cabbage Rose called de
Meaux, and R. *parviflora*, or Pompon de Bourgogne. Whether they occurred
as sports, or came from seed seems to be still a matter for conjecture; but,
whatever their origin, as garden plants they are a sheer delight. Centifolia
de Meaux was illustrated by Redouté under the title, R. *pomponia*—the name
de Meaux being thought to have some connection with the flower-loving
Bishop of Meaux, Doménique Séguier, who was translated to the see of
Meaux in 1637. He spent much time in his garden; and although no special
mention is made of this small rose growing there, it does commemorate
his name.

There are two forms of de Meaux grown still—the pink and the white.
The latter is the one we grow in our rock garden; but we were able recently
to add the other one. The inch-wide, perfect blooms of the pale variety
are really blush-pink, shading to a deeper tone in the centre of the numerous
petals, though they do fade out to near white in the hot sun. They are
deliciously fragrant, and the miniature foliage is in keeping with the rest
of the plant. Like its relatives, the tall Centifolias, de Meaux will stand hard
pruning, and can be well fed—for its size of course. Actually, the deep
pink form is even more appealing. We were sent the wrong plant by mistake, but were delighted to acquire it.

On a visit to Rome last year, it was enchanting to find we could buy
tight little posies of de Meaux and dark blue forget-me-nots, both in the
shops and on the street stalls. These lasted in water for several days in
spite of the heat. They are so popular arranged in this manner that the
Italians find them a profitable crop to grow. In 1854 Thomas Rivers, a
noted rosarian, wrote that children loved these Dwarf Provence Roses,
and called them, affectionately Pony or Baby roses. Grown on their own
roots, they made charming edging plants for their small gardens. Artists

have painted them on china; and, in *The Scented Garden*, Eleanour Sinclair Rohde mentioned these diminutive plants as having the same fascination for people as have paintings of children by old masters.

In 1814 a mossy form of de Meaux appeared in a garden at Taunton, Somerset. It was noticed by a Mr Sweet of the Bristol Nursery who bought the plant for £5 and afterwards sold plants of it for one guinea each. Very few roses would sell at such a price today. It was thought to have occurred as a bud mutation of the de Meaux which grew in this garden. Unfortunately this mossy gem seems to have disappeared, in spite of the fact that it had a great vogue for years.

The de Meaux roses have always been associated with R. *centifolia;* but R. *parviflora*, or the Burgundy Rose, has been linked in some books with R. *gallica* or the Provins Rose, though now we find it amongst the Centifolias. This famous miniature was illustrated in the Kreuterbach of Tabernaemontanus in 1664, and later, by Redouté, Parsons, and Andrews. In various areas in France it became known as Pompon de Bourgogne, Pompon de St Francis, and Pompon de Rheims—an impressive array of titles for such a very small plant. One old French writer described it as growing wild on the hills near Dijon, but this was proved to be incorrect, as it was almost certainly a chance seedling of garden origin. There are two forms of R. *parviflora*—one growing to eighteen inches in height and the other one being a little taller. The more vigorous plant was flourishing in the Roseta Communale in Rome: and we later saw it in England and Ireland, and heard of it growing in beds in a walled monastery garden at Assisi. The smaller variety is the one we grow, and it fits very neatly into a small rock pocket. A keen old-rose grower from Waitara, Taranaki, generously sent me this treasure. It has neat greyish-green leaves, is compact, and holds its tiny, full, deep tyrian rose blooms and fat buds quite upright.

There are two slightly larger forms of the Dwarf Centifolias; these were greatly admired by the late Constance Spry and used by her in miniature flower arrangements. Spong, with looser pink blooms, is a little larger than de Meaux; and Petite de Hollande is taller still. We grow all three here. Spong we admired when we saw it overseas and were able to acquire it on our return to New Zealand. Petite de Hollande is a first rate garden plant, bushy, with fresh green leaves very coarsely toothed, and small, full, rose-coloured flowers. These are held quite erect – a trait which is, unfortunately lacking in the large Centifolias.

All these roses originated in Europe; but by the end of the eighteenth century another race of small roses was introduced into the western world from China, having arrived there by way of Calcutta and Mauritius. These roses have an interesting history. During the Han dynasties, before the Christian era, ornamental shrubs, roses, and flowers were cultivated so extensively that, in the end not enough food was grown for the people. So a ban was placed on the growing of beautiful but non-productive plants for a considerable length of time. The history of the China Roses during this period is not known: but by 900 A.D. the double forms were being depicted on fans and screens, while in 965 A.D. the artist Huang Chuan made delicate paintings on silk of the Old Blush China which are preserved to this day. This gives some idea of the love of the Chinese for their smallest roses.

The first forms of R. *chinensis* to appear in England had pink and red flowers. They arrived during the stirring days of the French Revolution and, in a small way, caused a revolution in the rose world. Wars or no wars, the breeding of roses went on in France and England; and Napoleon, at Josephine's request, allowed English growers free passage back and forth to France, to carry with them the latest plants for his Empress's garden at Malmaison.

Parson's Pink, or Old Blush China, is an excellent plant in every way but rather too large for our small rock gardens, though we find it extremely useful elsewhere. However, its small red relative is a plant that pays dividends all year. This is the Crimson China or R. *chinensis* var *semperflorens*. It was introduced into England by the captain of one of the East India Company's ships who discovered it in a Calcutta garden, though it had come originally from China. When he sailed for home, he carried with him a bush of the new rose, which he tended carefully throughout the long voyage. On his arrival in England, he presented it to a director of his company, Mr Gilbert Slater. This keen gardener propagated it and gave it to his friends, calling it the Bengal Rose, though it later became known as Slater's Crimson China. At first, on account of its thin stems and small stature, it was thought to be delicate, and was treasured and coddled in glasshouses; but, to the surprise of all, it was found to be extremely hardy and strong. There are two distinct forms of this small rose in our garden —one having about fifteen petals, the other over twenty. This is one of the

ancestral China Roses, the form with fuller, more cup-shaped flowers showing a white stripe on some petals, being the rose known as Miss Willmott's
Crimson China. French breeders were quick to acquire plants of this
rose; and very soon new varieties began to appear. We owe these men
a great debt, as it was from these China Roses that most of the wonderful,
free-flowering modern roses came.

In 1814 the Crimson China was introduced into New Zealand by
the wife of one of the men brought out from England by the Rev. Samuel
Marsden, who established the first mission station in this country, at Oihi,
near the Rangihoua pa, in the Bay of Islands. Later, in 1822, when the
historic Kemp homestead was built at the head of the Kerikeri inlet, a
border of this small red rose was planted along the front of the house,
cuttings having been brought there from Rangihoua. These bushes are
still to be seen; and the two-storied house, now occupied by Mr and Mrs
S. Kemp, is being preserved as one of our historic homes, the oldest
surviving wooden house in New Zealand. The little red rose then travelled,
in a remarkably short time, far and wide over the country, as it rooted so
easily from cuttings. It is now to be found in most old gardens and cemeteries, as is its pink form—the two being referred to affectionately as missionary roses. On a very early grave, dated 1864, in the small cemetery
adjoining the old Bishop Selwyn Church at Howick, are bushes of the
wiry Red China Rose; while nearby, at Keppoch Lodge, the charming
home built by Captain Macdonald a hundred years ago, and still occupied
by members of his family, are more bushes of the red and pink China Roses,
as well as many other old varieties.

One of our plants comes from Highwic, an historic home in Gillies
Avenue, Auckland. Another plant on the rock garden came from Akaroa,
in the South Island, where the French were granted land. Here, over a
hundred years ago, they built their picturesque houses, established vine-
yards; and planted their gardens with fine trees and many roses. Soon
British and French settlers were living in harmony in this sheltered and
lovely spot. In the very early days, an Englishman who arrived from England brought with him many rose treasures, which he planted in his garden
up in Grehan Valley. Most of them have survived, even through years of
neglect, and one of our plants came from this garden, having been given
to us by a later owner. Still another plant was sent to us from the Studholme
homestead, Te Waimate, in South Canterbury. When the old house was

destroyed by fire—a sad fate which has befallen so many early wooden buildings in this country—bushes of red and pink China Roses were burnt to the ground also. But they survived this ordeal, having been planted on their own roots: fresh new growth appeared the following season and, when we saw these roses at a later date, they were certainly full of vigour. In sun or shade, China Roses thrive, and brighten our rock gardens for most of the year; but to give them a rest they are cut back quite hard at the end of the winter. This seems to rejuvenate the plants. The only thing they must have is plenty of moisture; for if too dry—and it can be dry in Auckland—they are inclined to mildew, a family failing.

Recently, a friend, who had been staying on the island of Savii in the Samoan group, told us about the bushes of the small Red China Rose she had seen growing in this tropical spot amongst the gay crotons, hibiscus, and golden alamandas. Apparently it and the Pink China flourish also on other Pacific Islands; and certainly we saw China Roses growing vigorously in Hawaii. It is possible that these wiry roses were introduced directly from China into these islands and not by way of Europe.

Several other red China Roses, bred about 1832, found their way to this country at an early date, and all are suitable for rock garden work. Fabvier, a favourite with us, was called after General Fabvier who fought under Napoleon, and later, for Greek independence. His namesake has vivid crimson-scarlet flowers with a distinctive white stripe down some of the petals. The Old Curiosity Rose, Roger Lambelin, inherits this touch of white from its small ancestor, but in the Hybrid Perpetual the white appears around the uneven edges of the deep crimson-purple petal. During the last century, Fabvier was highly regarded as a bedding plant because of its compact growth and cheerful appearance—the wide open flowers showing an abundance of yellow stamens, and a white base to the petals.

Another China Rose of the same period is Cramoisi Supérieur or Agrippina as it was first called. It can be kept bushy by close pruning, but will grow taller if trained against a wall. Our bush has now reached a height of eight feet where it is allowed to grow up a trellis in company with the pale blue, small-flowered *Clemantis campaniflora* from Portugal. The plant, if cut back regularly, will stay reasonably small and compact, though it would always be taller than Miss Willmott's Crimson China. We have seen this rose trained up and across a wide verandah—but this was not the variety Grimpante which we saw in England, and which has slightly larger and more velvety flowers than the ordinary form of Cramoisi Supérieur. Our form of this Red China Rose was growing in many South Island gardens; Larnach's Castle on the Otago Peninsula, just across the harbour from Dunedin, once boasted a border of these cheerful Red China Roses. The small, full, crimson flowers appear in clusters; and if spent blooms are removed regularly a constant show of colour results. This is a favourite rose in old gardens here, and was apparently very popular with early colonists in the United States of America, who carried it with them as they moved westward, and planted hedges of it. We saw Cramoisi Supérieur frequently in France and Italy, though it is the pink Old Blush China, not a red form, that is more often used for hedges on the Continent and in New Zealand.

Louis Philippe, a third Red China, was listed by a Nelson nurseryman in 1860; but, so far, Nelson old-rose growers have not found it again in that district. Its full, rich red flowers have rounded, incurving petals which fade to blush in the centre. This rose is not in our garden; but R. *serratipetala* is—a rose that appeared at a much later date in a French garden, and that bears a strong resemblance to Louis Philippe, except that the edges of its petals are deeply and attractively serrated. They are so alike, otherwise, that one could have occurred as a sport of the other.

When in Sydney recently we paid a visit to Professor Waterhouse, the great Southern Hemisphere expert on the camellia family. He and his charming wife entertained us in their unusual garden, one part of it being entered through a Moon Gate. Here a gay Chinese pagoda was surrounded by large bushes of camellias—shrubs of the Orient and some of the largest we had seen; but it was the plants bordering the wide, flagged pathway running up to shallow steps in front of the beautiful, shuttered, early colonial house, that caught our attention. Behind borders of lavender were rows of Red China Roses, which Professor Waterhouse told us were known in Australia as the Lady Brisbane Rose. It closely resembled our Old Crimson China but perhaps grew a little taller. We can find no reference to the Lady Brisbane Rose in any of our old-rose books; the name must have been given locally in honour of the wife of an early Governor of Australia.

Blooms of a fine single pink China Rose were sent up to us from Nelson recently. These were three inches across, with deep rose-pink petals showing a wide white zone round the stamens. Good green foliage set off the small, but attractive, flower sprays. Apparently, this plant is of low stature so should be a good subject for the larger rock garden, especially as it flowers very freely in the depth of winter. There were two single varieties of pale colouring, one with very small blooms and the other, like the one sent to us, having much larger flowers. This must be the old Single Pink China.

An interesting story is told of the finding of still another miniature China Rose. This was discovered in the Swiss village of Mauborget, where the inhabitants treasured it as a pot plant and displayed it in their windows. When a Dr Roulet was travelling through this district, he saw the rose; and was so delighted with his unusual find that he immediately got in touch with a M. Henri Correvon, who was an expert on rock gardening at the Geneva Botanical Garden. This keen gardener left at once for Mauborget; but, to his distress, he found on his arrival that the village had just been destroyed by fire – the roses with it. By great good fortune, the inhabitants of a neighbouring hamlet, Onnens, also had pots of the same small rose, and they generously supplied Monsieur Correvon with cuttings. These he carried back to Geneva where they rooted with characteristic ease. The plant was afterwards named R. *roulettii* in honour of its discoverer.

It is grown universally now; and its perfect, double blooms, of a deep rose colour, smother the compact plant not only in early spring, but also, on and off, all year. In our hot climate the plants do not grow as compactly as we saw them overseas, but a suitable semi-scree mixture helps to keep them dwarf. This is a plant we value very highly. Shirley Hibberd, writing in the *Amateur's Rose Book* in 1874, said that the man who can grow a fuchsia well, can do perfect justice to the Fairy Rose; and strangely enough, in this garden we find that the dwarf fuchsia species and miniature roses do seem to thrive together. R. *roulettii* is the only one of the original Fairy Roses we have; but we grow and love many of their descendants. These range in size from the three inch red Peon up to the eighteen inch white Pour Toi. Some of the intermediate sized roses, such as Oakington Ruby, a red sport of R. *roulettii*, Perla Rosa, Perla de Montserrat, and Perla d'Alcanada, are absolute gems for the rock garden; more and more of these useful little plants appear yearly on the market.

Towards the end of the eighteenth century, two keen Scottish rosarians became interested in breeding garden forms of R. *spinosissima*, which grows wild in the British Isles and Europe, particularly in sandy, coastal areas. Before long over two hundred varieties of these low-growing, ferny-leaved roses were available, some having been produced also in England and Northern Ireland. Comparatively few of these extremely easy and hardy plants are seen nowadays, though we saw some fine varieties in the old-rose garden at Kew. As newer and more spectacular roses appear, the old tend to be thrown out of gardens unless they are of patricular beauty or have great historical value. The highly fragrant blooms on these Scotch or Burnet Roses, as they came to be called, are not of great use as cut flowers because of their thin prickly stems; but the bushes themselves are ideal for planting along the top of low rock walls; as hedges on dryish banks, in association with heaths; or amongst rock work, for they will soon throw out runners amongst the stones and clothe the rock in natural manner. The ferny foliage turns plum colour as the weather cools, and remains on the plants all winter, only dropping when the new growth appears: while the shiny, round, black heps are an added attraction. In our small garden they have to be kept in check.

One of our plants of R. *spinosissima bicolor*, a gay thing with rich rosy-lilac flowers that pale at the edges and on the reverse of the petals, found its way under a rock wall, and came up, full of vigour, on the other side. However, a spade soon gets rid of these invasive shoots; and we then give them away, as friends are always anxious to make a home for them. Our plant of the low-growing R. *spinosissima myriacantha*, a form of the species with semi-double white flowers, came originally from the site of the old burnt-out freezing works at Reotahi, where it was discovered growing amongst rock and sand near the sea-shore in association with a dwarf blue bearded iris. This spot is not far from Waipu Cove where Scotch families, who had emigrated first to Nova Scotia in 1817, and then to Australia in 1850, finally came to settle in New Zealand about 1856, bringing with them the Scotch Roses which are to be found still in some parts of North Auckland. Many of Otago's old gardens have thickets of Burnet Roses; and this is not surprising as it, also, was settled by Scottish families early in New Zealand's history. The Double White, the yellow, and Townsend, are all very charming. In *Roses for English Gardens* by Gertrude Jekyll and Edward Mawley, there is a beautiful illustration of the Double White Scotch Brier growing on top of a low wall at Munstead, and Miss Jekyll used other forms and colours of the same rose as dwarf hedges, which were clipped over annually during the dormant period.

An old-rose enthusiast of Wanganui, who always took a keen inter-est in all horticultural matters, had a charming garden near the lovely Wanganui River. Here, amidst shrubs and clematis, she grew many of the older roses on her terraced banks; and it was through her generosity that I acquired my plants of the sweet Double White Burnet and the slightly taller-growing Townsend. The latter has creamy pink flowers, with a faint hint of yellow at their base, and it is now settling in well amongst rocks at the back of a small pocket garden. We still hope to find the dwarf rosy-purple William III and the taller *R. spinosissima andrewsii*. We admired this very fine rose when we saw it in the late Major Laurence Johnston's garden, Hidcote, in Gloucestershire. In H. C. Andrews' *Roses*, there are several illustrations in colour of soft pink Scotch Roses with larger, fuller flowers. These were lovely and we saw similar plants, unnamed, in the old-rose border at Kew.

People who have been interested in my articles on roses in old gardens, milling and mining settlements, and by the roadsides often send me plants or cuttings of roses that they grow and wish to have named. Several times, the same small rose has arrived—similar to one that was listed in New Zealand as Hermosa. Apparently, old growers and breeders must have had difficulty in placing two roses in a definite family; for in some books they are listed amongst the Chinas, and in others amongst the Bourbons. These are Hermosa and Mrs Bosanquet; and both were bred in France. The former is well known today, though it is over a hundred years old – a small busy plant with lilac-pink blooms a little fuller than those of one of its ancestors, Old Blush China.

A climbing form of this rose, Setina, was doing very well in France and England; and we grow here another dwarf Bourbon Rose bred from Hermosa which has even fuller flowers, and a still more perpetual habit. This is called Champion of the World, and a very fine garden plant it is. In 1860 a Nelson nurseryman, William Hales, published a list of roses, and included in it was the name Mrs Bosanquet. Ellen Willmott, in *The Genus Rosa*, described it as a useful, sweet and free-blooming rose, having very definite characteristics of the China family. As it was a popular and much loved plant, it would be surprising if it had disappeared from our old gardens entirely. When we were overseas, we did endeavour to check up on this rose, with no success. The only plant we saw of that name was in France; and it was in a dying condition, quite useless for identification purposes. This was a big disappointment, as no one in England could help us either. However, on our arrival home in the spring we found the first blooms of the new season out on our little plants—the best we had seen, in spite of an abnormally wet winter. The flowers grow in clusters on wiry, typically China stems; but the blooms are much fuller than those of the China Roses, being flat and quartered, and of a delicious shade of blush pink, deepening in the centre—in fact, they look like miniatures of the flowers of Souvenir de la Malmaison, another member of the Bourbon family. Remembering that there was a coloured illustration of Mrs Bosanquet in Dr Julius Hoffman's *The Amateur Gardener's Rose Book* we brought some buds and fully opened blooms indoors and placed them alongside this reproduction—the only picture of this rose that we have seen. The two were so alike that we hope now that we have found the old favourite of 1832. Mrs Bosanquet was called after the wife of one of the finest rose growers of that time, who owned a large private collection. We intend to send bud-wood to England later this year, and hope to get this matter finally cleared up by experts. At the present time, in the middle of an extremely dry and hot summer, the blooms are only half the size of those we saw in the spring, and are not opening so well. All are showing their China ancestry in the deepening colour of the outer guard petals.

If we had not seen those early flowers in their first spring glory, we might still have felt doubtful about this rose. When studying Mrs Gore's *Rose Fancier's Manual* at the Royal Horitcultural Society's Library in London, trying to find further information regarding Mrs Bosanquet, we did come across a description of another small rose of a similar type, Pompon de Wasennes; but as no one we spoke to in England had heard of it, either there or on the Continent, and as it was not listed in this country, we came to the conclusion that it was unlikely to have been brought out to New Zealand. However, whether our charming rose is correctly named or not, it is a firm favourite here.

In 1879, a long time after the introduction of Mrs Bosanquet and Hermosa, a dwarf rose appeared in the family of R. *sempervirens*—all the other offspring of this rose being rampant climbers. It has several names: Little White Pet, Belle of Teheran, and Little Dot, the last name being the one used in New Zealand. It is the second name that conjures up delightful pictures of the Middle East, though Belle of Teheran never grew in Persia,

France being the country of its origin as well as of all its large relatives. Its big clusters of small, tightly-packed, creamy flowers are exact replicas of those of its tall relative, Félicité et Perpétue. We grow it in the trough garden against a dark rock wall where it shows up splendidly, producing masses of flowers for months on end (unlike its summer-blooming ancestors), and this in spite of the southerly aspect.

Moss Roses have a great appeal to young and old, so we were very delighted when a friend from Gordontown, herself an enthusiastic and knowledgeable old-rose grower, sent us Little Gem. It was bred in England; and Dean Hole called it "a gem of purest ray serene – a ruby set with emeralds, having crimson flowers surrounded with green moss". Grown in a rock pocket, in not too rich a soil, Little Gem keeps very dwarf, even in semi-tropical Auckland. Being on its own roots, it is now beginning to sucker, and should soon fill its small bed. The unusual dianthus, Waithman Beauty, makes a fine edging plant round this small Moss Rose: the ruby-red flowers, with two flashes of white on each petal, tone beautifully with those of Little Gem, and give added colour to this pocket throughout the year. The full, rosy-carmine flowers and fat buds of Little Gem are a joy to behold, as they are held quite erect; but unfortunately, like its small relative de Meaux, it is summer-flowering only.

The plant collector, Robert Fortune, sent seeds of a form of R. *multiflora* from Japan to a French nursery some time after the middle of the last century. After they became established in France, they were crossed with the Dwarf Pink China Rose, R. *chinensis minima*. The result of this union between two widely differing families was another new race of roses, which quickly gained recognition and popularity. These low-growing plants were called Polyantha Pompons because of their many-flowered clusters of tight little blooms. The earliest plants raised were very small – admirable plants for the rock garden – and several of them were brought out here. These were Paquerette, the earliest; and a white form we do not grow; also, Anna Marie de Montravel, Golden Fairy and Mignonette. We treasure our plant of Anna Marie, and wish we knew something of the lady for whom it was named. It is an enchanting plant, with large clusters of small, violet-scented white flowers; and clean foliage of a metallic green. We came across this rose in a lonely spot in the middle of the wild Waioeka Gorge; but our plant came to us from Pompallier House, Russell, where Bishop Pompallier established a Roman Catholic

Mission to Western Oceania in 1839. As Anna Marie de Montravel was not bred till 1879, it could not have been brought out here from France by the Bishop himself, though he is credited with having brought out plants of the pink and red China Roses. Whether he did bring them or not, he certainly grew and loved these small roses; and, on an early visit to Akaroa, he took plants south with him. Old residents there still refer to the Crimson China as Bishop Pompallier's Rose.

Mignonette, another of this group amongst our rock garden plants, is a delightful, pale pink Polyantha Pompon which is charmingly illustrated, in standard form, in one of Gertrude Jekyll's books. In a country garden at Te Pora, Tokomaru Bay, we saw a fine collection of old roses; and nowhere in our travels did we see better specimens of Chapeau de Napoléon or the Duc de Fitzjames. It was one owner of this property who sent us little Mignonette. This sheep station is in the Poverty Bay area, so called because of the inhospitable treatment meted out to Captain Cook by the Maoris when his ship called in there.

A small, perpetual-flowering rose—another cross between R. *multiflora* and R. *chinensis*—is of great use to us as it can be used for edging as well as for the rock garden. It has single white flowers, pink tinged at first, which come in large sprays for such small plant. Except for its size and free-flowering habit, it is typical of the larger parent, even to the heavily fringed stipules. There is a similar plant with pink flowers: we saw it once in a Dunedin rock garden.

Next to Mignonette we grow Gloire des Polyantha, one of its seedlings, with larger, semi-double flowers of white and rose. This rose was sometimes used as the stock on which miniature standards of the smaller Polyanthas were budded. A close relative of Gloire des Polyantha – it, also, was bred from Mignonette and another, unknown rose – is Georges Pernet. The flowers of both roses are cup-shaped and semi-double; the colour of the latter is richer, tones of peach and apricot suffusing the pink petals. Recently we were sent a rose from Akaroa which appeared to fit this description of Georges Pernet, the blooms resembling in shape those of Gloire des Polyantha. Another old-rose grower thought it might be the Polyantha, Baby Betty, with flowers in the same toning. Now the two roses are being grown side by side; and later we shall have positive proof of their names. This Akaroa rose, being taller, is not suitable for a position on our rock garden; so we have planted it beneath R. *chinensis mutabilis*, both roses having blooms of similar soft subtle tones.

A keen Auckland rock gardener presented us with the scarce Gloire des Polyantha, and also with Perle d'Or, one of the famous Sweetheart or Buttonhole Roses, the other one being Cécile Brunner. Unfortunately, we grow only the climbing form of the latter plant; but, strangely enough, it has produced this season several very low-growing branches at its base, which are flowering profusely. From these we intend to strike cuttings and hope, by so doing to acquire also the dwarf form. In many parts of the country, a rose of the twentieth century, Bloomfield Abundance, is frequently mistaken for the much older Cécile Brunner; though there is a vast difference in their growth – Bloomfield Abundance producing much larger, lighter-looking sprays of small pink flowers with leafy calyx lobes – the flowering stems showing bracts instead of leaves.

The pale pink flowers of Cécile Brunner are even more perfect in shape than the salmon-yellow blooms of Perle d'Or; but both are popular here for bridesmaid's posies. Though it came into the country about the same time, the sulphur yellow Etoile d'Or is seldom seen, though it grows in an old garden in Hawke's Bay. R. *multiflora* was one parent of these roses, the others being Tea Roses. This accounts for the perfect shape of Sweetheart Roses blooms, as compared with those of Mignonette and Anna Marie de Montravel which were bred from the Dwarf Pink China.

In the rock trough are three interesting China Roses seldom seen, and rather unusual. Rival de Paestum is our only white China—really a creamy-white, with loosely nodding blooms and dark mahogany coloured foliage. This gem, which looks well against a background of volcanic rock, possibly rivalled in beauty the roses grown by Greek gardeners at Paestum, in the days of Nero's might. Indica Alba, Ducher and Irène Watts all China Roses, were listed here in early catalogues—the two former are pure white ones we do not grow; but the last named, a beauty flushed with pink and salmon, adorns our trough garden. Rival de Paestum was one of the parents of another rose we grow nearby. This is Madame Laurette Messimy with loosely semi-double blooms of rose and salmon flushed with yellow—a rose from which Irène Watts was bred. Queen Mab is further along the wall, a beauty with extra full blooms of a rosy-apricot, a vivid orange base, and dark reddish foliage. Unfortunately, the heavy petals cause the blooms to open badly in wet weather—a trouble which never occurs with the more loosely petalled Chinas. William Paul, who

▲ 13. Tour de Malakoff

► 14. Common Moss

15. Maréchal Davoust

16. Perpetual White
Damask Moss "sporting"
(also known as
Blanc Mousseau)

bred Queen Mab, considered that it would become an excellent plant for massing in beds; and also recommended it as a buttonhole rose. Mr A. W. Anderson, in his book *How we got our Flowers*, mentions that a visitor to William Paul's garden, on being shown this new China Rose, suggested he call it Queen Mab—the Queen of the Fairies. Mr Paul solemnly considered the problem; then asked, with all the severity of the upright Victorian, "Was she a good woman?" Queen Mab is rarely seen in New Zealand. Our plant was sent to us by an enthusiast who grows many old roses in her country garden near Pirongia Mountain. She discovered it in her district; and very aptly likened it to a Gloire de Dijon in miniature. Actually, although the same tones prevail, the colour is a little richer in the small plant. We sent this rose to an old-rose authority in England recently.

It never fails to amaze us that so many of these old treasures are still to be found throughout New Zealand; and that all give an excellent account of themselves when planted in a suitable environment, away from modern roses.

7

TALL CHINA ROSES AND THEIR TEA-SCENTED RELATIONS

'Tis the last rose of summer,
Left blooming alone,
All her lovely companions
Are faded and gone;
No flower of her kindred
No rose-bud is nigh,
To reflect back her blushes,
Or give sigh for sigh.

Moore

WHEN WE VISITED THE DUBLIN BOTANICAL GARDENS at Glasnevin, the first thing we saw as we entered the gate was a bush of Old Blush China in a small fenced enclosure. A plaque was attached to the railing, and on it was printed this verse from the song, *The Last Rose of Summer*, written by the Irish bard Thomas Moore. What a delightful tribute to a simple and modest little pink rose! We certainly agree with what Dean Hole wrote so long ago, that it deserved a place in the mixed garden and in the shrubbery, (the brave old Monthly, the last to yield in winter, the first to bloom in summer). Nothing pleased him more than the prettiness of a wayside cottage clothed with honeysuckle, jasmine, and China Roses, and fragrant with sweet-brier, wallflower, clove and stock.

Probably the most generally grown and most loved of all the China Roses is Old Blush, a form of R. *chinensis*. The late Dr C. C. Hurst, working on the evolution of these roses at the Cambridge University Botanic Garden, decided that there were characteristics of both the Crimson China and the wild Tea Rose of Burma in Old Blush China. He did not consider it a direct hybrid, but a plant that had been produced, after generations of crossings, by early Chinese horticulturalists.

This pink rose grows into an attractive bush, generally four to five feet in height, taller if it is given some support. It is covered for the greater part of the year with dainty, rosy-pink flowers in sprays. As these blooms deepen with age there are generally several shades of pink, rose, and pale carmine on the bush, creating a chintz-like effect against the green of the older leaves and the reddish-brown tones of the young shoots. The fresh scent, though not strong compared with the heady perfume of some old roses, is nevertheless very sweet, particularly now in mid-winter; but it is the generous way in which Old Blush produces its blooms during the cold season which is so appealing, as it is nearly always possible to fill a low bowl with its small flowers.

The following lines, written for the northern hemisphere, give a clear idea of the real value of this rose and the high regard in which it has been held:

> Roses blooming in December,
> Blooming on a cottage wall,
> Lovely are these simple flowers,
> Nature's kindly gift to all.
> How they cheer the winter weather,
> When the days are dark and drear. . . .

As soon as it was established in England that China Roses were really tough and hardy, not frail and delicate as was at first surmised, nurserymen and gardeners tried out plantings in newly settled, industrial areas. This was to see whether they would survive the effects of soot and fumes satisfactorily, before large rose-beds of newer and more expensive roses were laid out. Nowadays, when roses are so easily obtained and so inexpensive, most people would try first and worry afterwards.

It is amazing to find the Pink China Roses growing in such diverse ways. Hedges of them are quite common here—as they were in the south of France, especially in farming districts. We have seen them climbing up through felled trees to reach the sun, and growing as bushes on children's graves. On a steep hillside behind Pompallier House in Russell, overlooking the lovely Bay of Islands, a long pathway was edged with Old Blush China in memory of the French missionary, Bishop Pompallier, who loved the Red and Pink China Roses. They were planted in partial shade, beneath tall pines, but were flowering quite freely. In most old mission settlements bushes of the Old Blush China can be seen, and recently we heard of it growing in a small cemetery in the Te Akau district, just north of Raglan

Heads, where a Wesleyan mission was established about 1850.

Our bushes are growing in a pink, red and brown border where they consort very happily with a number of useful perennials and foliage plants. Another pleasant idea is to group bushes of Old Blush China with lavender and rosemary in front of a grey stone wall, the wall itself clothed with large-flowered clematis in shades of blue, mauve, and pink. There is no end to the number of ways in which this hardy and accommodating rose can be used, though it is no longer planted in conspicuous beds: its role is rather a quiet unassuming one.

One of the notable things about the China Rose is that the light-looking new growth springs right from a central basal point to fan out at the top in triangular shape. Another interesting feature is the fact that, whereas in the Damasks, Albas, Centifolias, and Tea-Scented Chinas the flowers tend to pale with age, those of the pure China types do the reverse —a pale pink bloom turning to rosy-red, and, in some cases, to deep crimson. This is a useful distinguishing feature, as it is typical of all Pink China Roses and many of their hybrids; it is also a tendency in some of our modern roses. As China Roses bloom practically all year, hard pruning at the end of the winter cannot be practised without sacrificing many flowers. Cutting off spent blooms, and the occasional removal of old wood right from the base, are all that is required to keep them healthy and floriferous. Mildew can be their enemy in Auckland's hot, humid climate; but modern sprays and plenty of water help to combat this unfortunate tendency. When these roses are found in a neglected state near roadsides or in old gardens it is noticeable that they are frequently heavily shaded at their roots with grass, weeds, and litter. This helps to conserve moisture in the ground around the bushes, and keeps the roses in good heart.

The history of the China Roses is interesting. Because of the difficulties encountered by Europeans in getting permission to explore the hinterland of China, the wild form of R. *chinesis* was not discovered as soon as the double cultivated forms. Dr A. Henry found it, in 1885, growing in a gorge at Ichang, in Hupeh. It was climbing up through trees with the aid of its wicked, hooked thorns. This tall rose, R. *chinensis spontanea*, had solitary, single, pink to red flowers, not the large flower sprays seen in the dwarfer forms introduced from Chinese coastal gardens—forms which had arrived in England at the end of the eighteenth century. We owe the old Chinese horticulturalists a great debt; for, without their painstaking work, we would not now be growing the Hybrid Chinas and Hybrid Teas in our gardens. They took a keen interest in selecting and perfecting the best varieties; and it was these, the double Red and Pink China Roses, that caused such a sensation when they reached Europe. Reading extracts from *The Gardener's Magazine*, published in England in 1828, we were amazed to learn the number and variety of China Roses growing in a Woking garden so soon after the introduction of the original types. There was the White Monthly Cluster, the Red Monthly Cluster, the Old Blush China, Barclay's New Purple China—probably the *purpurea* we saw overseas—the dwarf, small-flowered Chinas, and the Yellow Tea-scented China. This last, a famous rose, is no longer in existence in England though it still grows in its native haunts in Southern China and Northern Burma. There is no doubt that these small, wiry roses had a great impact on the rose world of those times.

For many years we have grown an unusual China Rose that we purchased in New Zealand, believing it to be Le Vésuve or Lemesle. Not only was it sold to us as such; but E. A. Bunyard, in *Old Garden Roses*, gives a description of a rose called Lemesle (Vesuvius) which fits our plant perfectly. He speaks of it as having a flower the size of Old Blush China, with pale pink central petals and dark exterior ones—the whole bloom finally turning dark red. The short red pistil, almost level with the disk, was another distinguishing feature. It was not till we were shown Le Vésuve in several English gardens that we realised there must be a mistake in nomenclature in either the English plants or the New Zealand ones. The rose we saw overseas had a large flower on a weak stem; and looked far more like a Hybrid China than the pure type. In fact, an American old-rose authority considers that Le Vésuve fits in quite well with a bed of Hybrid Teas. Our little rose would certainly look out of place in such company. English authorities are interested in it; so we are sending bud-wood overseas in July.

A rose found in Bermuda a few years ago, which was considered by experts to be one of the ancestral Chinas, appeared to be not unlike our rose: so we sent slides to the United States, where an American old-rose enthusiast had made this discovery. He did not consider that our so-called Le Vésuve resembled the rose he had found. In a copy of the small English journal, *The Rose*, the Bermudan rose was described as having a comparatively small flower, with ten to twelve petals that opened pale pink and grew to deep crimson. The accompanying black and white photograph of the rose in its deepest stage showed a bloom of similar form to our Le Vésuve, both in shape of bloom and size of leaf—the latter being larger and less pointed than those of Miss Willmott's Crimson China. On the other hand, Dr Gordon Rowley, writing on Ancestral China Roses in the *Journal of the Royal Horticultural Society*, in June 1959, does not mention any pink tones in the flower of the Bermudan rose, though the extra height and larger leaves are referred to.

One thing Le Vésuve and the Bermudan rose both have in common; they enjoy heat, and thrive in a sunny location. Both have small flowers, tallish growth, and stems and leaves showing the influence of tea-scented relatives. We shall look forward to getting a further report on the identity of this most attractive and quite unusual China Rose—as well as of several others which we wish to have named.

In a chapter entitled *Curiosities of Rose Growing* Shirley Hibberd writes: "there are on record many curious kinds of roses that, to the superficial, appear to belong properly to the land of dreams, but the wise man will not banish them thither in great haste". Certainly these freaks, some of them quite charming and delightful plants, do add a great deal of interest to a garden. There are the well-known Mosses to start with—those most appealing of roses—to say nothing of the rose named after Napoleon's hat, with its heavily fringed sepals shaped like cockades. There are the striped roses, fully described in another chapter, and the spotted Alain Blanchard, a lovely Gallica which we photographed at Sunningdale. The two Hybrid Perpetuals, Baron Giraud de l'Ain and Roger Lambelin always arouse special interest because of the white frosting round the uneven edges of their petals. There are rose freaks with green steeples in the heart of the flowers, as we have seen them on our bush of Tricolor de Flandre —in fact, one rose, called the Steeple Rose, is known to have produced a tier of steeples. Then there are the blue roses which have already been mentioned. Pliny spoke of black roses; and, centuries later, M. Villaressii, of Monza, in Italy, claimed to have produced black China and Tea Roses —though English growers were sceptical about them at the time, as none had found their way across to England. The darkest rose we have seen was the near black, Baron de Bonstetten, with another old Hybrid Perpetual, Empereur de Maroc, running it a close second. There is even a rose with variegated leaves, the Wichuriana hybrid Achievement, and lastly there are these three curiosities of the China family, R. *mutabilis*, the Changing Rose; R. *viridiflora*, the Green Rose; and R. *serratipetala*, with its carnation-like, fringed petals.

R. *chinensis mutabilis*, or Tipo Ideal as it used to be called—a rose that was painted by Redouté for *Jardins des Plantes*—has dainty, single flowers that change daily from soft yellow to buff-rose, and then to crimson before they finally fall. A large bush crowded with blooms, looks as though dozens of different shaded butterflies had alighted on it and were just going to fly off again at any moment. There is no definite information about the history of this changing rose, though in Roy E. Shepherd's *History of the Rose* he suggests it could be a sport of the variety *spontanea*. Its modern counterpart is the well-known Masquerade, though this is a heavier looking rose than R. *mutablis*.

Our plant, which is continuously in bloom, grows against a tall brick wall—the light, airy, chameleon-like flowers looking well against the background of reddish-green foliage and mellow brick. We keep this rose in a special spot, away from modern roses. It would look quite incongruous against them, the gaiety and lightness of effect being ruined. R. *mutabilis* has now reached a height of over twelve feet and is still steadily climbing. We have read of it reaching to the eaves of a tall house. It is a constant source of pleasure to us; so it was with great interest that we saw it planted below a balustraded terrace in front of our hotel at Stresa, on Lake Maggiore, in Northern Italy. These bushes were quite as tall as ours and equally floriferous, and had been artistically trained up beyond the terrace and balustrade on the tall iron light standards that flanked each side of the wide, curving steps. This hotel garden was full of interesting roses, and all were beautifully cared for. Many were trained up tall palms that flanked the paths running down to the lake, the palms and the roses growing quite happily together.

R. *viridiflora*, the Green China Rose, is known also, as R. *monstrosa*—being one of the rose curiosities. Where some of our friends admire its strange flowers, others dislike it on sight, and can find nothing to recommend it as a garden plant. It was known to be in cultivation as early as 1743; but it was not sold commercially till 1856. Like all China Roses, it does extremely well on its own roots, and soon makes a densely clothed, upright shrub from which flowers can be cut all year. Many deeply serrated, enlarged sepals make up this remarkable bloom. At first the colour is a clear, rich green; later, bronze and russet tones appear, and at this stage the flowers remain on the bush for weeks. They do not wilt or drop, are carried in upright sprays; and finally just dry off. It pays to cut a number of the older blooms from time to time, as this forces fresh growth for the winter. These flowers are lovely in green and white arrangements, with variegated foliage, or with other old roses. Charming unusual shoulder sprays or posies can be made with them, and they possess the great advantage of not fading or wilting easily. Tall fuchsias, such as the richly coloured General Montgomery, Aunt Juliana or Othello can be trained up behind the Green Rose to add interest; and a few carpeting plants, such as *Astilbe crispa*, *Viola hederacea* and *Primula juliana*, added underneath give colour at odd seasons. Lady's Mantle, *Alchemilla mollis*, with attractive feathery sprays of yellowish-green flowers and grey-green kidney-shaped leaves, is a good edging plant, toning well with the Green Rose, and its neighbour, the burgundy-red Cardinal Richelieu.

An uncommon rose, R. *chinensis serratipetala*, was discovered in a French garden in 1912; and given the name of Rose Oeillet de Saint Arquay. It grows more strongly with us than in the gardens we saw overseas, though our plant was sent out to us from England. It is as tall as the best form of Old Blush China, but the flowers are fuller, crimson on the outer petals with the inner incurving ones of a lovely soft shade of pink. Each petal is veined with a deeper shade, serrated and fringed like those of a picotee. These unusual features make another of the rose curiosities: and the fringing adds great charm to the flowers, which come in upright sprays. When in Honolulu recently, we were amazed to see a long hedge of a vigorous Red China Rose in front of breadfruit trees, crotons, and golden alamandas. It appeared to be the same as Louis Philippe, a Red China that was being sold in New Zealand by 1860. The blooms on this rose were identical with those of our R. *serratipetala*, except for the pinked petal edges: they were full, globular, and paler in the centre. We sent close-up studies of this rose in Honolulu to an English expert; and he was also struck by the resemblance between the two.

There is no definite record of R. *serratipetala* having sported from Louis Philippe. However, re-reading an article on Ancestral China Roses, we did notice that Louis Philippe was listed with the words "carnation sport" following it. Unfortunately, the writer does not say that this rose is synonymous with R. *serratipetala*. Still, this is a very interesting point, which we hope to hear more about later. The tropical heat and rain of Hawaii apparently suited this red rose, as there was no sign of mildew on these hedge plants, and they were very free-flowering. If we allow R. *serratipetala* to become too dry in the summer, it is a martyr to mildew: frequent heavy watering is essential to its well-being, particularly as our clay subsoil is inclined to crack during a period of prolonged droughts, even with the addition of plenty of compost.

In the days before the Revolution, French rose growers liked poetical names for their roses, such as Agathe Triomphe de Vénus, or Cuisse de Nymphe; but after the Revolution breeders offered their roses in homage to great men in order to seek their protection, men such as Napoleon and many of his generals and statesmen. Friends and relations were honoured in a similar manner; but dedicating roses to great men was a dangerous pastime, when fortunes were turning at the spin of a wheel. After the Battle of Waterloo, a sweet pink China Rose we grow, Napoléon, was hastily renamed Madness of Corsica—though why such a modest rose should have been called after such an aggressive tyrant is hard to imagine. I have before me some of the smallish blooms of Napoléon—a rose which was sold in Nelson in 1860, plants of it being sent to Government House and the Domain in Auckland the following year. It is not as tall-growing as the Pink China, but has more and paler petals,—these being shaded with rose. In typical China fashion, these blooms deepen in tone as they age.

Vibert was the first French rose breeder to sell roses commercially; it was he, also who rescued thousands of rose bushes and took them to safety on the Marne, when the Allies were preparing to march on Paris in 1815. He bred, in 1825, a rose from a China-Bourbon cross that was to become famous as a stock rose, and also as the parent of a great number of red Hybrid Perpetuals. This was Gloire des Rosomanes, a rose which was greatly esteemed in its day, and which was grown very extensively in the south of France. At La Mortola, on the Italian Riviera not far from the French border, we saw tremendous bushes of this semi-double, brilliant red rose, looking very effective on the steep Mediterranean hillside. In its early days it was cultivated in pots so that these could be sold, laden with flowers, at Christmas time. Mrs Earle, in *Pot-pourri from a Surrey Garden*, called it a good rose for a warm wall or a pergola because of its rich, velvety-red flowers – this colour being transmitted to its descendants in full measure. Actually we saw very little of Gloire des Rosomanes in

England; and, so far, we have not found it in New Zealand, though it may be in the country, as so many red China Roses do flourish here. We procured our bud-wood from an old-rose nursery in England. Gloire des Rosomanes is used very extensively as a stock rose on the Pacific Coast of the United States, where it is known as Ragged Robin; and Mr Hunter of the Plant Diseases Division of the Department of Scientific and Industrial Research, in Auckland, is anxious to experiment with it as a stock. It may succeed up here in the north, where the climate is mild, as it has been so successful in California.

A charming rose, Fellemberg, which Miss Willmott described and Alfred Parsons illustrated so well, in *The Genus Rosa* as R. *chinensis multiflora*, was known in France as La Belle Marseillaise. This was another China-Multiflora cross. Fellemberg as well as Gloire des Rosomanes, was a great seed parent, and was used most successfully for producing new red varieties – our ever blooming Gruss an Teplitz being one of the offspring of these two. Fellemberg later enjoyed great popularity in England, where it was considered one of the freest-flowering of all roses. Though it is now listed amongst the Chinas, Rivers, in *The Rose Amateur's Guide*, called it a dwarf Noisette. It is far from dwarf with us. We grow it up a white trellis against the house, where its large corymbs of glowing rose-crimson flowers look most effective for months on end, being particularly fine in the autumn, when the flowering sprays seem to be longer and stronger. Tall-growing, large-flowered modern fuchsias in tones of carmine, rose, and lavender make ideal companions for this generous rose. In George Taylor's *Book of the Rose* he describes what he calls an impressive shrub, which he saw growing in a Huntingdonshire garden. The owner told him that it was Fellemberg, and that it had been a large plant twenty-five years previously, when he took over this property. In all those years, it had never failed to be smothered with flowers; and he suggested that the health and vigour of this rose was due to the fact that it was growing on its own roots. Except that it is more vigorous than the true Chinas, Fellemberg resembles this side of the family rather than the Multiflora. On a visit to Lady Londonderry's famous garden, Mount Stewart, which is situated on Strangford Lough, some miles south-east of Belfast we saw, as we left the Shamrock Garden to enter the West Sunken Garden, an old Irish yew, round the base of which were planted South African bulbs, and the China Rose, Fellemberg. The rose had hooked itself on to the tree and had climbed right up to the top: the glowing flowers looked beautiful against this sombre background.

We are always pleased when a rose we have brought out from England not only lives up to a good reputation, but even exceeds it. Such a one is the Hybrid China, Général Schablikine—a very desirable rose in every way. Clean, healthy stems and foliage—the latter a fresh blue-green—and abundant bloom, even in the depth of winter, characterise this ninety-year-old rose. Even in these days of beautiful, mid-twentieth century innovations this is a rose that can unashamedly hold its head high; which it does literally, as the flowering stalks are firmer than those of most members of this interesting family. The double, almost quartered blooms of rose, flushed with salmon and buff, come on erect, well spaced sprays which make a wonderful indoor decoration when the cold weather sets in. We do not prune Général Schablikine except to cut flowers for the house, and to remove from the base periodically the oldest branch. Neither does it require much spraying; which is a great point in our humid climate. It is trained, with other old roses, along a white trellis on the western side of the house. Pink and cream fuchsias are planted between the roses on this wall, and considerably enhance the general effect. Pastel, Pink Quartette, Crinoline, and Marie Louise are excellent fuchsias for such a position.

Marie Louise is also the name of one of our Damask Roses, and we were most interested recently to discover how many roses bear the same name as fuchsias, even some of those in our own garden. Among them are the Damask, Rose of Castile; two Albas, Maiden's Blush and Joan of Arc; the Moss, Zenobia; the Bourbon, Champion of the World; the climbers, Cloth of Gold, Electra, Penelope, Ramona and Flora; the Teas, Général Gallieni and Nancy Lee; the Hybrid Perpetual, Commandant Félix Faure; the modern roses, Queen Elizabeth and Mission Bells; and the miniatures, China Doll and Frosty—some tall, some short, some old, some new, but all of them interesting plants.

One winter, when motoring from Christchurch to Dunedin, we saw the gayest rose growing through a low, white picket fence, on to the roadway. The lady who owned this cottage garden did not know its name though she said it had grown in that spot for many years. So far, it is the only plant of its kind we have found, and we could only surmise at its name until we saw the China, Madame Eugène Resal overseas, and realised it was the lovely rose we had seen at Makihikihi. We are thankful that our colour slides of this China Rose turned out so well; for the cuttings, so generously given, failed to strike after being carried round the country for three weeks—this was before we learnt the art of sealing them in polythene bags. Madame Eugène Resal has vivid, semi-double flowers of a rosy-flame colour, shading through to orange round the clear yellow stamens. The bud and the foliage are both delightful. In fact, we are most impressed with the quality and number of leaves on this plant in such cold weather. We grow its parent, Madame Laurette Messimy and its grand-parent, Rival de Paestum—actually, it is a sport of the former rose, which is rather amazing, as it has more substance in its petals and richer colouring than has Laurette Messimy. A month ago, on a trip to the South Island, we saw this rose again. The garden and picket fence were neglected, the cottage gone, and the China Rose was looking very sick. On our return trip some poor cuttings were gathered; and these struck, so a charming rose has been saved for posterity.

A rose with a romantic association, having been named in honour of Louis XVIII's mistress is the semi-double, coppery-pink Comtesse du Cayla. The base and reverse of the petals on the nodding blooms are lightly tinted with yellow. Though our plant came from a Waikato nursery, this China Hybrid grows in many old gardens in this district. One elderly friend, who had a large, typically twiggy bush of Comtesse du Cayla, always had a bowl of this warm-coloured rose on her table in winter. If picked in the bud, it lasts fairly well indoors in cool weather; and can look most attractive when arranged with coppery-toned foliage. We grow it against a rock wall on which are trained soft creamy-pink fuchsias; and during most months of the year one or other, or both, of these plants are in flower.

Over the years we have grown a great number of Tea Roses in this garden; but, as our interest in old roses increased, we were anxious to include amongst their number the ancestors of many rose families and so make our collection more complete and comprehensive. With this end in view, we gradually eliminated, here and there, roses that were not signifi-cant. Either they lacked historical interest or we had too many of the same type in the garden, and naturally retained those that for colour, or per-fection of bloom, appealed to us most. This was the case in the Tea Rose family. Though we finally discarded Safrano, for instance—one of the earliest Tea Roses to be brought into the country, and the one most frequently seen in old gardens—we did grow it and other slightly later ones for a number of years; and were able during that time to study and photograph them for our slide library. So in one way, we feel, they are still with us: and can thus be included amongst the roses to be described in this chapter.

The history of these Tea Roses is fascinating. They were bred from the small Red and Pink China Roses and the Pink and Yellow Tea-scented Chinas. The advent of the wiry China Roses into Europe has already been described; but the two more delicate, Tea-scented Roses, which arrived a little later on the scene, were destined, also, to cause a stir in the rose world. It is sad that they have not survived the rigours of life in a new environment. These were two forms of R. *indica odorata*. Both were natural hybrids of R. *chinensis or indica*, and two Burmese roses—R. *odorata gigantea* and R. *odorata ochroleuca*, which grew in the warm valleys of Southern China as well as in Burma, in close proximity to true forms of R. *chinensis*. From these four plants, the two small Chinas and the slightly larger Tea-scented Chinas—all of which survive in their native lands—many lovely, perpetual-blooming roses were bred, their free-flowering habit being a rich inheritance from their Far Eastern ancestors.

Present day botanists have proved that in R. *indica odorata* or R. *indica fragrans*, as illustrated by Redouté, there are many characteristics of R. *chinensis* though the former has a different habit of growth, the new shoots springing mostly from the branches, and not always right from the base as is the case with the true China Rose. The smooth leaves are larger; the wood is not as thorny and grows more strongly, while the flowers are much bigger and fade as they age. In R. *chinensis* this habit is reversed and acts as a sure means of identification; for in mature blooms the colour darkens by several shades. However, both roses have one fault in common, and that is a tendency to have weak necks and hang their heads— a fault that is frowned upon by modern growers and gardeners.

R. *odorata gigantea*, one of the parents of R. *indica odorata*, and the grandparent of our fine Tea Roses, is a rampant grower, covering vast areas in Burma, its native land. We do not grow this rose, though we treasure two of its evergreen, free-flowering, and extra vigorous children – the Australian-bred cherry coloured Nancy Hayward, with glowing single blooms, and the rosy Lorraine Lee. However, we hoped to see and photograph R. *odorata gigantea* in either the British Isles or on the Continent, as we knew of various gardens in which this immense rose flourished. Unfortunately, we never found it in flower, but we were able to admire the magnificent bronze-green foliage, and large heps the size of apples. These are collected and sold in the bazaars at Manipur, since the Nagas relish their sharp flavour. Dr Rowley, who was connected with the Bayfordbury Research Station in Hertfordshire, kindly gave us some fine slides of the six-inch, creamy-white, single flowers to bring home with us; and these also give a good idea of the beauty of the yellow buds and very prominent stamens. We saw one plant there—it reached to the eaves of a lovely old brick building beside the formal rose garden. We also saw this tremendous rose—the most vigorous in the world—in the late Sir Cecil Hanbury's garden, La Mortola, on the Italian Riviera, and at Mount Stewart, Lady Londonderry's wonderful garden on the shores of Strangford Lough, where it partly covered three sides of a large pergola framing a sunken garden. A related form, with smaller, whiter blooms, *R. cooperi*, was, to our delight, in full bloom in Rome, where it covered an archway in the Roseta Communale. Another variety was described by Ellen Willmott and illustrated by Alfred Parsons, R. A., in *The Genus Rosa*, under the title *R. chinensis* var. *grandiflora*. This rose, considered to be a natural hybrid of *R. odorata gigantea*, is not listed today; but Canon Ellacombe, who wrote *In a Gloucestershire Garden*, grew it at Bitten, and gave a charming account of its healthy green foliage, and large, single, white flowers flushed with pink at the edges of the petals.

It is of great interest to us to know that the descendants of these large Burmese Roses were Hume's Blush Tea-scented China—so called after the man who imported it from the East in 1809—and Park's Yellow Tea-scented China, which was introduced in 1824 under the auspices of the Royal Horticultural Society. The latter was thought to be a cross between *R. chinensis* and *R. odorata ochraleuca*, a yellow-flowered form of *R. gigantea* that was discovered in Manipur later than its hybrid, Park's Yellow China. This rose was painted by Redouté from a plant growing in the Empress Josephine's garden at Malmaison. Both the pink and the yellow forms of the Tea-scented Chinas acclimatised well in France, where breeders soon saw their great potentialities. However, growers of new varieties were at first far from successful in the British Isles; and this was put down to the rigours of the climate; but later it was discovered that those budded on *manettii* stock, and subsequently hard pruned, generally failed to make good bushes. So other stock, such as Multiflora de la Grifferaie, and forms of *canina*, *rubiginosa* and even *banksiae*, was given a trial, with much better results. Plants were developed, also, on their own roots; and though this way proved tediously slow, it did in the end produce sturdy and long lived shrubs, especially when pruning was cut down to a minimum. Many of the grand old Tea Roses seen in our gardens have been developed in this manner and huge bushes, producing flowers over many months, have resulted. Still later, particularly in France, it was discovered that, by budding the more delicate Teas on earlier and hardier forms of the same rose family, successful results were obtained. Lamarque, a favourite here, and Solfaterre, were used as stocks for such varieties as Maréchal Niel and Gloire de Dijon. They proved their worth, since hardier strains resulted.

Fine Tea Roses have graced our gardens for 150 years. Few are listed today, but a large number were catalogued by the old New Zealand nurserymen, and good specimens are still to be found in early gardens and cemeteries. Each year, more of these roses disappear as large gardens are cut up and roadways widened. This is one of the prices we pay for progress. Before too many are destroyed, let us describe some of the brave bushes that still survive in many parts of New Zealand.

One of the earliest Tea Roses was raised in England in 1838, by crossing Smith's Yellow Tea with Park's Yellow China. This was bred in Devon by a Mr Foster, and was named appropriately, Devoniensis. For a long time it was considered to be the best English-raised Tea Rose, but we were surprised to hear that it had deteriorated in that country, except in very mild and favoured localities. Actually, we cannot call to mind seeing one bush of this rose in the British Isles, which rather bears out this statement. Twenty years later a climbing form appeared, which is still to be found in many New Zealand gardens—the low-growing, bushy Devoniensis being seen less frequently.

Three particularly fine climbing specimens come to mind. One is growing in an old garden in Wanganui; another, a tremendous plant, very free-flowering and healthy, is growing in the garden of one of Auckland's historic homes, Highwic; still another is growing in a field at Waipawa. When this last-named home was established in Hawke's Bay 100 years ago, the four-acre garden was planned in the traditional English style, part of it being a formal area surrounded by trees and shrubs. Over an iron archway the climbing form of Devoniensis was planted; and, though this portion of the garden was abandoned long ago and the arch has since rusted away, this Tea Rose—which would now fill a large room—is still standing as it grew, quite unsupported, the tremendous branches holding it erect. It has not been pruned for a very long time; so has spread in all directions, sharing the honours in this field—where stock now peacefully graze—with other old Tea Roses and a yellow Buttonhole Rose. In this garden Devoniensis is one of the earliest roses to come into flower.

Because of the creamy colouring and rich texture of the large, full, rather flat blooms, this English Tea Rose is sometimes referred to as the Magnolia Rose—a name which suits it well. The splendid reddish-green foliage acts as a fine background for the pale beauty of the flowers, which are sometimes tinged with a soft buff at the base of the thick petals. At one time Devoniensis was used as a stock on which to bud more delicate Teas; and was found to be eminently satisfactory for this purpose. We have often tried to grow this hardy rose from cuttings; but so far, we have been unsuccessful—which is perhaps just as well, as space would not permit us to do this splendid plant justice now the garden is fully established.

In New Zealand, wherever there are old gardens and settlements, huge, hoary bushes of the early yellow Tea Rose, Safrano, are sure to be seen. One of the parents of this early rose was the famous Park's Yellow Tea-scented China. At one time Safrano ranked high as a florists' flower, because of its lovely bud; but modern roses have quite ousted it from this position. It still gives a good account of itself in many districts where early settlers were established. If left completely unpruned, and given the support of a hedge, Safrano will grow to a tremendous size, as we saw it in the Gisborne district where it was mixed up with Catharine Mermet—a creamy-pink Tea Rose. The hoary branches of the two roses were carrying an amazing amount of bloom for such neglected plants. In the rays of the setting sun, the flowers of Safrano glowed—the apricot-buff petals with a sulphur-yellow base being washed with rose on the back.

On another trip, we saw a splash of yellow roses behind a weather-beaten country store. When we asked the owners—one tall and thin, the other round and jolly—whether they knew the name of their rose, the jolly one put back his head, roared with laughter, and said, "The rose! We couldn't tell you. We're far too busy to worry about roses here!" A young man, then appeared on the scene; he lived nearby and volunteered to show us the yellow rose. We went to the back of the store, struggled

17. Irene Watts

18. Rival de
Paestum

19. Mrs Bosanquet

20. Hermosa

through a tangle of ginger plant, tu tu, and bindweed, and climbed a high pile of rubble behind a tumbledown shed in order to view this treasure, which turned out to be an ancient bush of Safrano. On a later trip to the same district, we were interested to see that new owners were having the old store repainted; the rubbish, the shed, and rose had all disappeared. Another bush of Safrano grew in a hedge near the Taurikura Post Office and Store, not far from Whangarei Heads. In a Whangarei old-rose garden, Pa Mairie we saw a sulphur-yellow sport of Safrano, Isabella Sprunt, which was also a popular Tea Rose. These early yellow roses were, at one time, grown extensively in the South of France; they did remarkably well in that mild climate. In fact in the early part of the last century, yellow Tea Roses were in great demand in the markets, where they were sold in pots, sometimes in bush form, and sometimes as low standards. The heads of these plants were partially enveloped in coloured paper in such an elegant manner that buyers found it hard to resist them. One small enclosed garden at Versailles was planted entirely with yellow Tea Roses; and Safrano, being one of the earliest, must have been amongst their number. In Italy also, about the same period, these new roses flourished and added much to the variety and beauty of the autumn garden.

Safrano was the parent of many yellow to coppery-toned Tea Roses, one of which was Madame Falcot, a particularly free-flowering autumn rose, a little larger and of slightly deeper colouring than its parent. The bud of Madame Falcot, plants of which grow in the Panmure district, is charming; so when this rose, in turn was crossed with R. *multiflora*, a famous button-hole rose, Perle d'Or, was produced. Some time later, another rose, which was in this country at an early date, the rosy hued Madame de Tartas, also was crossed with R. *multiflora*, another buttonhole rose, Cécile Brunner, resulted from this union.

A hundred years ago, a pure white Tea Rose, Niphetos, ranked high as a cut flower because of its elegant tapering buds and tulip-shaped, lemon-tinted flowers. It was generally grown under glass in England, as it was not a robust plant out-of-doors, and the blooms damaged easily. Both the bush and the climbing forms were available here, and grew well outside in milder areas, as we saw them growing up in the North. But it had never been as universally grown and loved as its offspring, the Hybrid Tea, Mrs Herbert Stevens, whose white flowers are in great demand by florists during the winter months. One old lady told me that she had a steady source of income from the blooms of this free-flowering rose. We find it a great asset in our white garden; two tall standards, at key points, produce hundreds of flowers each season. We have now discarded our climbing Mrs Herbert in favour of Lamarque; but we did once see this rampant form making an amazing picture, as it climbed up through old lichened apple trees which were in flower and fruiting at the same time. Beneath the trees, pink and white belladonna lilies were in bloom; while white geese, dark blue swamp hens, and black cattle grazed amongst the large leaved taro and arum lilies.

A rose which combines the desirable qualities of sturdy growth, healthy, persistent foliage, lovely flowers, and the habit of blooming almost continuously, certainly merits a prominent position in any garden. Such a one is the old Tea Rose, Souvenir d'un Ami, which was bred in 1848 in France by Beluze, who raised the famous Bourbon, Souvenir de la Malmaison. Rivers, describing Souvenir d'un Ami, said it would be hard to imagine a more beautiful rose. It was sent to us as a rooted cutting many years ago; it is now a seven-foot shrub, and a real garden treasure. The mature leathery leaves, which show a purple sheen on their undersides, particularly in the autumn, roll under slightly at their edges—these features are characteristic of the rose and are an aid in identification. The smooth young stems are practically thornless, the fat, globose heps being depressed on top, unlike the pear-shaped ones of the China Roses. The large, slightly cupped flowers are quite circular in outline—their colour is a soft rose slightly flushed with salmon, with a deeper tone in the outer petals. In the autumn, the general tone of the rose darkens by several degrees until it matches the rosy-carmine colour of its immediate neighbour, Papa Gontier. The first and last blooms of the season are particularly lovely—after a very hot and dry summer the bush is an absolute picture, with its biggest crop of flowers for the year. Even in the dead of winter Souvenir d'un Ami brightens the garden with its cheerful blooms. Lightly pruned after each burst of flower, mulched with compost or farmyard manure, and well watered, this stalwart Tea Rose astonishes all who see it. A white sport of American origin, Souvenir de S. A. Prince or The Queen, was being sold in New Zealand at the turn of the century; but so far we have not seen it in any garden.

Madame Bravy, or Alba Rosea, one of the early Teas and a rose that became famous as one parent of the first Hybrid Tea, La France, is to be found in some of our oldest gardens. One garden at Mangonui, in the far north, has a beautiful bush of this rose, as well as numerous other Moss, China and Tea Roses; and a very large bush of the pink R. *multiflora cathayensis*. Madame Bravy has creamy-white, globular flowers flushed with a delicate pink. It is a glistening, lovely rose. The leaves on the plant we photographed were a shiny, rich green, and very healthy, in spite of being absolutely neglected. A dwarf-growing rose, Nancy Lee, was bred from Madame Bravy. This had delightful buds, and small, highly-scented blooms in a delicate and lovely shade of satiny-rose. Recently a Mangere friend, who owns a very fine garden, brought me blooms of a rose which fit this description; so we hope that it will be possible in the future to name it definitely.

From the Massey College rose garden in Palmerston North we received cuttings of Madame Lambard and Marie van Houtte; and, in exchange, we sent down bud-wood of some of the Alba Roses. Sad to relate, this garden is no longer in existence. The late Mr Frank Mason of Feilding, one of our fine old rosarians, who took a keen interest in the National Rose Society in this country, was instrumental in helping to establish these trial grounds at the College. Madame Lambard, a Tea Rose which Gertrude Jekyll praised very highly in *Wood and Garden*, has full, salmon-rose blooms with a hint of buff at the base of the petals, and thinner leaves than those of Marie van Houtte, though both have one parent in common, the rosy Madame de Tartas. The other parent of Marie van Houtte is Madame Falcot; so this large-growing and large-flowered rose is closely related to the small Sweetheart Roses.

We photographed some good blooms of Marie van Houtte that were brought to us in Gisborne. They had been gathered from a huge, sprawling bush growing at the back door of an old shingled farmhouse. Forty years ago there was no road into this property; and, twice a year, all stores had to be taken in, across a swift river, by bullock teams; and yet roses were planted in this lonely spot and must have brought cheer and beauty into the lives of the original owners.

Madame Bérard, an earlier rose than Marie van Houtte, and also a very strong grower, did well in this same Gisborne district where it hung down from the top of a clay bank. The large, well-filled, cupped, salmon-yellow flowers, with a deeper pink in the outer petals, were an inheritance from its famous parent, the Tea-Noisette, Gloire de Dijon. Its other parent was Madame Falcot. Another fine specimen of Marie van Houtte was growing in the garden of the historic Kemp home at Kerikeri in the Bay of Islands. Judging by our coloured slides of this Tea Rose, it must have been in perfect condition when we saw it—the leaves being clean and glossy and the pale yellow flowers quite unblemished. These blooms are streaked with red on the outside; and the inner petals are often faintly flushed with rose. Still another rampant plant of Marie van Houtte was growing in a ninety-year-old garden overlooking the Bay of Plenty, a few miles beyond Opotiki. We were privileged to hear something of the old days in this area from an elderly lady, who had lived there most of her life. She is being cared for by her niece, who kindly showed us round the garden, where we saw many old roses: the Pink and Red Chinas, Moss Roses, Multiflora de la Grifferaie, Madame Plantier, Souvenir de la Malmaison, Marie van Houtte, Paul Neyron, La France, Comtesse Riza de Parc, Maman Cochet, Antoine Rivoire, Gruss an Teplitz, Frau Karl Druschki, Lady Hillingdon, Souvenir de Madame Léonie Viennot, Mrs A. R. Waddell—one of the parents of Albertine—and many other bush roses, as well as *multiflora, sempervirens* and *wichuriana* ramblers.

A friend told us of a large, sprawling Tea Rose that was growing up through native trees on the site of the Buried Village in the Rotorua district. When Mt Tarawera erupted in 1886, the whole top of this vast mountain was blown off, the country for miles around being devastated, and the village buried to a depth of over six feet with volcanic ash and rock. Here roses flourish, the old Tea Rose at the rear of the Museum being very healthy and having full, flat flowers of salmon-rose. Marie Ducher was being sold in the Auckland district at the turn of the century; and Ellwanger's description of this rose fits that of the Tea Rose growing on the site of the Buried Village. Another interesting Tea Rose, Jean Ducher, was bred a little later than Marie Ducher, and was listed in the same catalogue. We feel sure that a large bush of Jean Ducher grows in a Remuera garden, within a mile of the old nursery that stocked this Tea Rose. The nursery is no longer in existence; but this hardy, vigorous, French-bred rose is thriving still, and producing its richly tea-scented, globular blooms throughout the year. These flowers are a soft salmon shading into yellow, and later the tone of the whole rose changes to peach—a lovely colour combination, and one that is delightful under artificial light.

The lower and less strong-growing Madame Hoste has been sent to us on several occasions as the more vigorous Marie van Houtte—in fact, we have a plant of it in the garden at present, though we are not going to keep it, owing to its predilection for mildew, and the fact that the pale yellow blooms seldom open perfectly and fade to a weak colour very quickly. On the other hand, we were sorry cuttings of Perle des Jardins failed to strike. The flattish blooms on this straw-yellow rose with an orange heart are carried on stronger stiff stems, the deeply serrated, dark shiny foliage being particularly fine. A climbing form, as well as a saffron-orange sport, Sunset, were also on the market in New Zealand. Two *wichuriana* ramblers we admire greatly, the single Jersey Beauty, and the double Gardenia, inherit their large creamy-yellow flowers from their parent, Perle des Jardins.

In its day, Étoile de Lyon, which we saw growing in the lovely garden surrounding the old Mission House at Tauranga, was considered to rival the straw-yellow Perle des Jardins. This tall rose, with handsome dark reddish-green foliage and brownish-red young shoots, carried the large, full flowers of a rich yellow shaded with orange, very erect. This is a rather unusual trait in Tea Roses, which, more often than not, have weak necks and a tendency to hang their heads. There is a fine coloured illustration of Étoile de Lyon in *The Amateur's Rose Book* by Shirley Hibberd, which was published in 1874.

In no old garden have we seen more old Tea Roses than at Pa Mairie in Whangarei. As well as all the Tea Roses mentioned previously, there were tremendous bushes of the creamy-buff, rose-flushed Anna Olivier and its richly toned sport Lady Roberts. Both these roses, once very popular in New Zealand, have long pointed buds; but their full flowers hang down on weak necks. Further over were two vigorous red Tea Roses seldom seen, though both were sold in Auckland at the end of the last century. These were Souvenir de Thérèse Levet, which has fine buds and unusual metallic, brownish-purple shading on the older petals and Christine de Noué, with rosy-crimson petals shading down to salmon. The owner of this old garden found these two red roses indispensable on account of their tremendous growth and free-flowering habit. Francisca Kruger, dark of stem and leaf, grew on a nearby bank. This firm favourite has full, flat blooms richly shaded with yellow and copper-pink on a flesh ground. In *The Amateur Gardener's Rose Book*, by Dr Julius Hoffmann, there is a splendid illustration of this subtly-toned Tea Rose.

The lovely, but extremely variable, Comtesse de Nadillac also graced this Northland garden. Not a large grower compared with many of these free-flowering old roses, the Comtesse de Nadillac needs shelter and care to give of its best, as its thinnish petals are easily damaged. The distinct and effective globular blooms have pale coppery-yellow outer petals, the inner unevenly indented rosy-salmon ones lighting up an attractive flower. The third of a trio of metallic-toned roses, Comtesse de Caserta, is a good pillar rose as it has a strong tendency to climb. The medium-sized, cupped blooms of coppery-pink shading down to yellow, have thick petals of camellia-like texture – very effective in a garden. Not far away from these exotic beauties was a dainty, modest-looking rose, Madame de Watteville. Low-growing, its creamy, cup-shaped, fragrant blooms, edged with carmine-rose, made an appealing picture. Maman Cochet, a real old garden stalwart and a great favourite in older gardens such as Pa Mairie we have not grown, though its parents, Madame Lambard and Marie van Houtte are both in the garden. Maman Cochet was considered one of the finest Tea Roses of its day. A pointed bud, which opens in tulip form, and flesh-pink colouring shading to salmon-rose, describes the bloom of this well-loved rose. Five years after its introduction it sported and produced White Maman Cochet – the best White Tea of the period. A tremendous bush of the rosy-crimson Mrs Edward Mawley sprawled down from the top of a bank. The blooms are not unlike those of Madame Lambard; but the foliage is very different, with wider, greener leaves of firm texture, these being much more resistant to mildew than the thinner ones of Madame Lambard.

A rose we looked for in vain in this Whangarei hillside garden was the lovely Catharine Mermet which we found growing up over a tall hedge in the Gisborne distsict. This full, pale-pink rose has a creamy-yellow tint near the base of the petals, some of which are flushed with lavender. Several fine sports of Catherine Mermet were introduced into New Zealand, though they are not roses we know. These were Muriel Graham, a pale cream just flushed with rose; Bridesmaid, a clear pink considered by older rosarians to be better than the parent; and a lovely pure white, The Bride, a very popular rose in its day.

Papa Gontier, a rose we grow as a large shrub next to the tall Souvenir d'un Ami, and also up a fence, to provide colour at the rear of the pink border during the winter months, is quite common in New Zealand. It strikes readily from cuttings and is highly valued for its winter-flowering qualities. It is much more wiry and thorny in growth than Souvenir d'un Ami; and not as easy to handle, though it is a decorative garden rose and a most useful one for indoor arrangements. A friend, who gave me Papa Gontier, grows it magnificently in several spots in her garden. One bush climbs up a trellis against her white, blue-shuttered house, where the semi-double, loose, rosy blooms, carmine on the reverse of the petals, look gay and very charming on a cold winter's day. One of Auckland's fine historic homes, has an old archway separating two parts of the garden; the arch is completely covered with this bright, winter-flowering Tea Rose, while alongside grows a tremendous bush of the climbing form of Devoniensis. At Sunningdale in England, and also in Rome, we admired a newer rose bred from Papa Gontier and the tall Himalayan Brier, R. *microphylla*. This rose, August Roussel, had loose sprays of semi-double pink flowers; and appeared to be an excellent pillar rose.

Most unusual, irregularly shaped blooms give the Tea Rose, Général Galliéni an air of distinction. The French general after whom it was named was responsible for the defence of Paris at the beginning of World War I, and helped to check the German advance at the Battle of the Marne. Friends who sell winter blooms consider it a valuable rose for this purpose, their two enormous bushes producing hundreds of flowers at a time when many other roses are having a well-earned rest. These blooms change colour with the seasons. In early winter, they are a very dark red shadowed with purplish-brown, and are rather similar in colour to one of the parents —a rose we used to grow—Souvenir de Thérèse Levet. Earlier in the season, the colour is quite bright, the inner petals being a rich buff-yellow, and the outer ones a bright rosy-red. In fact, if a spring bloom and a winter one were placed side by side, no one could be blamed for imagining they came from different plants. Smooth green stems and leaves, with an overall bluish sheen, complete the picture of a most unusual, easy, and healthy rose.

On one trip to Russell we were privileged to talk about the early days with a ninety-year-old resident. We sat on her wide verandah, looking across the bay to the historic Treaty House at Waitangi, and she pointed out a tall date palm which she had grown from a stone, and which bore fruit. Then we strolled round the old garden—she still did her own housework and gardening—while she pointed out some of her well-loved roses. Not all were from the earliest days of the colony however, though the

China and Moss Roses were there, as well as Captain Christy, Gruss an Teplitz, Cécile Brunner, Frau Karl Druschki, and Général Galliéni, besides a mass of climbers and ramblers.

Another Tea Rose that begins flowering towards the end of the winter is the climber, Souvenir de Madame Léonie Viennot. In town and country alike its multitude of flowers make gay splashes of pink which are particularly welcome in late winter and right through till the main rose season opens; but woe betide the unwary who prune this rose hard. It flowers only on the older wood; which is why the often neglected plants to be seen throughout the country bloom so freely. The flowers are variable in form, and not always perfect in shape; but even these imperfections can be glossed over when it is possible, in the depths of winter, to gather a bowl of cheerful rosy-yellow blooms. This old rose adorns farmhouses, barns and fences: there are three fences covered with its strong-growing bushes in our own Auckland road. It is probably correct to say that the great majority of these bushes have been grown from cuttings, which will account for their general health and vigour. We trained our plant against the white carport trellis behind the rose and pink camellias, Lady Claire and Peach Blossom.

In the Lisbon Botanical Garden, Portugal, in 1898, several crosses were made between R. *odorata gigantea* and certain old Tea Roses, which resulted in producing some fine climbers. One of these, Belle Portugiase or Belle of Portugal, is well known in Auckland, a particularly large and free-flowering specimen being grown at Bayswater by Mr J. M. F. Connolly, President Emeritus of the National Rose Society of New Zealand. It has large foliage like that of its Burmese parent, and long pointed buds which open to flesh-pink, tea-scented flowers. The rather semi-double blooms are inclined to be weak in the neck, though highly decorative indoors; and resemble very closely, except in size, the illustration by Redouté of R. *indica fragrans* or *odorata*—another rose related to the Burmese climber, and also, itself, a parent of many Tea Rosea. Belle of Portugal is a better garden plant than an exhibition rose, as the drooping flower heads would debar it from doing well on a show bench. La Follette, a rich toned edition of it has the same parentage; and both are a glorious sight on the French and Italian Rivieras early in the season, as they love a warm climate. Perhaps this is why the paler one flourishes in Auckland.

The name Peace is associated in all our minds with one of the most talked about and highly commended of all our modern roses; but there was another rose called Peace which was bred in England in 1903. This was a Tea Rose, full and flat in shape, the flowers being of a lemon-white shading to pink on the edges. Strange that two roses of such different breeding should have rather similar colouring and identical names. As both appeared on the scene after major wars, the matter of nomenclature is perhaps not so surprising. The pink toning of the petals deepens in both cases when the weather is hot and dry—in fact, in the earlier Peace a flush appears all over the blooms in late summer. It is in the winter months that this rose attains its real beauty, as then the colouring is clear and exquisite. Such a free-flowering bush always catches the eye as the pale flowers shine out against a background of dark reddish-green foliage. In our own neighbourhood there are no less than three large bushes of this prolific rose. One of them came originally from another early settled part of the country, Katikati, not far from Tauranga.

A mere forty-nine years old is Lady Hillingdon, which originated from a cross between two of our roses, Papa Gontier and the pale yellow Madame Hoste. Most gardeners are familiar with its rich nankeen-yellow flowers and dark, reddish-brown foliage. The form most commonly seen is the climbing sport; and, as the flowers of Lady Hillingdon have in large measure the Tea family's weak neck this is the ideal manner in which to grow it, so that the blooms can be seen to advantage. The loosely filled flowers are an inheritance from Papa Gontier. We wanted a position in our pergola for Mermaid and a yellowish Hybrid Musk: so Lady Hillingdon was given away several years ago; but we can admire her still as there are a number of bushes in this vicinity.

The day of these Tea Roses is undoubtedly passing, and it is quite understandable that people planting new gardens should prefer the excellent modern roses available in such variety; but there is an undoubted fascination in the history of these long-lived, stalwart roses that have given so much pleasure over the years.

Its beauties charm the gods above;
Its fragrance is the breath of love;
Its foliage wantons in the air,
Luxuriant, like the flowing hair,
It shines in blooming splendour gay,
While zephyrs on its bosom play.

Anon

T HE FASHIONABLE ROSE OF THE EARLY DAYS OF QUEEN
Victoria's reign originated on a mountainous island 500 miles east of
Madagascar, in the South Indian Ocean. At that time, the island, now called
Réunion, was known as the Isle of Bourbon. It was part of the Mauritius
group, first discovered by the Portuguese, and later settled, for a time, by
the Dutch. It then became a colony of France, and was taken over by the
British Government in the early part of the nineteenth century.

French farmers on this island grew rose hedges round their fields.
No roses were native to the southern hemisphere, and it is fascinating to
imagine the early arrival of these plants in their new home, so far away
from their natural habitats. For there were two roses, quite dissimilar, but
both perpetual-flowering, which were introduced into Mauritius some time
during the latter part of the eighteenth century and which flourished and
increased amazingly on this sea-girt land. One was Parson's Pink China.
This rose must have been carried safely by ships of the French East India
Line over that long route from the Far East. Plants transported in those old
sailing vessels were often given a rest ashore in such places as the Botanical
Gardens of Singapore and of Calcutta (though we saw no trace of any of
these China Roses when we visited the Singapore Gardens recently). Thus
they were able to survive the rigours of the trip. Mauritius, also, came to

be used as a stopping off place for roses being sent to Europe; so it is probable that some of these plants remained on the island to form the nucleus of rose hedges.

The other rose introduced was the Pink Autumn Damask, a form of *R. damascena bifera*, or the Four Seasons Rose. Arab dhows, sailing down the eastern coast of Africa from the Persian Gulf, carried this famous rose southward; it survived through equatorial heat to flourish exceedingly under conditions far removed from those of its native land.

While the China Rose has small, smooth, persistent, dark reddish-green foliage, spaced curved thorns on wiry stems, and loose, semi-double flowers, the Persian rose has large, soft, deeply-serrated, pale green leaves; thicker stems heavily clothed with straight thorns; and tight clusters of double flowers, the buds of which have longer calyx lobes than those of the China Rose. The Autumn Damask suckers freely, making an easy and natural method of increase, while cuttings of the Pink China strike readily; but, as the seeds germinated well, seed was generally used by the farmers of the Isle of Bourbon for stocking their nursery beds with hedging material. It was in one batch of seedlings that a Monsieur Perichon noticed a rose with different leaf growth. He removed the small plant to his own garden to study it more closely. The first blooms were distinct from those of any rose growing at that time, on the island.

In 1817, the French Government sent a botanist, Monsieur Bréon, as Director to the Royal Botanic Gardens on the Isle of Bourbon. When he was shown the new rose, which was to become known as Rose Edouard, he realised at once that it must be a natural hybrid between the two hedge roses used by the farmers. A specimen of this historic rose has just been sent us by Dr B. P. Pal, director of the Agricultural Institute, New Delhi.

Various dates, ranging from 1819 to 1822, have been mentioned in old rose books for the arrival in France of the earliest Bourbon Rose. William Paul, when writing the first edition of *The Rose Garden* in 1848, said that Monsieur Bréon grew plants of Rose Edouard and then, in 1819, sent seeds of it to his friend, Monsieur Jacques, the Duke of Orléans' head gardener at the Chateau Neuilly, near Paris; and that it was Jacques who raised the next generation of the Bourbon Rose. One of these plants was then named Rosier de l'Île Bourbon, its common name being Bourbon Jacques, in honour of the man who raised this, as well as another new race of roses, the Sempervirens Hybrids, of which Félicité et Perpétue is a well known member. On the other hand, six years later, when Thomas Rivers wrote *The Amateur's Rose Guide*, he stated that this second generation rose was raised in Mauritius by Monsieur Bréon; who then sent plants as well as seeds to Monsieur Jacques. This was in 1822, about the time that the Bourbon Rose was said to have arrived in England from France.

A hundred years later the late Dr C. C. Hurst, of Trinity College Cambridge, began his treatise on *The Origin and Evolution of our Garden Roses*. His findings agreed with those of William Paul, so it does appear that the plant called Rosier de l'Île Bourbon was raised in France. Before long it was being distributed to French growers; and a little later still it was sent across to England. About 1824 His Highness the Duke of Orléans, afterwards to become King Louis Philippe, gave permission for the celebrated painter, P. J. Redouté, to visit his garden, in order to paint the new rose. Either Redouté or Thory, who wrote the text for his book *Les Roses*, called it R. *canina bourboniana*—a strange title, the name for the whole group now being R. *bourboniana*. This early Bourbon had attractive semi-double flowers of a rosy-red; and was soon in great demand for outdoor gardening.

From this time, till well on in the century, French breeders produced a great number of new and lovely Bourbon Roses, most of the earliest varieties being rose or rosy-lilac in colour; but in 1843, Souchet of Paris produced plants with deep red and red-purple flowers. These, though very attractive, were not perpetual-flowering, having been derived from the non-remontant Gallicas. From other crosses came the first white, and blush-white varieties. The only record of a yellow Bourbon occurred much later when the pale-toned Souvenir de la Malmaison threw a sport in 1888, which was afterwards given the name of Kronprinzessin Victoria.

William Paul gave impressive lists of Bourbons; but of all these names only five appear amongst the twenty-five roses of this class which are catalogued today. These are Bourbon Queen, Great Western, Coupe d'Hébé, Louise Odier, and Souvenir de la Malmaison, all roses we love and grow. There were two border-line roses, Mrs Bosanquet, bred in 1832, and Hermosa or Armosa, in 1840, which were listed sometimes amongst the Bourbons, and sometimes amongst the Chinas. They were small; but had fuller flowers than those of the China Roses, though the blooms were not as large as those of all other Bourbons.

All old-rose books spoke of Mrs Bosanquet in such glowing terms that it is surprising to find its name no longer figures in catalogues, though that of Hermosa, and its climbing sport Setina, still do. However it is amongst the Chinas, not the Bourbons, that Hermosa is now placed; and certainly, except for the extra fullness of the flowers, it does resemble more closely that side of its rose family. Between 1834 and 1840 this little gem appeared independently with four different breeders; so it is understandable that plants of Hermosa, if collected from different places, can vary slightly and cause a little confusion. We are sending bud-wood to England this winter of the charming small rose we feel sure is Mrs Bosanquet – a rose that was listed in New Zealand as early as 1860. So perhaps, before long, it will be once more available to old-rose lovers.

Coming to the Bourbons we grow and love, it seems right to begin with a description of Bourbon Queen, or Reine de l'Île Bourbon, as it is listed in *The Old Shrub Roses*. The date given is 1835, which is very puzzling. Mr Thomas has grave doubts about this plant being true to name, as it does not match up entirely with early portraits of that rose, neither is it perpetual-flowering. However, our plant surprised us this season by producing, for the first time, good autumn flowers—whether this will occur again is problematical. It may just have occurred because of the unusual climatic conditions prevailing this year. On the other hand Bourbon Queen is apparently well established as such in various large collections in England and can be seen, as we saw it, on many a cottage wall. We grow our plant, imported from England, with other shrubs on a sunny bank; but it does grow in some early gardens here, as we have since discovered. This rose has medium-sized, circular, slightly cupped, open blooms of a rose-carmine, that assume a lilac flush and faint veining as they age. The individual flowers of the Boursault Elegans, which came to us from an old farm on Banks Peninsula, are not unlike those of Bourbon Queen, both roses being first-generation hybrids from Parson's Pink China; and both showing the odd white stripe on the petals that is typical of China Roses. A plant of Bourbon Queen in full flower is a fine sight, as the blooms come in tight clusters all along the arching stems, which are well clothed with dark green, leathery, and deeply serrated leaves. When these branches are allowed to hang down freely from a wall or a bank, they make a charming picture in the garden. What a pity Bourbon Queen is generally summer-flowering only—a characteristic of many of this rose family, particularly the earliest ones.

Queen of the Bourbons, a lower-growing rose with full, quartered flowers of a blush-salmon tinted with fawn; Bonquet de Flora, which was a favourite of Dean Hole's and had rose-coloured blooms; and Baronne de Noirmont, also rose-coloured, were all listed out here a hundred years ago. Where are they now? It is possible that some of them do still exist in old neglected gardens. Wherever there is progress, and population is increasing, many large gardens are cut up, and old roses in them swept away to make room for newer ones. This is reasonable and right, as so many old roses are only summer-blooming; but the best of the old roses are still worth a place in any garden, amongst their number being some of the perpetual-flowering Bourbons. The Nelson district is a fruitful hunting ground, as many famous roses were in cultivation there by 1860. When the French explorer Dumont d'Urville daringly took his corvette *Astrolabe* through the tricky waters of what was to become known as French Pass, he discovered a quick route through to Nelson between the mainland and the island which now bears his name. It was interesting to read in Thomas Rivers' book, published in 1854, that Souchet, a Parisian rose-breeder, had named one of his rich, red-purple Bourbons, Souvenir de Dumont d'Urville. What interests us more is the chance that an old dark, reddish-purple Bourbon, which we have seen in three of our earliest gardens, could be this rose. Unfortunately, we were not able to get confirmation of this overseas.

Great Western, the first transatlantic steamer, also had a Bourbon Rose named in its honour. This was in 1838, when no other dark-hued varieties had appeared. Unfortunately this strong, tall-growing rose flowers only in early summer; but the blooms, richly fragrant, full, globular and of a deep crimson marbled with maroon-purple, are worth waiting for; and are followed by striking red heps. One old book mentions that all the progeny of Great Western retained the fine foliage and good branching habit of the parent plant and that it was a rose which thrived exceedingly in the cool, moist atmosphere of Scotland. Since it is a good seed bearer, some fine roses were bred from this immensely vigorous and very handsome Bourbon, one of which, the modern shrub rose Poulsen's Park Rose, grows in our garden. A lovely Hybrid Perpetual, Comte de Montalivet, which was bred in 1846, and was out in New Zealand at a very early date, could be a relative of Great Western. When we compared the coloured plate of this rose in the first edition of William Paul's *The Rose Garden*, with blooms of our rich, purple-red Bourbon, they were strangely alike; but so far we have not found a bush of the Comte de Montalivet in any old garden we have visited, though we still hope to do so. Rose collecting is an interesting hobby with many surprises: several unknown roses have been sent up to us from Nelson recently.

A rose which has given us great pleasure each season since we imported it from England, is the Bourbon, Coupe d'Hébé. It is growing up against one of the pillars on a pergola and is allowed to spray out freely, showing off the fine, strong foliage, and marvellous sprays of richly scented, globular, rose-pink flowers. These have wavy, crimped edges to the petals, and a great depth of colour in the heart of the blooms. If this were a perpetual-flowering rose it could be ranked as one of the finest pillar roses. As it is, it makes a magnificent show in the garden for several weeks, during which time it is greatly admired both for the colour and scent of the full blooms, and its luxuriant foliage. Long sprays can be cut for the house: they last well in water, and look almost more attractive as they fade to a lavender-rose. As soon as Coupe d'Hébé has finished flowering the old wood is cut out. New strong shoots very quickly put in an appearance; the bush is then a mass of rich green foliage, each leaf having seven leaflets. No further pruning is required until after the next year's flowering, unless a little shortening of some branches is advisable.

Over the years, we have been sent cuttings of Souvenir de la Malmaison from many parts of the country. This was the first Bourbon Rose to be planted in our garden, and is still one of our favourites. M. Jules Gravereaux, of the Roseraie de l'Hay, called it the Queen of Beauty and Fragrance; it well deserves this charming name, and the special spot allotted to it in this famous rose garden. One story of how this rose acquired its name is given in several books. Having been sent as an unnamed seedling to Malmaison, it was seen and greatly admired by a visiting Grand Duke of Russia. He was so impressed with this blush-tinted Bourbon that he asked to be allowed to take plants of it back with him to Russia, and to name it Souvenir de la Malmaison. On the other hand, A. W. Anderson, in his interesting book *How we got Our Flowers* mentions that it was named by Béluze, its breeder, to commemorate the famous garden with which he was connected. Of moderate growth, this rose requires to be placed near the front of a border if it is to be seen to advantage. In our experience, it does better on its own roots, and strikes readily from cuttings. Souvenir de la Malmaison is exceptionally free-flowering, an inheritance from its Bourbon-

Noisette parent, the lovely lilac-rose Madame Desprez, a rose we admired overseas. The blooms are extra large for the size of the plant, and generally appear in small clusters. Their soft, blush-white petals are quartered, and stand out well against a background of leaden green leaves. Shirley Hibberd, speaking of quartered roses, said that many were so lovely that it would have been better to burn and forget show rules than to lose roses such as Souvenir de la Malmaison. This is the rose seen so frequently growing on children's graves in old cemeteries all over the country. In the graveyard surrounding the tiny old St Stephen's Chapel in Judge's Bay there are two fine spreading bushes of Souvenir de la Malmaison. The first stone chapel having been destroyed by a storm in 1843—the very year this rose was bred in France—a wooden one was built later for the use of the Maoris, who used to beach their canoes in this pretty, sheltered little bay and camp on the shore. The chapel is of historic interest; for in 1857 the deed for the Constitution of the Church of the Province of New Zealand was signed on a table which now forms the altar.

Several graves in the Grafton cemetery are adorned with flourishing bushes of Souvenir de la Malmaison and it grows, and flowers very freely, on a baby's grave in St Mark's Churchyard. There is scarcely a month throughout the year when this bush is not covered in bloom—wonderful in a very old plant. A young friend who lives in the Gisborne district showed me fine plants of this same Bourbon which she had grown from cuttings collected from a derelict garden near an old abandoned farmhouse. We have frequently seen Souvenir de la Malmaison surviving under similar hard conditions; and it never ceases to amaze us that bushes, so neglected, should still be capable of producing blooms of fine quality. On the site of an early schoolhouse near Waipu, which had been destroyed by fire many years previously, we could trace the direction of an old curving pathway by the shrubs which had bordered it. These included flowering bushes of Souvenir de la Malmaison, the white Noisette, Madame Plantier, philadelphus and camellias.

The smaller and more perpetual-flowering of the Bourbons need hard pruning; the stronger growers, strangely enough, should be pruned rather lightly. In 1893 Henry Bennett, of Shepperton, England, put on the market a climbing sport of this old favourite, Souvenir de la Malmaison. We find it very vigorous; but though it flowers freely along the branches, the large, flat, short-stemmed blooms are inclined to ball and discolour in cold, wet

▲ 21. Old Bush
China

► 22. Général
Schablikine

▲ 23. Souvenier d'un Ami

▼ 24. Bourbon Roses

weather. In 1859, a French nurseryman, Jacotot, used the dwarf form of this lovely Bourbon to produce the glorious Tea-Noisette, Gloire de Dijon, which inherited the flat, scented, quartered blooms of its fine parent. In 1950, in the Irish garden of Lady Ardilaun, Souvenir de la Malmaison threw a sport—a singularly lovely single rose with warm yellow stamens, and thick petals of palest pink, the outside being of a deeper tone. This was named Souvenir de St Anne's after the garden in which it originated. We saw and admired this rose in English and Irish gardens, but we do not grow it in Auckland nor have we seen it elsewhere in this country.

What's in a name? With all the romantic and fine-sounding titles bestowed upon roses during the nineteenth century it is odd that a Mr Blair, of Stamford Hill, should have produced two sister seedlings and called them Number 1 and Number 2. Stranger still that they are still known by these numbers. The first was a rose of no great interest; but Blairii No. 2, bred in 1845, is a lovely thing, though not perpetual-flowering. Dean Hole remarked that it would soon cover the side of a large house; and he spoke of an old cottager who always referred to this Bourbon as Bleary Eye. Gertrude Jekyll, who had grown it successfully for fifty years, valued it as a free pillar rose. We grew it along the balustrade of the terrace in front of the house; but with its vigorous growth and horrid thorns, it quickly outgrew this intimate spot; and had to be removed to a safer spot on a boundary fence, where its long, mahogany-coloured shoots could cause no damage. Rambling over this wire fence, which tops a seven-foot rock wall, it has now hooked itself on to the branches of a nearby purple-leaved prunus. There it creates a charming picture in early summer, when, with its companion rose in the same colouring, François Juranville, it cascades down through the tree and over the rock wall. If pruned when most roses are cut back, it will not flower; but it is safe to thin it out immediately after the blooms have faded, though it resents too much cutting away. The large flowers have a rare charm, the pink colour deepening towards the centre of the delicately veined petals.

Many seedlings of Louise Odier—bred a few years later than Blairii No. 2—were listed in France during the first ten years of its existence, which shows the impact this Bourbon must have had on the breeders and nurserymen of that time. It is not surprising therefore to find that it is still being sold, and as highly esteemed as ever. Catharine Guillot, rose-coloured; Comtesse de Barbantane, blush shaded with rose; the salmon-rose

Modèle de Perfection; and Baron Gonella, light silvery-pink shaded with violet-rose, were all seedlings of Louise Odier. The two former roses were listed in early Auckland rose catalogues—the Comtesse de Barbantane having as its other parent the historic Bourbon, Reine de l'Île Bourbon. The parent rose, Louise Odier, is familiar to many New Zealanders, both as a garden plant and in pictures. Her full, circular, cupped blooms of bright rose have a rich fragrance, and are set most attractively amongst fresh green foliage. In our humid climate most of the Bourbons require regular spraying to keep them clear of mildew; but they are all well worth the trouble involved. Old rose books recommend frequent waterings with liquid manure during the growing season, and well worked and enriched soil if the autumn flowering is to be good; Louise Odier responds well to such treatment. Actually, this rose, Souvenir de la Malmaison and the lower-growing Champion of the World, are all excellent autumn roses; and, for that reason, are valuable garden plants. Louise Odier grows alongside the pergola, being trained on to the low trellis which links the posts near ground level. Around the rose is a carpeting of low, pink ageratum; while the glossy-leaved climber *Pandorea jasminoides rosea-superba* grows nearby, the colour of its rosy, red-throated flowers toning perfectly with the others. This flamous, free-flowering Bourbon was given to us many years ago by Mr G. A. R. Phillips of Paraparaumu, the author of *Aristocrats of the Flower Border* and other books.

Because it arrived early in New Zealand and is to be found frequently in old gardens, mention must be made of the Bourbon, Charles Lawson. This is a vigorous climber with masses of large, loosely-filled, rose-coloured flowers, the petals of which are veined and deeper in tone on the back. In a lovely hillside garden on the outskirts of Wanganui, Charles Lawson is trained along the front of a wide verandah that goes round three sides of the old, white-gabled house; its companion rose there is the largest plant of the China Rose, Cramoisi Supérieur that we have seen.

In Auckland, some of the Bourbons are not as perpetual-flowering as we should like: they tend to produce blooms spasmodically after the first magnificent show is over. Some others, of course are summer-flowering only. But of those that bloom consistently, Boule de Neige, which we grow in our white garden, is one of the best. It was bred in France from Blanche Lafitte, an earlier blush-white Bourbon, from which came also Perle des Blanches, another early introduction into this country. Perle des

Blanches is rather similar in flower and leaf texture to Boule de Neige, which has medium-sized, full white flowers that reflex into a ball. The petals have a waxy appearance; a good bloom, when it first opens, has rather the look of a formal camellia. The handsome leaves are thick and dark in colour and set off the fat, red-tinted buds and pale flowers excellently. Boule de Neige is a tall grower, the small flower sprays appearing at the tips of long branches; but far more bloom is produced if the stems are arched over, since flowering shoots appear along the whole length of the branch.

There is a great deal to be said for a thornless rose; so we look upon Zéphrine Drouhin with real affection, particularly at pruning time when we have just finished coping with a really prickly specimen. Such a rose has decided advantages when planted near a house or alongside a pathway. Zéphrine Drouhin makes a spectacular shrub in wide mixed borders, and also an excellent pillar rose. In one garden we saw it growing among clear blue delphiniums and silver-foliaged plants, and it looked a picture. Our plants are placed at the back of a pink border and, though the spring show is all that could be desired, any later blooms come intermittently, though we do get some flowers right into the winter. We did think that the bushes we saw in England produced particularly fine flowers. These are semi-double, uneven in shape, and of a vivid rose-pink, the base of the petals being white. In this century, Zéphrine Drouhin produced a pretty, pale pink sport which was named Kathleen Harrop. This does not flower well later in the season, but an old-rose grower in Auckland gets lovely blooms on her bush in early summer. Mt Stewart, a National Trust Garden in Northern Ireland, has a series of gardens within the garden proper. Two of these, the Italian and the Spanish gardens, are separated by a broad grassy walk adorned, at regular intervals, by tall pillars topped with monkey pots. The Bourbon Roses, Zéphrine Drouhin and Kathleen Harrop, are planted against and trained up the pillars—the rose and pink tones alternating and looking most effective.

The late Constance Spry, as well as being one of the foremost floral artists in London, was a greater admirer of old roses and grew them extensively both at Winkfield Manor in England and in her smaller Scottish garden. One of her favourites for including in a period arrangement of old roses was the Bourbon, Madame Lauriol de Barny, which was bred nearby a hundred years ago. V. Sackville-West, in *Even more of your Garden*, said she wished she could find out who Madame Lauriol de Barny was in real life, to have such a sumptuous flower, with all the rosy lavishness of the Second Empire, called after her; and suggested that someone ought to write the biographies of persons who have had roses named in their honour. It would certainly make interesting reading. A number of our Bourbon Roses are grown in a fairly narrow border against the brick base of a terrace facing due north, getting all the sun there is. This necessitates frequent watering and mulching; but we use carpeting plants as well, to shade the roots and hide any ugly legginess towards the base of the bushes, since this border is in a very prominent position. Between each rose we have planted the attractive but low-growing, pink-flowered *Veronica speciosa variegata*, which is interesting throughout the year. The still lower-growing *Veronica spicata rosea* is used in a narrow border in front of these roses. This is a fine perennial—easily grown, free-flowering and always fresh looking, even in the hottest weather. This repetitive planting is effective; and does not detract from the taller roses behind, which can be admired from the lawn, as well as from the raised terrace above.

In this same bed we grow Adam Messerich, Commandant Beaupaire, Lauriol de Barny, Madame Pierre Oger, Madame Isaac Pereire, La Reine Victoria, Madame Ernst Calvat and last, but not least, the rosy-lilac Champion of the World, a three-foot rose which fills in delightfully the far end of the border where it narrows towards wide steps. Lauriol de Barny is one of the most attractive of all these beautiful roses; but unfortunately she is very susceptible to mildew, though her neighbours are not. In Auckland this Bourbon soon reaches up to the iron terrace railing, where its sprays of large, full, richly-scented, silvery lilac-pink blooms can be fully enjoyed. These flowers are of singular beauty, their delicate loveliness being a constant source of pleasure in the spring.

In my grandmother's home, I can remember being allowed to see, but not to touch, an arrangement of waxed flowers and fruit that reposed on an ebony stand inside a glass dome. Last year a clever floral artist created, with real flowers from my garden, a copy of one of these artificial posies. We chose one or two lovely buds of the pink Moss Rose, Salet; and, to accompany these, blooms of the two Victorian Shell Roses, La Reine Victoria and Madame Pierre Oger. The former has completely globular flowers in a subtle toning of rose and silver, the thin, shell-like petals being paler within. Sacheverell Sitwell, in *Old Fashioned Flowers* calls both this rose and its creamy-pink sport, Madame Pierre Oger, period pieces; placed under this glass dome, they certainly looked it.

Few roses can be more appealing than these two Bourbons; and fortunately they are fairly free-flowering. Both grow into reasonably tall bushes which, if desired, can be arched over to produce more blooms on shorter stems. In very hot seasons Madame Pierre Oger blushes all round the edges of her pale, shell-like petals, with remarkable effect. Black spot and mildew have, in the past, marred the leaves of these roses in our humid summer weather; but ample water, combined with newer sprays, now appears to be keeping them healthy, for which we are very thankful, as they are amongst our favourites. We blamed our climatic conditions for these complaints; but the late Constance Spry mentioned having the same trouble, even in the cool, moist climate of Scotland. On the other hand this, and several other Bourbons, looked extremely healthy when we saw them in the old-rose border in the Savill Gardens, Windsor Great Park.

A striped rose Commandant Beaupaire, grows in this same terrace bed; and further along is that sumptuous beauty, Madame Isaac Pereire. Eleanour Sinclair Rohde, in *The Scented Garden*, said that the scents of summer flowers are rich and joyous; and sweetest of all are the scents of old roses. Her favourites amongst the Bourbons, in this respect, were Souvenir de la Malmaison and Madame Isaac Pereire.

My earliest recollection of a rose, and it is still very vivid, is of this carmine-red Madame Isaac Pereire growing against a wall in my parents' Southland garden, with banks of red paeonies nearby. In our hot climate, and probably because of the very sunny position, this rose does not produce her best blooms till later in the season; but in the very late autumn, and after the first heavy rain for some time, she flowers magnificently, the blooms being of fine colour. Constance Spry was a great admirer of this rose, and used it in many floral arrangements; but with her, also, it did better in the cool, moist climate of Scotland than it did in England. This is probably why it grew so vigorously south of Invercargill; and why its scent there was so unforgettable. I have only to inhale this rich perfume to be wafted back to my childhod. Madame Isaac Pereire was probably named after the wife of one of the Pereire brothers, who were great, though unorthodox, financiers and bankers during the Second Empire, when Louis Bonaparte, Napoleon III, was on the throne. The Pereires' adventurous methods finally lost them the support of orthodox finance, and caused their downfall, since Napoleon III was not strong enough to help them.

After the introduction of Madame Isaac Pereire, this richly-coloured rose produced, first in France and later in the garden of an Irish priest a pale pink sport which become known as Madame Ernst Calvat. Rich, reddish-purple foliage distinguished this new rose. It has been one of the slowest to settle down in our garden, probably because the *canina* stock on which it was budded would keep sending up greedy suckers. We have now overcome this nuisance, and already the vigour of the plant is amazingly improved. Foliar feeding has proved very beneficial; and this year we have had lovely blooms all along the arched-over stems particularly in the autumn. The flat quartered blooms are of a subtle shade of soft rose-pink; very attractive in the garden, and charming in the house.

Peter Lambert, of Germany, who bred some unusual roses, was responsible for the introduction of a modern, dark-flowered Bourbon, Zigeuner Knabe or Gipsy Boy. This sumptuous, free-flowering rose we photographed at Sissinghurst Castle, and also in Queen Mary's Rose Garden in Regent's Park, where it was allotted a bed of its own, not far from a lovely planting of the Shell Rose, Madame Pierre Oger. We were also so interested to see one of its parents both in Rome and England—the old Multiflora Hybrid, Russelliana or the Scarlet Grevillia. Another of Peter Lambert's roses, Adam Messerich, is trained along our terrace rail, being by far the most vigorous of all the Bourbons growing in this sunny border. This is a descendant of the rose-pink Louise Odier and, like her, is free-flowering, though far more rampant in growth. In fact it is definitely a climber, and a very strong growing one, with fine foliage. The sprays of bright, rose-coloured, semi-double blooms smother the plant in spring; and are produced generously off and on all year, especially if we arch over the long, whippy branches. In many respects this rose reminds us of the Boursault family. The young shoots of both are flexible and not very thorny; their clear green leaves are quite alike; while the buds of both have long, elegant calyx lobes, the flowers, in each case, being loose and floppy. The Bourbon, Adam Messerich, is a valuable plant both for garden and cutting. It is possible during most of the year to gather sprays with really long stems; these look lovely in tall bowls of mixed flowers and last well as each bud opens out in water. The colour of the newly opened blooms is a vivid rose; but pales to a lavender-rose in the hot sun.

We grow two other striped Bourbons, one on top of a brick wall, where we can look up at the rich purple and blush blooms. This is Variegata di Bologna which, with Honorine de Brabant, is described elsewhere. Honorine de Brabant is the most free-flowering striped member of this lovely family, as well as the healthiest; and it is a joy when there is sufficient bloom for a bowl to be filled with these richly scented, subtly toned roses.

A much more common rose, though a very useful one for odd corners, hard conditions, and hedges, is Gruss an Teplitz, or Greetings to Teplitz, which was bred about 1896 by a Hungarian rose-grower Geschwind, from a number of famous roses, several of which are in our garden. These are Fellemberg, a seedling of which was crossed with Papa Gontier, the progeny of the union then being crossed with Gloire des Rosomanes, to produce this red rose. We grow all three, and all are remarkably free-flowering, so it is no wonder that Gruss an Teplitz, their offspring, gives such a consistent display of bloom throughout the year. From the window in front of my writing table, I look out on a plant of this hardy red climber, which is trained rather loosely on to a trellis on top of a low bank. From this elevated position the long swaying branches, clothed with claret-coloured young growth, hang down gracefully. Many people must know its weak-necked, scarlet-crimson, velvety textured flowers, as it grows all over the country in old gardens and hedges. It strikes remarkably easily, like two of its famous relatives, Fellemberg and Gloire des Rosomanes.

Gruss an Teplitz will climb, and does with us; but it can be kept as a large shrub if pruned differently. Climbing roses are useful here, as we have adopted perimeter planting and find it a good method in our moderate sized garden. Both our plants came from the South Island; one from an old garden in Akaroa, and the other from a famous South Canterbury garden, Te Waimate, but it has been sent to us for identification from many other parts of the country. Even in the depth of winter, cheerful sprays of bloom are to be seen on this useful and easy rose.

These beautiful and historic roses add richness to any garden; and each new season, as the Bourbon Roses come into bloom, we feel more than ever grateful to those horticulturally minded seamen who so carefully cherished the two old roses that were carried safely across the sea to their new home on the Isle of Bourbon in the South Indian Ocean, there to become, in time, the parents of these garden treasures.

PORTLAND ROSES, HYBRID PERPETUALS, AND SOME EARLY HYBRID TEAS

Then gather the rose in its fresh morning beauty

Tasso

A CHARMING ROSE, JACQUES CARTIER, WHICH CAME TO us originally from an early garden in Ellerslie, and which we found years later in another old garden at Oakleigh, south of Whangarei, was given to us by an Auckland friend. Its identity puzzled us until we read Graham Thomas's description of the Portland rose family—a small family, but a very charming one of compact, moderate growth, rich scent, and perpetual-flowering habit. A ruff of leaves round the short neck below the fat buds is a distinguishing feature. We were able to confirm our naming of this rose when we saw a bush of Jacques Cartier in an English nursery, and were able at the same time to photograph the original Portland Rose, which was thought to have been bred in Italy from the Scarlet Four Seasons Rose, Slater's Crimson China, and R. *gallica officinalis*. This red rose arrived in England at the beginning of the nineteenth century and was being grown in a French nursery in 1809: it was named after the Duchess of Portland, an enthusiastic gardener and rosarian of that period.

Jacques Cartier, the first Portland Rose to be planted in our garden, was grown from cuttings. It is an admirable rose for the smaller garden, being compact as well as perpetual-flowering. The stiff stems are beautifully clothed with persistent and handsome foliage—the flowers being held quite erect. These generally come in clusters of three and are packed with small, reflexing, rosy-pink petals that surround a button eye. A picturesque ring of light green leaves frames the flower head, which has the short neck of the Portland family. The full, flat buds of this rose, encased in long, leafy sepals, are beautiful as they open to show a depth of colour in the heart of the flower. We have placed Jacques Cartier alongside the upright-growing, small-flowered, pink fuchsia Bon Accord, in a large pocket at the top of the rock garden – the ground beneath being carpeted with low-growing ericas and pink polyanthus.

It is always interesting to discover something about the person after whom a rose has been named. Jacques Cartier was called after a famous sixteenth century navigator who came from the French seaport of St Malo. His exploration of the Gulf and River of St Lawrence proved of great geographical importance, and ensured that his name would never be forgotten. When in Canada recently we flew over the Jacques Cartier channel on this vast waterway and later crossed a spectacular bridge, which bears his name. Because of our love for this old rose we were delighted to see these memorials to an adventurous sailor.

After acquiring and successfully growing this splendid rose, our interest in the group was so stimulated that we imported two more Portland Roses, both of which have turned out to be excellent plants, healthy and rewarding in every way. The hundred-year-old Comte de Chambord was also known as Madame Boll. It was bred by a New York rose-grower, Daniel Boll, and named after his wife. He did not, however market this rose, which was distributed by Boyeau in France, who named it after the Comte de Chambord. This French nobleman was a grandson of Charles X, and a son of the Duc de Berri who was assassinated on the steps of the Paris Opera House. Some years later the Comte's mother travelled in disguise from Marseilles to the royalist stronghold in the Vendée, hoping to organise an uprising in his favour. The few followers she was able to rally were defeated; but she fled, and for some time evaded capture. Her son never reached the throne of France; he passed most of his life in an Austrian castle, a devout and unambitious man, the noblest and last of his line. So our beautiful rose was called after two very dissimilar people.

It is an excellent plant, and thrives in the pink border next to its relative, Baronne Prévost. The abundant, clear, rose-pink petals of this lovely flower are slightly waved at the edges. This enhances the beauty of a richly scented bloom, and makes it a showy rose in the garden. We have placed Blanc de Vibert, an earlier rose bred by the famous Frenchman whose name it bears, in our white garden, where its pale green leaves and double, green-centred, white flowers are an asset. This Portland Rose flowers very well, and has grown taller than the others; this may be due to its rather sheltered position. In France and in England we admired other members of this grand family—the rose and purple striped Panachée de Lyon; Céline Dubois, another white; Pergolèse, a rich rosy-magenta; and Madame Knorr with looser blooms. They appear to be very well-liked overseas: when we tried to procure plants of Panachée de Lyon and Pergolèse some years ago, we found that they were sold out for the season. We have become very attached to our Portland Roses over the years: they are so easy to cultivate, so generous with their lovely flowers, and so decorative in the garden.

The first Hybrid Perpetual—the deep red Rose du Roi—was bred in 1816 from the earliest Portland Rose. When Rose du Roi first appeared it created a great deal of popular interest in France and, later, in England; it was soon being used by growers to breed a new race of larger-flowered and stronger-growing Hybrid Perpetuals—Rose du Roi itself having blooms of only moderate size. Three years later, it produced a purple sport which was called Rose du Roi à fleurs pourpres. A Waitara friend, with a lovely garden, grows this old and unusual rose; and we saw it again at Sissinghurst Castle where it made an excellent photograph. We were glad to be able to add slides of these roses to our collection, as neither of these early Hybrid Perpetuals grows in our garden, though a number of their descendants do.

Hybrid Perpetuals are roses of complex origin—Portlands, Hybrid Chinas, Noisettes and Bourbons having all contributed something to their creation. Until the arrival of the Hybrid Teas in force, the sturdy, large-flowered Hybrid Perpetuals dominated the scene, and became the leading garden roses of their day. At that time systematic rose breeding was not practised; and, as thousands of new roses were being produced yearly, many of them were of inferior quality, or very similar to other varieties. H. B. Ellwanger, writing in the *The Rose*, said that the drawback to purchasing fresh roses in those days was the fact that large numbers of new sorts were not sufficiently distinct from known varieties to prove of any value. This was notably the case in France, more so than in England, where greater care was exercised. Ellwanger then goes on to give lists of roses, the flowers of which bore such a strong resemblance to each other that it was difficult to name them correctly. The number of red Hybrid Perpetuals was legion. Many of these have been sent to us from country districts for identification; but unless we actually know the rose well, we always hesitate to name them from written descriptions, since these vary so tremendously from book to book. In Curtis' *Beauties of the Rose*—a rare book—five well-known rosarians gave their description of each illustrated rose; and seldom did their ideas coincide. This being the case, how hopeless for an amateur to try to sort out such a tangle a hundred years later. On the other hand there are roses so distinct amongst the Hybrid Perpetuals that identification is easy. These are the heads of certain types or families, roses such as Baronne Prévost, La Reine, and Général Jacqueminot.

In an early New Zealand rose catalogue eighteen Hybrid Perpetuals, as well as many other roses, were listed; and quite a number of them were sent up from Nelson to the Domain and Government House, Auckland. These are the names of the Hybrid Perpetuals sold in New Zealand by 1860 —some of them not many years after they were first introduced: Auguste Mie, Baronne Prévost, Comte de Montalivet, Duc d'Aumale, Edward Jesse, Earl Talbot, Géant de Batailles, Général Jacqueminot, Lady Sefton, La Reine, Lord Raglan, Madame Laffay, Madame Rivers, Queen Victoria, Rivers, Robin Hood, Triomphe de l'Exposition, and William Jesse. Excellent blooms are produced on the neglected plants of William Jesse in Grafton cemetery: one bush grows up through arum lilies and dog-daisies. Of this original number, only three are still on sale: Baronne Prévost, La Reine, and Général Jacqueminot; and all grow in our garden. Many of the others are to be found throughout the country, mostly in early gardens, and a certain number in the oldest cemeteries. By 1875 many more interesting roses had been added to this list. In fact, it would be safe to say that the best of the different groups of Hybrid Perpetuals found their way to this country, even though transport was such a problem.

Baronne Prévost, one of the original Hybrid Perpetuals, and the head of a small line, was the first of this French family of roses to be sold commercially in any quantity. Others had been bred between the introduction of Rose du Roi, and this fine rose; but none had so captured the public fancy. Baronne Prévost is still listed in old-rose catalogues, which says a great deal for its hardiness, beauty, and general garden usefulness. Our plants came from small cuttings that were sent to us some years ago, and have grown into free-flowering, strong-growing bushes. The thick, thorny, upright stems of this robust rose are well clothed with dark green, rather coarse leaves. Fat buds appear in tight clusters—too tight sometimes for all the extra large, flat, deep rose-coloured blooms to open properly—so a little disbudding is advantageous, if perfect flowers are desired and not just a mass of colour. In a quiet corner of the Boboli Gardens in Florence, a large statue of Jove presides over a series of box-edged beds and borders in which are planted bushes of this early Hybrid Perpetual, Baronne Prévost, the Pink Four Seasons Rose, R. *damascena bifera*, and pink and red paeonies. All these tones of pink, rose, and red, the green of grass and edgings and the whitish statue backed by tall sombre trees, made a very charming picture and brought to mind a poem written by Sappho 600 B.C., which ran:

> Would Jove appoint some flower to reign
> In matchless beauty on the plain,
> The Rose (mankind will all agree)
> The Rose the queen of flowers should be

So we were enchanted to find Jove gazing down from his raised platform on to two of our favourite roses—the only ones, along with paeonies, growing in that interesting spot. The lovely Portland Rose, Comte de Chambord is the only one of Baronne Prévost's descendants in our garden and a most attractive rose it is too.

Laffay, one of the finest French breeders of Hybrid Perpetuals, and the grower who raised the first large-flowered variety in 1837, five years later introduced a rose he named La Reine, the Rose of the Queen—a Hybrid Perpetual that held pride of place for many years. In *Beauties of the Rose*, Curtis, describing La Reine, said that "a greater sensation had rarely been excited amongst florists than was caused by the announcement of the Floral Queen, to which title its style of beauty lays no mean claim." The form of the rosy, lilac-tinted La Reine is globular, very double, and massive. The singularly stiff reflexed edges, contrasting with the glossy pale pink of the back of the petals, give character to a perfect bloom which retains its shape till the last.

A characteristic of La Reine, and of most of its progeny, is the triangular shape of the smooth calyx, which tapers down to join the stem. This feature is quite a help when trying to place members of La Reine's family, a number of which grace New Zealand gardens, and all of which give a splendid account of themselves. Anna de Diesbach, Paul Neyron, Auguste Mie, and François Michelon are all interesting roses; but of this quartette, the only one in our garden is Paul Neyron. The first time we saw La Reine, the handsome blooms were beautifully arranged in a low bowl. Since then we have found that these full flowers last extremely well when cut with long stems, better than many first-class modern roses; the stems are particularly firm, so hold the enormous flower heads quite erect. We have had them last over a week in water when gathered late in the season: and after being indoors for a day or two the petals assume lilac tints which are attractive. Our bush was given to us by an Auckland friend who had treasured it in her garden for a very long time.

An old red Hybrid Perpetual, which we have found on an early grave in Grafton cemetery, was one which reached Auckland by 1861. This Géant de Batailles or Giant of Battles, a dark-foliaged, low-growing, erect rose, the head of its family, has medium-sized crimson flowers which fade out in the hot sun. Some old growers say this is a good autumnal rose; and if it is, the rose in the cemetery cannot be the Géant; but other writers mention it as being free-flowering only in spring and early summer, not later in the season. This particular old Hybrid Perpetual never gets any attention; it has to struggle up through grass and dog-daisies, only to be cut back in early spring when pathways are scythed. Most of the rose has suckered out beyond the grave. Lord Raglan, a descendant of Géant de Batailles, and another low-growing rose which arrived out here at a very early date, is probably in this cemetery also. I say probably, because there are a number of red Hybrid Perpetuals in the vicinity, none of which flower after early summer, and all rather alike. The very dark burgundy-red Emperor du Maroc, another relative of the Géant, is not in Grafton cemetery; we know it only from the garden of a friend.

The famous Général Jacqueminot, or General Jack as it was affectionately called, was considered a most valuable acquisition in its day, since so many rich, crimson roses were bred from it. Gloire des Rosomanes, an old stock rose, is thought to have been one of the parents of the Général. This red Hybrid Perpetual has more slender stems, and is less vigorous and robust, than the earlier types such as Baronne Prévost, Jules Margottin, and La Reine; because of this it is quite suitable for a pillar rose. At the time of its introduction popular taste demanded crimson roses, so Général Jacqueminot quickly became a garden favourite, as did many of its descendants. Some of these—Beauty of Waltham, Camille Bernardin, Marie Baumann, Charles Lefébvre, Alfred Colomb, and Duke of Edinburgh, arrived out here in the early days; and still exist in odd gardens.

Jules Margottin, head of still another family of Hybrid Perpetuals, is a rose well suited to the cottage garden, with its faintly scented but poorly shaped blooms. A hardy rose, it is not particular as to site or soil, is very free-flowering, and good in the autumn; but is rather a martyr to mildew. The green stems are covered with red thorns; the large, rosy-carmine flowers are somewhat flat in shape, though more irregular in form than those of Baronne Prévost. A great number of Hybrid Perpetuals are descended from Jules Margottin; and many of them found their way out to this country, the most generally known being Magna Charta, Edward Morren, John Hopper, and Madame Gabriel Luizet. The last two were popular in English and French gardens. Jules Margottin was raised at Bourg-la-Reine, near Paris, not far from where the internationally famous Roseraie de l'Hay is now situated. The village nearby was so proud of this lovely rose garden, which was drawing visitors from all over the world, that in 1910 it requested that its name be changed to L'Hay-les-Roses. Our large plant of Jules Margottin was grown from cuttings which were sent to us from the country; when the bush was moved three years ago, we found that a small piece of root left in the ground had begun to grow, and was throwing up a vigorous new shoot. This shows the great hardiness of some of these old varieties.

Several other Hybrid Perpetuals such as Victor Verdier, Sénateur Vaisse, Charles Lefébvre, and Duke of Edinburgh were all heads of families; but they are roses we neither know well, nor grow. However certain members of each group are represented in New Zealand.

A rose which grows in the old Grafton cemetery had puzzled us considerably until we sent slides and pressed specimens to an English old-rose authority. Apparently, it is Triomphe de l'Exposition, a Hybrid Perpetual that was supplied to Auckland by a Nelson firm in 1861. The rose was bred in France just five years before its introduction into New Zealand. The flat arrangement of the many narrow petals, the button eye, and the crimson-purple tones give this old scented rose the look of a Gallica; and it must be closely related to this family as it is summer-flowering only. Triomphe de l'Exposition has dark, pointed leaves, tinged with red round the serrated edges and on the back: the young growth, of a yellowish-red tone, is a distinguishing feature. In the old cemetery this rose reaches only to the top of the iron railings which surround the graves over which it suckers; a yearly cutting back with a sickle, and no tall support, keep it low-growing. However, given the support of a high fence or tree it will soon climb up to ten feet, as it does in one early Auckland garden as well as in our own. It grows in Avondale, also; and we have learnt that it grew in the Karangahape area, before that district became commercialised.

Some really sumptuous roses of deep maroon-red to velvety, blackish-purple are to be found amongst these fine old roses. They are roses of good petal texture and strong stems: if well fed and watered after the first flowering—an essential with such vigorous bushes—they will give another, though less spectacular, display in the autumn.

Prince Camille de Rohan, with full, fragrant, circular blooms of rich, velvety-red, shaded with maroon and purple, is planted on a raised bank in front of a high fence. Some of the long, strong stems are trained along the heavy wooden trellis behind the rose; while others are pegged down towards the front of the bed. In this way masses of glorious blooms are produced, generally in groups of three. Other roses, of equally luscious colouring, are grown nearby— roses such as the maroon and blush-striped Bourbon, Variegata di Bologna; the two old Gallicas, Tuscany and Tuscany Superb, with velvety-maroon blooms; Roger Lambelin, maroon-edged with white; and Gruss an Teplitz, velvety-crimson with deeper shadings. These roses are interplanted with long-spurred aquilegias, a strawberry-coloured, low-growing foxglove, *Digitalis mertoniensis* and *Salvia pratensis tenera*, with flowers ranging from deep blue to rosy-purple.

A low brick wall, supporting the sixty-foot raised bed, is clothed along its entire length with a variety of plants which break the severity of the long expanse of brick. As purple roses look well near grey foliage, we have used our own *Senecio greyii*, the Tasmanian *Calocephalus brownii*, *Convolvulus cneorum*, *Teucrium fruticans azureum* from the Atlas Mountains, with its royal blue flowers, the English lavender, Munstead Dwarf, the French lavender, stoechas, perpetual-flowering carnations, weeping rosemary, and a variegated wallflower to trail over the edge. The part nearest the house and kitchen is planted with useful herbs—sweet marjoram, lemon thyme, and the common sage—all of which have attractive colour-ing, particularly so in the case of the sages *aurea variegata* and *tricolor*. Even deeper in tone than its glorious ancestor, Prince Camille de Rohan—a rose which is always greatly admired by garden visitors—is the blackish-maroon, purple-tinted Baron de Bonstetten. The blooms, of a sombre rich-ness, are held erect on firm stems; and though we do not grow this sumptu-ous beauty, we saw last year a large bowl entirely filled with these fine flowers. It was so unusual and so magnificent that it commanded a great deal of attention.

The blooms of one of our lovely Hybrid Perpetuals, Reine des Vio-lettes, could easily be mistaken for Gallica flowers, if separated from their smooth leaves and stems. The deliciously scented, flat and quartered blooms open rosy-cerise with a button eye; but this colour changes soon to violet, grey, and rosy-purple. Much as we admire this rose, we have not been altogether successful with Reine des Violettes, though it does seem to improve as the season advances. Ours was an imported bush; so it may be that the vigorous *canina* stock, which will throw up strong suckers, saps its strength to a certain extent. We are now planting cuttings; if these strike we may find that this old-fashioned but charming rose will do better on its own roots.

For many years we had searched in vain for the unusual Hybrid Perpetual Baroness Rothschild (1867), which was being sold in this country during the latter part of the nineteenth century. Quite unexpectedly, an old rose was brought to us recently by a fellow rosarian; he had seen it in an elderly lady's garden in our own city and, when she heard of our interest in old roses, she kindly offered us the plant. Comparing it with a clear illustration in *Roses for English Gardens* we realised at once that it was the Baroness Rothschild, a rose rather reminiscent of the Portland family with its compact, upright growth, stiff short-jointed, green stems, and full of foliage around the shapely, non-fragrant, shallow, cup-shaped blooms of a clear rose-pink. These flowers generally appear singly and are held quite erect. Several white sports of Baroness Rothschild were sold in New Zealand in the early days.

The term cabbage rose is a misnomer when applied to the thin-petalled bloom of R. *centifolia*, but there is a rose in this garden which does justify such a title. This is the extra large-flowered Paul Neyron—a descendant of the lovely La Reine—and a Hybrid Perpetual well-known in New

25. Mme. Pierre Oger

26. Mme. Isaac Pereire

▲ 27. Baronne Prévost

▼ 28. Jacques Cartier

Zealand, as well as in England and France. An excellent way of producing masses of flowers on these strong-growing roses is to arch over some of the stems and peg them down. When this is done they send out flowering shoots along the entire length of each branch. It was interesting for us to find that this method of training Hybrid Perpetuals was being used extensively in Rome, Paris, and parts of England. At Roseraie de l'Hay the branches of Paul Neyron and many other sturdy roses were attached to horizontal wires only two feet above ground level, and were flowering profusely and producing good quality blooms. At Sissinghurst Castle Miss Sackville-West had similarly trained a large square bed of Ulrich Brunner—a rose related to Paul Neyron; the whole area, the size of a large room, was very effectively covered with the rosy-red blooms of this vigorous Hybrid Perpetual. Elsewhere we saw the lovely rosy-flowered Mrs John Laing treated in the same manner. Unfortunately we do not grow this fine rose; but Ulrich Brunner flourishes with us, and both were popular plants in our older gardens.

Roger Lambelin, the Old Curiosity Rose, inherits from one parent Prince Camille de Rohan, its rich deep-maroon colouring: while the white frosting round the edge of the dark petals comes from another relative, the low-growing China Rose, Fabvier. This, however has its white markings down the petals, not round them. All three are favourites here, Roger Lambelin being one of the roses planted on a raised bank with other richly coloured varieties. While we were in England we saw, for the first time, another deep-toned Hybrid Perpetual with a white edging to its petals. This was the handsome Baron Giraud de L'Ain, a much more vigorous and sturdy rose than Roger Lambelin, which is not a very robust plant with us.

Some years ago we were given a rooted cutting of Commandant Félix Faure. This Hybrid Perpetual was called after an amiable man-of-the-world who was President of France in 1894. It is a richly scented, velvety, dark red rose, shaded blackish-brown on some of the petals. At its best Commandant Félix Faure is really beautiful, but so far this rose has not grown as vigorously as most of the family. It may give a better account of itself next season; it has now suckered, and the new growth looks particularly healthy. Nowadays, whenever we are given cuttings or plants of old roses, we make a note of the name of the donor, as this adds to our interest in particular roses. Unfortunately, when we first started collecting we were not so methodical, and are therefore not able to give some donors their due; this applies to Commandant Félix Faure.

Not long ago, a Gisborne old-rose enthusiast found an interesting Hybrid Perpetual growing in a hedge by the roadside. Looking through a recent American rose catalogue we were interested to see a very clear illustration of a rose named Clio, which resembled the one recently discovered in this country district; later, we found that Clio had been sold in Auckland in 1900. This information confirmed the identification of a very robust Hybrid Perpetual of double, globular, blush-pink blooms. The thick stems were closely covered with strong thorns, and the leaves, which grew well up to the flower head, were dark green and coarse, after the style of those on the early Hybrid Perpetual, Baronne Prévost.

Three very familiar Hybrid Perpetuals in New Zealand gardens—though not in our own collection—are the purple-crimson George Dickson; Henry Nevard, a fine rose we know from a neighbour's garden; and the crimson Hugh Dickson which we saw represented by a magnificent specimen alongside tall bushes of the rosy-purple *Rhododendron ponticum* in front of an old church in Cheshire.

Frau Karl Druschki, or Snow-Queen as many visitors to the breeder's garden felt it should be called, was raised at Trier, in Germany, by Peter Lambert early in this century. It still ranks as one of the finest white roses. Its Hybrid Tea ancestry is strong but, because of its stiff, upright growth, large leaves, and huge flowers, it is still listed amongst the Hybrid Perpetuals. Frau Karl was bred from a cross between Merveille de Lyon, and the lovely Hybrid Tea, Madame Caroline Testout—a very popular pink rose in this country. It was called after the wife of the President of the German Rose Society in 1900; and quickly gained popularity in Europe, North America, Australia and New Zealand. A rooted cutting of Frau Karl was sent to us from Akaroa several years ago: the original plant was grown in the old Church of England cemetery in that early settled township on Banks Peninsula. We planted it in our white garden; but it had to be moved two years later, when it threw out tremendous long shoots and quite outgrew its allotted position.

Frau Karl is now trained along a high wire fence at the rear of a yellow and white border, in front of a tall, dark-green hedge which makes an excellent background for the snow-white flowers. These large blooms, with pink-tinted buds, show beautiful yellow stamens when fully open, and are just as effective indoors as semi-double white paeonies, though they lack their scent. A shrub rose, Karl Foerster, which grows in our white garden, was bred from Frau Karl and the Siberian *spinosissima*, R. *altaica*. An enthusiastic Gisborne old-rose grower, who has made some fine public plantings in that town, sent me a rose, Sachsengrüss. This is called the pink Frau Karl, and has similar large flowers, but in a uniform soft pink shade. It is listed as a Hybrid Tea, though it has the stiff stem, large rounded leaves, fat buds and big blooms of the Hybrid Perpetual family—a family which, strangely enough, did produce one or two miniature varieties.

It would be a pity if we entirely lost sight of these old garden stalwarts with their robust and vigorous habit, their general hardiness, and interesting as well as beautiful flowers. Many of them have been cherished for over a hundred years; and though, with some exceptions, they cannot compete with modern roses as regards continuity of bloom, there are many that still merit inclusion in a garden where space permits. It would be fascinating if we could look ahead, even fifty years, and see what the rose-breeders of the future have in store for us; but in the meanwhile, let us enjoy those that we have, old and new, and feel thankful to the men who have given so much to the rose world over the last hundred years.

Just after the middle of the nineteenth century, a new race of roses appeared—the fine Hybrid Teas which, a hundred years later, are still holding a dominant place in the rose world. They were created by the fusion of the continuous blooming Tea Roses with the sturdier, larger-flowered Hybrid Perpetuals. We grow, or have grown, only a few of the earliest Hybrid Teas, though many were introduced into New Zealand. Looking back, we find that those of which we have had personal experience were all pink-toned roses, several being popular still.

A rose that became universally grown and loved was the historic La France, bred in 1867. At first it was listed as a Hybrid Perpetual; and it was not until many years later that the National Rose Society of England named it a Hybrid Tea. La France has large full, fragrant flowers of silvery-rose deepening to rose-pink on the outside of the petals. A climbing sport appeared later. Captain Christy, another well-loved old Hybrid Tea, has open cup-shaped blooms of a pale flesh-pink. This charming rose grows splendidly in North Auckland. A Whangarei old-rose enthusiast treasured a climbing form of Captain Christy which was trained on the wall of her house, as it was on so many other homes of earlier days.

Three more pink Hybrid Teas that were destined to become very popular had one parent in common and were bred by the same French grower. The well-known Madame Caroline Testout grows vigorously in many parts of New Zealand. It has large, globular, well-filled blooms of centifolia pink with shell-shaped petals. This is a decorative rose both in the garden and in the house. The breeder, who at first had not been very impressed with his creation, presented this Hybrid Tea to a French dress designer: she gave it her own name, and launched it so successfully in France and England that it became popular immediately. Two famous roses were derived from Madame Caroline Testout—the white Frau Karl Druschki and the flame-coloured Madame Edouard Herriot. We were interested to see the climbing form of this grand Hybrid Tea trained against many a high brick wall in France and England. Not as vigorous as Madame Caroline Testout, but an attractive rose in many an old garden, is Antoine Rivoire with its wide flowers of creamy peach-pink shading down to yellow at the base. The third of this trio, which were all bred within a few years of each other, is Madame Abel Chatenay. The beautifully formed, full, sweet-scented flowers of this fine climber are a rosy-carmine tinted with salmon, the colour paling on the outer petals. Our large plant was removed in mid-summer to allow a new fence to be erected, since we thought we could easily replace the rose: however, we found sadly that we could not.

Hybrid Teas have proved excellent garden plants throughout their long reign of popularity, and their day is far from over, in spite of the fact that many of their descendants, the modern Floribundas, have equally large and showy flowers. Hybrid Teas have taken pride of place at rose shows since shows were first inaugurated, and still continue to do so. Spectacular colour-breaks from orange through the flame shades down to subtle lavenders and browns help to keep public interest in this large rose family; many breeders are also striving to bring back the rich scents that were in danger of disappearing. More helpful still is the fact that more and more disease-resistance is being bred into the Hybrid Teas—a fact that is going to be to the ultimate advantage of all rose growers.

Health's blushing Rose the virgin streaks,
And paints the down on Venus' cheeks

Anacreon

STRIPED FLOWERS HAVE A DEFINITE DECORATIVE VALUE —a fact which was appreciated by the painters of the Old Dutch School, who used such blooms to add character to their rich and lovely flower studies. But, for sheer charm, striped roses have a graciousness and a softness not possessed by the stiffer blooms of such flowers as camellias, dahlias and carnations. There were varieties of polyanthus, also, with green striping on the lower flowers, and still more unusual auriculas. Now, new and unusual zinnias and petunias have put in an appearance; these have stripes and bizarre markings in extremely rich colours; but none have the quiet appeal of the roses. Most of these striped roses have occurred as sports on self-coloured bushes, and, if grown on their own roots, are liable to revert back again to the original type. Such sporting occurred in our own garden last year, and we noticed the same abnormality again this season.

The term sporting, when applied to flowers, denotes a change in colour, not in form, as is the case with Moss Roses. Often you will see just one branch on a rose bush producing a bloom of an unusual tone. For example, a solitary white flower, or even one that is striped, may appear on a bush of pink roses; and a striped variety may suddenly reproduce the self-coloured bloom from which it originally sported. From such a branch, it is possible to create a new rose—though there is no certainty that it will not revert again in the future. At some time in their history, most ancient rose families have produced striped sports—the Gallicas having been particularly prolific in this respect. All the old garden roses of the nineteenth century—the Portlands, Teas, Hybrid Perpetuals, and Hybrid Teas—have thrown striped varieties which have added greatly to our garden treasures.

The oldest striped rose on record, and still the most widely grown, is R. *gallica versicolor* or Rosa Mundi, sometimes called the Rose of the World. It occurred as a sport of one of the earliest known roses, R. *gallica officinalis*, a form of the ancient R. *rubra*. Returning Crusaders were probably responsible for introducing this striped rose into England, the self-coloured rose from which it sported being indigenous to the Holy Land. Edward Bunyard, in *Old Garden Roses*, mentions that it was in cultivation before the sixteenth century; and this is confirmed by other authorities, who say it was growing in the Woodstock garden of Fair Rosamund, mistress of Henry II—the name Rosa Mundi possibly having been an adaptation of Rosamund. Whatever the real date of its origination, it certainly has been in cultivation for several hundred years, and has come down to us unchanged through the ages. It is a short, upright-growing shrub well suited to a front position in an informal border. As it flowers only once a year it is advisable to add more colour to the area by the use of carpeting plants and dwarf shrubs such as fuchsias, azaleas, and ericas.

Rosa Mundi improves when well established; and responds to an annual dressing of compost. After flowering, spindly wood should be removed from the base of the bush; it often does good to shorten the remaining branches in spring. Our budded plant does not sucker, as did many we noticed overseas; they had spread into wide thickets and, in some cases, had partly reverted to the un-striped crimson form. These Gallicas were wonderfully effective in many English gardens; and we were charmed with those we saw at Newby Hall in Yorkshire; at Hidcote in Gloucestershire; and at Highdown in Sussex. It is interesting to see these two roses, R. *gallica officinalis* and R. *gallica versicolor*, growing side by side. The fairly large blooms are semi-double, and open rather flat to show a cluster of yellow stamens. As the flowers are held upright, and the bush is low, these little sprays of blossom make a pleasing picture. Rosa Mundi has a pink flower, heavily striped and splashed with carmine. The fat buds, with short calyx lobes, are typically Gallica; and, in themselves, are not as attractive as the buds of the Albas or the Damasks, though they open out delightfully. The rose makes an excellent low hedge, which benefits by being clipped over with shears at the end of the winter, just before the new growth commences. There is a glorious coloured photograph of such a hedge in the *English Home and Garden's* Special Garden Number. This was taken at Kiftsgate, the late Mrs Muir's lovely garden near Chipping Camden in Gloucestershire. Mrs Muir died just after our arrival in England; it was a great disappointment to us not to be able to see this wonderful old-rose garden.

There are more striped roses amongst the Gallica group than in any other rose family; and one of the best, if not the very best, is Camaieux, an early nineteenth century introduction. This has slightly taller growth than Rosa Mundi, with the same rough, dark leaves. The flowers, however, are very full, cupped at first and later reflexing to show an informal but charming bloom, with golden stamens interspersed amongst the curled, centre petaloids. The colour is a pale pink, so heavily striped with purple-shaded carmine that it gives the impression of being a deep toned flower, though this varies a little according to the season. As it ages, the whole bloom fades to blush, shaded with soft rose and lavender-grey. This is its most beautiful stage; and one feels it should adorn a large, romantic hat, or a soft dove-grey room decorated in the French style. Camaieux has taken to popping up in odd corners of the garden; but it is such a charming plant that we forgive its invasive habit.

Perle des Panachées or Cottage Maid is another French rose introduced a little later than Camaieux. The breeder, Monsieur Vibert, was responsible for putting on the market many unusual and interesting roses, including a number of striped ones. Cottage Maid has fairly full, cupped flowers with a cream ground and broad stripes of a deep carmine-pink. The leaves are small and rough to the touch; and the growth is erect though not very tall. We find it a useful plant when grown in association with Village Maid, a Centifolia, and Rosa Mundi, because it comes into flower when the other two are just past their best.

Tricolore de Flandre has fuller, though smaller, flowers than those of the lovely Camaieux, and the petals are narrower, rolling back at the edges when the bloom is fully open. In this rose the striping has more purple in it, the ground colour being the palest blush-pink. Last season some of the blooms produced a freakish green bud, known as a steeple, in the centre where the pistil should have been. From a distance, it looked like a large green eye. Whether this abnormality was the cause of the rose sporting, we do not know; but we did notice that on one branch of Tricolore de Flandre the blooms had reverted to what must have been two of its ancestors. We were able to recognise these sports, one resembling the buff, rosy-mauve Jenny Duval, and the other the slaty-purple Belle de Crécy—both roses we grow in the garden. One sport on a bush at a time is quite common; but two is definitely unusual, so we took slides of these freak blooms, and sent them to Graham Thomas, author of *The Old Shrub Roses*, who was most interested. While we were in England, Mr Thomas showed us Georges Vibert, another compact Gallica rather reminiscent of Tricolore de Flandre.

Oeillet Flammand, a striped French rose, was highly recommended in old books, though it is not listed nowadays. We had hoped to see it in France, but did not come across it in any of the gardens we visited in that country. If it is discovered again, enthusiasts are sure to bring it back into circulation, as its double flowers, white striped with rose, were highly decorative and resembled variegated Flemish carnations. At Sunningdale we saw the striped Moss, Oeillet Panachée, not a very showy plant; but it was better in Rome, and interesting as being the only striped member of that family.

The Gallica, Rosa Mundi, and *R. damascena versicolor*, or York and Lancaster, are striped roses of great historical interest—the former being a sport of the Red Rose of Lancaster, and the latter, a much taller rose with a smaller flower, being associated with the Wars of the Roses. We were told that this old rose suvives in an early churchyard at Te Uku, on the southern side of Raglan harbour. When the original church was pulled down, most of the old roses were cleared away—the only one remaining being a bush of York and Lancaster. It was in this area that Methodist missionaries carried out their work from 1835 onwards—the Church Missionary Society having elected to care for the heavily populated Waikato area.

One of our oldest Hybrid Perpetuals, Baronne Prévost, derived its flat flowers from Gallica ancestors – a family always prone to throw sports. Probably that is why, only three years after its introduction, Baronne Prévost threw a striped sport, Panachée d'Orléans. We saw this rose on the Continent; it has white markings on a rose-pink background.

At a later date, a second sport appeared, which reversed the striping, having rose stripes on a white ground. Judging by the illustration of this rose, Madame Désirée Giraud, in the *Amateur's Rose Book* by Shirley Hibberd, which was published in 1874, the bloom was very reminiscent of a stiff and formal camellia. Strangely enough William Paul, writing in one of his editions of *The Rose Garden* towards the middle of the nineteenth century, speaks of the need for striped Hybrid Perpetuals; and suggests that some of the Gallicas with this unusual marking on the petals should be crossed with Hybrid Perpetuals in the hope of producing new and unusual roses. As a number of roses have sported in our garden, we always hope that Baronne Prévost will do what she did so many years ago, and produce, once more, some striped blooms.

Another of Vibert's roses, *R. centifolia variegatu*, is commonly called Village Maid—not to be confused with Cottage Maid, a Gallica. It is blessed with two other names as well, Belle des Jardins and La Rubanée. It grows into a vigorous, thorny shrub, taller than the Gallicas, and suckers freely if on its own roots. Village Maid flowers freely, the blooms, globular in shape, coming in clusters early in the season. In fact, it is generally our first striped rose to flower. The marking on the blush-pink petals is lilac-pink, though this varies in some districts. We noticed one year that the colour was particularly good on some bushes growing by the roadside not far from Mangaweka, in the centre of the North Island. This is a useful cut flower, as the blooms come on long firm stems. Two other Centifolias, both of rich rosy-purple colouring, having marbling on their petals, though not definite striping. One is the lovely Tour de Malakoff, and the other, Robert le Diable, with smaller, less showy blooms.

We have a great affection for our Bourbon Roses; but wish that they all bloomed perpetually. Three of them are striped; and very charming roses they are, though only one of them blooms continually. Commandant Beaupaire, a rose with a military flavour to its name, has distinctive foliage, the pale green leaves being long, narrow, and pointed—an inheritance from *R. moschata*, one of the parents of the Noisette Rose used in the breeding of some of the Bourbon Hybrids. This striped rose flowers well in the spring; but is disappointing later in the season, for it then produces few, if any, blooms. The rich stripes of pink, carmine, and purple make these full, fragrant, semi-globular flowers very spectacular: they have greater depth of colour than any other striped rose, and are always exciting when first seen each season. The disease-resistant, pale green leaves are an added attraction, for they set off the flowers to perfection.

A sport from Commandant Beaupaire, with the same unusual leaves, is called Honorine de Brabant. This is a valuable garden plant, as it is healthy, has a mass of beautiful foliage in a lovely shade of green, and flowers consistently throughout the season, unlike the rose from which it sported. The fragrant, globular blooms of blush-pink are not only striped; but are stippled as well with a fresh carmine-rose. The late flowers, which generally come in sprays of three, are extra fine as regards colour and size, the carmine tones being more pronounced in the autumn. During its early flowering, *Rhododendron* Pink Pearl makes a fine background for this useful rose, the pale pink fuchsia Bon Accord, looking delightful in the foreground. Unfortunately, in this hot climate all our Bourbons require regular spraying; but if this is finely applied it does not disfigure the leaves.

Some writers say that old roses require no spraying, and this is certainly true of some of them; other writers mention that, though some are susceptible to mildew and black spot, these blights will not kill them and they will flower again the next season just as freely. Certainly, the nearer the roses are to true species, the less prone they are to disease, and many are completely healthy and free of all ills. Plants like these are a joy to any gardener, though their blooms are fleeting compared with those of a Bourbon Rose. However, when rose breeding was at its height in the middle of the last century, many roses were produced without any thought being given to disease resistance, though their flowers were beautiful and are still considered so today. Present day breeders are alive to the necessity for creating strong strains which they can label disease resistant. This augurs well for gardens of the future when it may be possible to discard sprays altogether. However, when we can fill a bowl with richly scented, subtly toned old roses for the house, we are inclined to forget the trials and tribulations of growing them, and think only of their beauty and their great historical interest.

The third of this trio of striped roses is Variegata di Bologna, a very remarkable plant. The sprays of full, scented, globular flowers have rich purple stripes on a blush-pink ground—a most arresting combination. Visitors to the garden always pause when they see this rose, as it is so very different. Some find it beautiful: others are not so sure. Unfortunately, both here and in England, it is a martyr to black spot; but modern trends in spraying greatly assist in checking this distressing tendency. In *Summer and Autumn Flowers* by the late Miss Constance Spry there is a coloured illustration which shows how very effectively the blooms of this Bourbon can be used in a flower arrangement.

The first Portland Roses were bred before the Hybrid Perpetuals arrived on the scene; but others kept appearing all through the nineteenth century until, in 1895, a lovely striped variety, Panachée de Lyon, was produced. When overseas we admired this compact, upright-growing rose, with pink flowers striped with crimson and purple, and ordered it for our own garden. All the Portland Roses have fine foliage: and in some there is an attractive ruff of leaves just below the flower head. Those we have in the garden gives us endless pleasure and very little trouble.

A Californian old-rose specialist called a Hybrid Perpetual, Ferdinand Pichard, the "pick of all the striped roses". This is a comparatively modern, tall-growing rose with fine foliage and double flowers of pink, heavily but irregularly striped with crimson. A rich scent adds to its attractions. We often peg down the long stems of Hybrid Perpetuals, as this makes them throw flowering shoots along the whole length of their horizontal branches. The striped Ferdinand Pichard reacts very well to such treatment, producing far more blooms than it would do otherwise.

Before leaving for overseas, we made a list of old roses growing in New Zealand, the names of which needed some clarification; and one of these was Wick's Caprice, a sixty-year-old Hybrid Perpetual. A North Auckland rose enthusiast, now breeding new varieties, sent us an interesting rose which she had collected from a milling site in the Hokianga area, and we were later shown the same rose which was supposed to have been growing in an old Tauranga garden for eighty years.

Now the age of a rose is one guide as to its identity, for a rose bred only sixty years ago could not possibly have been growing in a New Zealand garden eighty years previously. Some rose friends here wondered if it could be Wick's Caprice, so we were most interested to see a bowl of this rose displayed at one of the early fortnightly shows, sponsored by the Royal Horticultural Society at the New Hall. It had full, heavily scented blooms of a definite lavender-rose striped with white. This was interesting as the rose sent to us for identification was very different. It had fewer petals, these being notched and uneven at the edges—at the centre were glistening petaloids resembling some of our native shells in shape. The blooms were held quite erect, on firm stems. At first, the colour was palest blush, washed rather than striped with a deeper pink; but, in our hot sun, the colour faded quickly, leaving the flower an off-white.

Since we returned home, another bloom of the same rose, coming from a different part of the country, was sent to us for identification. This—a winter bloom—had definite carmine markings on a blush-white ground instead of being washed and faintly striped with pink. It was most attractive. We are now going to send bud-wood to two English experts to see if they can help us to name this rose, which has obviously been in the country for a considerable time. Because of its firm, upright growth—the flowers are held upright also on short stiff stems—it appears to be related to the Hybrid Perpetuals; so it will be interesting, later, to get a report from overseas authorities who have seen it in flower.

Though most rose families have produced striped varieties, it was not until a few years ago that we saw a striped Tea Rose. This was Anna Charton, first bred in 1896; it was being sold in New Zealand within a few years of its introduction. This cream rose, well striped with carmine, was growing in the same country garden which we saw our first plant of Lamarque, and several other old roses. Rainbow, a rose and carmine striped sport of our much loved Papa Gontier, was also brought into the country fairly early.

There is a new rose, Modern Times, a Hybrid Tea, which has pink stripes on a carmine ground—the darker shade predominating. This present-day rose, though an attractive plant, lacks something of the charm of the really old striped roses, which had luxuriant foliage set closely round the flowers. In the modern rose the bloom is held away from the widely spaced leaves—though this is a useful point when flowers are being cut for the house. We finally, though reluctantly, discarded Modern Times as it did not fit in happily with the other roses near it. As with all sports, it occasionally reverts back to the self-colour. Stripes have appeared in other modern roses, though none of these are in our garden.

Striped roses are flowers that either appeal to you or which you dislike intensely, and it is interesting to see people's reaction to them. The fact remains that, whether you like them or not, they do add variety and interest in a garden. To those of us who love them they have an irresistible charm and are a never ending source of joy. Of them all, the oldest, Rosa Mundi, is still one of the best.

I saw the sweetest flower wild nature yields,
A fresh-blown musk rose!

                              Keats

THE MUSK ROSE, R. *MOSCHATA*, WAS THE ROSE OF THE
Persian poets, the rose whose praises were later sung by Shakespeare,
Bacon, and Keats. It was also the rose from which the famed attar of
roses was distilled, and sold, at one time, for six times its weight in gold.
Musk Roses graced old Persian gardens; and probably grew in the Hanging Gardens of Babylon, built by Nebuchadnezzar for his bride. From
Persia, the Musk Rose spread to all the countries surrounding the Mediterranean, even as far south as the Atlas Mountains of North Africa. From
there the Moors took it to Spain; and a Venetian, visiting Granada early
in the sixteenth century, admired the carefully tended and well-watered
gardens filled with fragrant myrtle groves and sweet Musk Roses. These
roses must have reached England also at about this time, since Gerard,
writing in his Herbal in 1596, speaks of the Persian roses as blooming in
July, with great clusters of flowers weighing down the branches. The
Italians knew it well; and we read of gardens filled with Musk and Damask
Roses, violets and narcissus, groves of citron and orange, and beds of
sweet smelling mint, rosemary, and lavender. An Englishman visiting
Persia over a hundred years ago was given breakfast at a beautiful spot
near the Hazir Bagh or Thousand Gardens, near Shiraz; and was amazed
and delighted to find that he was sitting on a stack of roses over which

a carpet had been laid. Truly a perfumed feast!

The Persian Musk is only one of many forms of R. *moschata*. Members of this family appear also in other parts of Asia Minor, in northern and southern India, and in China. In fact some writers consider China to have been the cradle of this, as well as many other roses, and suggest that it gradually spread westward, suiting its growth to the different climatic conditions elsewhere. The Musk Roses must be a glorious sight growing free and unrestrained on the hills and valleys of central China, in the foothills of the Himalayas, and on the Persian mountains. Their praises have been widely and highly sung: so it is no wonder that they should have been brought out to New Zealand in the early days of the colony.

The Persian Musk is a magnificent rose and we shall never forget the first time we saw it, cascading down full of flower from the top of a tall tree at Te Waimate, a sheep station in the foothills of the Southern Alps. Until that moment, we had seen no roses grown in this free manner, and the unrestrained beauty of the heavily laden branches was unforgettable. The same rose, growing on an open site on a hillside behind Thames, formed a tall, arching shrub; for it climbs only when given the support of a tree or a high wall. In this spot, near the head of the Firth of Thames, Musk Roses were scattered over the sparsely tree-clad and steep, rocky slopes, in great frothing mounds of milky white. Persian writers describe bushes of R. *moschata* in full flower, as looking like "snow on the mountains", and that is how they appeared to us with the afternoon sun lighting up the mass of pale flowers. Later, in the autumn, the same bushes were barely recognisable from a distance, though we found that the heps of several varieties were lovely, the colour shading through greeny-orange to orange-red and the shape ranging from round to oval. Small thorns are spaced along the green branches, which are well clothed with the distinctive long, narrow, pointed leaves of this family. The large, loose-looking sprays of bloom carry many small, single, white flowers and the slender buds open at intervals, so the bush is in bloom for some time.

When Thames was in the throes of the gold rush, miner's cottages clung to some of the steep hillsides. The son of one of the early settlers is said to have taken cuttings of these roses with him, as he tramped over the hills, and planted them here and there amongst the rocks and scrub. This would account for the numerous bushes of Musk Roses growing in rather inaccessible spots in this locality. What is quite amazing is the fact that it is not only the small-flowered form which is to be found in this mining district; there are several other types as well, with larger single flowers and even double ones—all scattered throughout one area, not far from where the rich gold deposits were found and mined. We saw only one plant of a larger-flowered form of R. *moschata*, a beautiful rose with three-inch, single flowers and mealy, purplish young shoots, much deeper in tone than those of the small-flowered Persian Musk. This was a native of southern India, R. *leschenaultia*, and a close relative of the handsome Himalayan Musk.

A little further up the hillside was a huge bush of R. *moschata grandiflora* —not a true *moschata*, but a cross between the Musk Rose and R. *multiflora*. J. A. Pemberton, who produced many lovely Hybrid Musks and was a great admirer of this rose family, describes *moschata grandiflora* as "unrivalled among the wild roses of the world for outdoor cultivation". The green arching stems, bronze on the side exposed to the sun, and the large leaves, dark and shining, are almost evergreen. In this rose, the thick creamy-white petals of the large, single bloom are faintly flushed with pink at first, as are the buds; and a ring of prominent orange stamens forms the centre of the flower. In full sun, on a steep hillside, this Hybrid Musk was throwing its rich growth over native shrubs and other Musk Roses, and was full of bloom and perfectly healthy in spite of years of neglect. Nearby, and cascading down out of tall trees, were several tremendous bushes of a Double Musk. These were obviously of hybrid origin, as the blooms were a little larger than those on the bush of R. *moschata plena* which we were shown at the Bayfordbury Research Station in Hertfordshire.

After several exploratory trips in the same neighbourhood, we made an interesting find higher up this rocky and scrub covered face, not far from a small creek and near the site of an old quarry. This was no less than a Double Pink Musk, similar to the double creamy-white one we had found lower down the hillside on an earlier visit. The perfect, two-inch blooms, of a soft salmon-pink, were very lovely though the plant itself was neither as vigorous nor as floriferous as the white form. We think, from what helpful Thames residents have told us that the single Musk Roses must have been planted at a much earlier date than these charming double forms. We feel fairly certain that these were hybrids of the strong-growing Himalayan Musk produced by Paul & Sons of England; though unfortunately we saw neither of them overseas. They were Paul's Himalayica *alba magna* and Paul's Himalayica Double Pink; but we did see Paul's beautiful Tree Climber, with masses of very small, double, blush-white flowers, growing up through two trees—one with dark, bronzy foliage, and the other with variegated leaves—in a garden, near Woking, in Surrey. This was a garden filled with old-rose treasures and marvellous foliage plants, all grown in an informal manner in a natural, semi-woodland setting.

Even this does not exhaust the list of roses we found on this exciting Thames hillside. Two Wichurianas, that we had not found elsewhere, carpeted the ground between some of the Musk Roses, trailing thin stems over grasses and low-growing coprosmas, their glossy, bright green leaves and pink and white flowers looking fresh and lovely. We were interested also in a tremendous bush with darker foliage; since its smallish, double flowers of a soft, nankeen-yellow, had a definite musk fragrance. We wondered whether it could be the early Hybrid Musk, Elisa Wherry described by William Paul in *The Rose Garden*. Since then we have grown and studied this old rose, and feel fairly certain that the name must be correct, as the plant shows a definite resemblance to the Musk family. In our own garden we grow another hybrid, Princesse de Nassau, which not only has the long narrow leaves of the Musk family, but also exquisite blooms which open from typical, slender buds shaded with pink, into cupped, semi-double flowers of creamy-yellow. These soon fade to near-white, the yellow stamens turning brown as they age. Though the flowers are smaller, they closely resemble those of a later Hybrid Musk, Penelope. The charming Princesse de Nassau was sent to us from Dargaville. It arrived in Auckland on a hot summer's day, quite dry and looking rather sick. We soaked it for twenty-four hours in water sweetened with honey, and to our amazement it survived. Thereafter it settled in quickly and grew at a tremndous pace, keeping up with its companion on a pergola, the glossy-leaved, buttery-yellow Mermaid. The two roses now make perfect companions, with their shiny healthy foliage and toning yellowish flowers. This Hybrid Musk was sent from England, the original plant having grown over a gateway of a farm at Odiham, near Basingstoke. One of Queen Elizabeth I's hunting lodges was situated on this spot; and traces of a bowling green, surrounded by lime trees, can still be seen there.

While in England, we made a point of seeing two roses, bred in 1835, from a cross between the Persian form of R. *moschata* and R. *multiflora*. They were the rampant growers, Madame d'Arblay and The Garland,

▲ 29. Comte de Chambord

▼ 30. Rosa Mundi

▲ 31. Perle des Panachées

▼ 32. R. *moschata*

which were described in several of Gertrude Jekyll's books, and which were grown in many delightful ways in her garden at Munstead. We saw plants of both these roses at Sunningdale Nurseries in Surrey, and later at Sissinghurst Castle. Miss Sackville-West had trained The Garland and R. *filipes*, a Chinese Musk, up old fruit trees in her white garden, and both these lovely roses were cascading down in lacy, white showers when we saw them in June. The Garland has very small, semi-double flowers, buff-coloured in bud, but opening a creamy-white, the stamens turning brown as they age. At one time, we mistook our Hybrid Musk on the pergola for this rampant climber, as the flowers, photographed in black and white, do look rather alike, except for the size of the blooms.

Some of these Thames roses, which strike readily from cuttings, are now well established in the garden; and we find them highly decorative, as well as perfectly healthy for the bushes need no spray throughout the year. When they have flowered, we thin out a number of older stems, as this encourages the development of splendid new shoots. These Musk Roses are planted at the back of a long shrub border above the tennis court, and the branches are trained to spray out through the wire netting and to hang down over a twelve-foot rock wall, where their beautiful flower clusters can be seen to great advantage, and their thorny stems can do no harm.

Further along this same wall is R. *brunonii*, the Himalayan Musk or R. *moschata nepalensis*, a very vigorous handsome rose. We have grown it for quite a number of years now, the original plant having been sent out from England; each season it increases in size and beauty, till we marvel anew at its prodigous growth. It is recommended only for the larger garden, but we planted it at the back of a shrubbery where it is well out of the way. At first it was trained on to a ten-foot netting fence, but each year it throws out wonderful new growth. The branches hook themselves on to the nearby trees where they can spread out and down over the tennis court, but well above the heads of the players. R. *brunonii*, called after a celebrated botanist, Robert Brown, has very beautiful long grey-green leaves, the young shoots being tinted with dusky pink. These leaves alone justify its place in the garden; but the flower sprays are magnificent, each bloom being larger and of firmer texture than those of the Persian Musk. It flowers for several weeks; tall white foxgloves and white forget-me-nots round its base make a pleasant contrast to the rounded clusters of bloom. Only once have we found this rose in a country district, and that was on a lonely farm down the Wanganui River. A ship's captain had retired to this spot in a pleasantly wooded valley, wishing to be far away from the sea and had surrounded his home with a lovely garden. Several interesting roses were growing there, including tremendous bushes of the grey-foliaged Himalayan Musk.

In two overseas gardens there were impressive plants of this same Musk Rose. One was growing mixed up with the rampant Chinese Gooseberry, *Actinidia chinensis*, alongside the pleasant river Vartry, which flows through Mr E. H. Walpole's Irish garden in the Wicklow Mountains. We were told that at the end of the last century, R. *brunonii* had covered the roof of an old kiln house near their home. When this building was pulled down, the rose was removed to its present position. Many New Zealand trees and shrubs also grow splendidly in this warm, sheltered spot, protected from cold Irish winds by the heavily wooded hills which surround the park-like garden.

Another beautiful plant of the Himalayan Musk was seen at La Mortola, the late Sir Cecil Hanbury's garden at Ventimiglia, on the Italian Riviera. Here, R. *moschata nepalensis* and R. *moschata grandiflora* were growing up and over a tall, classical belvedere; while a little further over we saw a rampant Musk, new to us, cascading down over a high rock wall in a shower of blush-pink and white against a background of tall dark cypress trees and the deep blue of the Mediterranean. This unusual Musk was a variety bred in the garden and named R. *brunonii* var. La Mortola—a form with semi-double flowers tinted with palest pink and buff.

When travelling from Auckland to Gisborne through the wild Waioeka Gorge, we came across some unfamiliar Musk Roses growing in rugged, hilly country beyond the Gorge. One solitary plant was seen far below the roadway: this had sprays of semi-double, slightly cupped, white flowers with seven to ten petals, and was an exciting find. The bush was growing along a typical wire fence bordering an area of native bush, with no other garden plants nearby. How or when this Musk Rose arrived in such a spot we do not know; but each time we make the trip we get fresh pleasure from its blooms. Judging by a coloured illustration in *The Genus Rosa*, we feel this must be R. *moschata* var. *nastarana*, also named R. *pissardii*, in honour of a Frenchman who went to Teheran in 1880 as gardener to the Shah of Persia. The blooms of this rose vary from white to pink, one writer likening them to the sweet flowers of the Dog Rose. This form, growing between the Waioeka Gorge and Otoko, was white; but later we found another bush near Owhango in the King Country, which had a pink tint round the edge of the petals, and long, narrow, slightly shiny foliage. This fine specimen was growing up through tall trees by the roadside; and swayed down from the topmost branches, creating a delightful picture. While in England, we saw a twentieth century Musk Hybrid that had been bred in the Lester Gardens, California. This was named Francis E. Lester; and the flowers, though slightly deeper in tone, were strangely reminiscent of those of the old Musk Rose growing alongside the Owhango cemetery. It has been thought that the garden form of R. *moschata*, known as R. *nastarana* or *pissardii*, could have been a natural hybrid between the Pink China Rose and the Persian Musk—the pink-edged blooms and smoother foliage bearing out this supposition. Though one parent of the Californian rambler, Francis E. Lester, was certainly R. *moschata*, the name of the other one has not been verified.

The Owhango Musk hybrid with the pink-tinted flowers was found again rambling through trees in a lonely spot near the Wanganui River. This was at Aukopae, the site of one of the original landing stages used by the settlers in the days when all goods had to be transported up from the coast in boats, and then carried inland by pack-horses. An old schoolhouse nearby is now used by the New Zealand Canoeing Association as a resting place. The spot is surrounded by tall trees and bracken, through which struggle several forms of R. *wichuriana*, as well as this uncommon Musk Rose.

It is a tremendous thrill to find new varieties in such out-of-the-way-places, and we always wonder how they came to be growing there. Another semi-double, blush-pink Hybrid Moschata, which has since been cut out, used to grow in the Bay of Plenty: but now only our colour slides remain to remind us of a charming rose. Photography is a great help when it comes to comparing the flowers and foliage of roses such as these, all belonging to one of the great rose families. The blooms, buds, foliage, and even the thorns, must be taken close to the camera, so that even such details as pubescence on a leaf will show up clearly.

R. *helenae*, the Chinese Musk, was discovered in 1907 by the explorer E. H. Wilson, when he was collecting plants in China. It was called after his wife: but he named it also the Hardy Musk Rose; and hardy it certainly is, as our imported plant proves. We have trained it up a twelve-foot fence where its strong but slender stems have attached themselves to wires. It is closely allied to R. *moschata*, though the leaves are smaller and darker. The fragrant single flowers are white with bright yellow stamens, followed later by scarlet fruit. A charming variety, Patricia Macoun, was derived from R. *helenae*: we had the pleasure of seeing this rose at Sunningdale in England.

A climbing rose which came to us from Ilam, a well-known rhododendron and azalea garden in Christchurch, puzzled us for some time until we saw similar plants in France and England. These we photographed, bringing home slides to compare with those of our rose. This proved to be another form of the Musk Rose discovered in China by E. H. Wilson, and named R. *longicuspis*. It has reddish-brown stems, small thorns and very shiny foliage, the sprays of flowers appearing on short stems along the arching branches. In Queen Mary's Garden, in Regent's Park, London, spectacular use was made of R. *longicuspis*. It was grown against tall, stout, pillars, the stems being trained along great loops of heavy rope. This could hardly be seen when the branches were smothered with silky, white flowers. Since then we have discovered that this rose grows in an Auckland garden. We were interested to see two hybrids of it while in England: one was the semi-double R. *recta*, with blush-pink blooms; and the other was Wedding Day, a rose bred by Sir Frederick Stern at Highdown near Worthing. This famous gardener had crossed R. *longicuspis* with R. *moyesii*, another Chinese species, producing a vigorous climber with creamy-white flowers occasionally tinged with pink. It was growing over one of the outbuildings at Highdown; and, also, most effectively up through a tree near a bed of that many-coloured eremurus for which this garden is famous.

One of the roses we had hoped to see in full flower at the Villa Taranto, on the shores of Lake Maggiore, was R. *soulieana*, another rose allied to R. *moschata*. Unfortunately it was just past its best, though a few blooms were still out; but it must have been a remarkable sight about a week previously, when it flung a mantle of white blossoms over the top of a tremendous pergola for quite a distance, rivalling in beauty the snow-clad mountains in the background. The grey-green foliage of this rampant Chinese Rose is very distinctive, especially in the young growth.

I have left to the last a favourite of ours: the Snow Bush, R. *dupontii*.

Monsieur Dupont, Director of the Luxembourg Gardens in Paris during the Napoleonic Wars, created many roses with fine or unusual foliage, R. *dupontii* being one of them. This wonderful climber adorns the end of our carport, sharing it with R. *fortuneana* and the fragrant *Stephanotis floribunda*, the Madagascan jasmine. The three flower at different times, so there is always something of interest for us to enjoy in this corner of the garden. We have edged the semi-circular bed at the base of the wall with the charming old, white, green-eyed dianthus of 1730, Charles Musgrave.

R. *dupontii* is a cross between the rampant Musk Rose and the low-growing R. *gallica*. From its French parent, it inherits its coarse, rough leaves—which are wider than those of R. *moschata* and its bristly and prickly stems. Its climbing habit and the large, single, white flowers, faintly edged with pink, come from the other side of the family. This fine plant is a beautiful sight in full flower, with the dark stone wall behind it, and later its colourful autumn heps. On its own roots, R. *dupontii* suckers very freely; so adequate space must be allowed if it is to be grown in this manner. At Beccles, an old-world garden near Bulls, and in a charming hillside garden on the outskirts of Wanganui, R. *dupontii* is a sheer delight, as are many other old roses in these same gardens. Many years ago, when visiting Geraldine in the South Island, we came across an old shed which was literally sagging under the weight of a tremendous bush of R. *dupontii* —a bush that must have been in this early established garden for very many years, judging by its great size.

These members of the Musk Rose family give us endless pleasure. Their historical and geographical associations are fascinating: they are easy to grow, perfectly healthy, and charming, as well as fragrant, in the garden. They flower only in the summer; but give a spectacular display when smothered with hundreds of blooms in every stage of growth. Their hybrids have given garden lovers some of their most perpetual flowering and useful shrubs; so it is no wonder that these Musk Roses are held in warm affection throughout the rose-loving world.

. . . Thro' twilight pale,
She climb'd and climb'd, and peeped into the dim
Nest of the nightingale

Lytton

R OSES THAT CLIMB, TRAIL, OR RAMBLE, GENERALLY
produce masses of blooms, large and small—some for a short but
glorious season, and others for months on end—and they are amongst
the most worthwhile of garden plants. On the whole, New Zealanders do
not grow so many climbing roses as Europeans, whose gardens we admired when overseas: nor are such roses used here, to any extent, for climbing up through trees—a delightful way of training some of the flexible
types. For the most part, they are to be seen growing against fences, or
over archways and pergolas in association with other climbing plants,
though in some parks and gardens the garland method of training roses
on chains hung between stout posts has been used most attractively. On
the whole, not many roses are grown against houses in New Zealand:
this is because the majority of houses are built of wood in this timber-rich
country. Such wooden houses need constant painting, so that climbing
roses would often be distrubed. But in Britain where most of the houses
are built of stone or brick, roses are grown up to the eaves, softening the
hard lines of many of the buildings.

It was not until we visited the internationally famous garden of
Roseraie de l'Hay near Paris, that we realised in how many different ways
climbers and ramblers could be trained. Everywhere we looked we could

see some fresh method of growing them. A huge metal clover-leaf, on top of a tall, stout post, was garlanded with trails of the exquisite Blush Rambler. Graceful Wichurianas cascaded out from large, stone, pedestal urns. The tripod method, which is well-known in New Zealand was much in evidence; and there was one most unusual structure, up which roses were trained on wires to look, from a distance, like a floral maypole. From a strong base, stone was beautifully moulded till it came to a narrow neck about eight feet from the ground. This device stood in a pool of water surrounded by a low coping; and outside this again was a narrow garden bordered with grass. Small-flowered white Multifloras and Wichurianas were planted at intervals round this circular plot, then twined round the wire supports up to the apex of the central column, the whole creating an arresting and unusual picture. Green wooden trellis fences of different shapes and heights outlined some of the boundaries; many of them had semi-circles of trellis placed on top at intervals to give extra height. Free-flowering roses were so beautifully trained against these fences that very little of the woodwork was to be seen. Screens of other types had been built to segregate various individual gardens: some were made of tall wooden uprights linked together with loops of heavy rope, others were joined by rustic supports at three levels for the horizontal training of roses. It was here that a large collection of Multiflora Hybrids had been planted, and we were particularly interested to see these plants, as so many of them are to be found in old New Zealand gardens and by our road-sides. We were also delighted to have our naming of these roses confirmed. The Wichurianas were also very numerous; and we were able to identify many we had found out here.

Climbers and ramblers are of great value in a garden such as ours, where perimeter planting is practised, where all roses are grown as shrubs, climbers, or rock plants; and where there are no formal rose beds. They give an amazing amount of bloom, clothe walls satisfactorily, act as wind-breaks; and create a cool green background for the white garden, when semi-evergreen types are used. We train other free-growing roses through trees and tall shrubs, where the support of a tree encourages tremendous growth. Even the wild Dog Rose and the Sweet Brier will climb when growing in amongst trees, though they are compact plants when out in the open; and very charming they look, too, as they hang down from the tall New Zealand kanuka, both in the spring when covered with fresh pink flowers, and in the autumn, when smothered with heps.

Our own climbing roses start blooming right in the middle of winter, and many carry on till the cold weather sets in again. They come from Japan, Korea, China, India, Persia, Europe, the British Isles, and North America. Many of them are the wild types from which originated the Hybrids that we grow, also: and practically all of them do well in this part of the southern hemisphere far from their native haunts. We shall deal in the next chapter with those types generally seen growing semi-wild. We found them, for the most part, in old gardens.

If the winter has been mild, the first climber to flower is generally R. *sinica alba*, or *laevigata*, a native of China. As its name implies, it is at home in moist ground and, if allowed to dry out, it is rather prone to mildew. Unfortunately its season is short; otherwise it would rank as one of the finest white climbers. The large, five-petalled, slightly cup-shaped flowers come singly from each leaf axil. They have prominent yellow stamens which turn brown rather quickly. The flower stem and calyx tube are both densely hairly; and each shiny, light green leaf has three leaflets, the centre one being elongated. The new stems, with wicked hooked thorns, can climb well over twenty feet during a year: in fact, one particularly rampant branch leapt over a high trellis and made its way up over *Eucryphia nymansensis* and *Hoheria alba variegata* and even reached out across a driveway into a neighbour's oak tree.

This floriferous rose is spectacular in full bloom; and lasts well indoors, each bud opening out in water. Its common name, the Cherokee Rose, is misleading since people imagine that it must be a North American rose. It reached the United States only in the latter part of the eighteenth century, where it was grown along the river banks in the eastern part of the country, and quickly became naturalised. Women belonging to the Cherokee tribe of North American Indians garlanded their hair with its lovely blooms and it is now the state flower of Georgia. We saw it grown in a delightful manner at La Mortola on the Italian Riveria, just across the border from France. The whole garden is terraced and commands a fine view over the Mediterranean. Wide flights of stone steps, with heavy balustrades, are used to link up one level with another; and adorning either side of one of these pathways was a mass of white wisteria interwoven with the Cherokee Rose. This was a wonderful way of growing it: the blooms shone out against a dark background of yews and the blue of the sea—a truly delightful and colourful composition.

The only other time we have seen this combination of the single white Cherokee Rose and the white wisteria was in a lovely eighty-year-old hillside garden at Putiki, Wanganui. There was an extensive planting of single and double pinky-mauve primroses underneath these white-flowered climbers; further on beneath a tangle of Yellow Banksia and mauve wisteria, the ground was carpeted with the wild English primrose and white violets.

R. sinica alba was one of the first Asiatic roses to be introduced into England. It arrived there in one of the English East India Company's ships in 1696, but only does well in the south of the country. There is an exquisite pale pink hybrid, *R. sinica anemone*, which was bred in Germany in 1895 – the other parent being *R. odorata*, a rose from southern China and northern Burma. With us, this is not as vigorous as the parent, but it also flowers very early, even occasionally in midwinter, if planted by a warm wall. The large single flowers have a crinkled edge to the petals. These have deeper rose-coloured veining, and a silvery reverse, and they, also, appear singly in the leaf axils. In Ellen Willmott's book *The Genus Rosa*, there are two very fine coloured illustrations of the white and pink Cherokee Roses painted by Alfred Parsons, R.A. At Bodnant, in Northern Wales, home of Lord Aberconway, there is a very fine specimen of this rose covering a low rock wall. It was in full flower at the time of our visit. In 1915 this pale pink rose threw a vivid cherry-red sport, which became known as Ramona or the Red Cherokee. It, too, has the same attractive silvery reverse to the petals. Our plant should have been put in a warmer position where it would have flowered more freely, but in other Auckland gardens it does tremendously well, making a grand splash of colour early in the season. Last year we were amazed to see that one bloom on the Pink Cherokee was half cherry-red and half pink; but that was as far as it got. We had begun to wonder if the rose was going to sport again, as several roses of other types had already done so in this garden. Some of the large-flowered clematis such as Barbara Bibley, Lawsoniana, and Comtesse de Bouchard make lovely companions for these roses. The roses look better when grown in association with other climbers, as they are not heavily leaved.

R. banksiae or Lady Banks Rose was named in honour of the wife of Sir Joseph Banks, a keen horticulturalist and a Director of Kew Gardens, who encouraged and helped young plant collectors, and sailed with Captain Cook on the *Endeavour* during the voyage to Australia and New Zealand. It was from Sir Joseph Banks that Banks Peninsula in the South Island acquired its name. Banksia Roses flower very early, the double white, violet-scented, and extra rampant form coming into bloom with us before the better known and slightly larger-flowered double yellow shows any colour. On the Continent we found it was the white form, more than the yellow, that was commonly grown; and we were absolutely amazed at the size of many of the specimens we saw. At La Mortola the Banksia Roses had climbed through trees to a tremendous height; and Gertrude Jekyll described these Riviera beauties as "flinging their sprays of blossom down from the highest to the lowest branches, with never a pruning knife or gardener's shears to mar their native grace". I am afraid that we do have to cut our plants back immediately after they flower; but they are very quickly clothed with an abundance of shiny new foliage on long graceful stems, which will bear the next season's flowers.

When in Italy recently we saw the cool green and white garden of the Villa d'Este which is situated in the heart of the ancient town of Tivoli. Many beautiful trees provided the various tones of green, and a multitude of fountains, shooting, spouting and cascading, provided the white. Tremendous bushes of the Double White Banksia hung down from the high walls; and, in the main courtyard, and in another intimate garden adorned with statuary, we saw standards of the old white Hybrid Perpetual, Frau Karl Druschki. As we drove out from Rome, we saw many White Banksias adorning houses and roadside hedges; and there were tremendous bushes of it in full flower on either side of the gateway leading up to Hadrian's Villa. Other old roses had been planted along one of the ancient walls centuries after Hadrian's time, though a fine form of the Dog Rose we saw growing near the ruins of the baths could have grown there in the days of that much-travelled man. In ancient Rome we saw many high blocks of modern flats with potted plants of the Banksia Rose, in full flower, cascading over the balcony railings. One morning, in a busy street, we saw a young man pedalling his way through the milling crowds, with a trailer attached to his bicycle. In this box-like contraption were four tall potted climbing roses in full flower; they were probably on their way to adorn some quiet balcony, and one of them was the Double White Banksia!

In the Chinese provinces of Yun-nan, Shensi, Sze-chuan, and Hupeh, these lovely climbers grow wild; and in the gorges of the Yangtse River near Ichang they form great cascading bushes. On one of his trips to China, George Forrest, the plant collector, came across the Double White Banksia not far from this same gorge, making a remarkable picture. He wrote:

"I saw it in absolute perfection in the Lashi-pa Valley. Can you imagine a rose mass a hundred or more feet in length, thirty feet high and twenty through, a veritable cascade of the purest white backed by the most delicate green, and with a cushion of fragrance on every side? One such sight as that, and it is only one of many, is worth all the weariness and hardship of a journey from England. Looking down on the Lashi-pa Valley, which is a circular basin, backed on the east by the massive peak of the Li-chiang, one could see hundreds of those huge flower clumps showing up white, even at a distance of four or five miles, like bosses on a green shield. What a pity one can only bear away mind-pictures of these scenes!"

Apparently, there are some very huge specimens of this same rose in warmer parts of the United States; we have photographs of one vast plant in Arizona, covering an area of 2500 square feet. The original plant came from Scotland. Farrer, writing of one of his trips to China, likens the bushes "to heaps of snow, with an intoxicating scent of wine, and violets and pure warm sweetness."

The Double Yellow Banksia Rose is scentless; but the flowers are a little larger and fuller than those of the white; and one writer mentions it as being a glorious sight when seen cascading through the rosy-magenta of the Judas tree and bougainvillea on the south coast of France. On one trip in our own country, we came across a plant of the Double Yellow Banksia growing in a vastly different way. In a field adjoining a Maori pa, we saw what looked like a huge, glowing, yellow mushroom. Cattle grazing in the field had eaten away all the lower growth, leaving the plant standing starkly on a pedestal base of its own stems. Another fine specimen of the Double Yellow Banksia grew up through a tall poplar tree alongside the Old Mill House in Akaroa. This was the site of New Zealand's first flour mill; the mill itself, built nearly 120 years ago, no longer survives. Traces remain of the race that led water from a sparkling stream to drive the wheel, and three huge walnut trees, planted when the house was built, almost dwarf the old building. Red China Roses grow by one doorway, the ground beneath the trees being carpeted with periwinkles, honey-suckle, daffodils, and old-fashioned aquilegias.

Another fine specimen grew along, and almost enclosed, a wide verandah surrounding another early house in the French part of Akaroa. This was the home for nearly a hundred years of a lady who loved her roses; she was credited with having received a plant of the Crimson China from Bishop Pompallier, when he travelled down from the Bay of Islands to pay a visit to Banks Peninsula. After her death the house changed hands and many old roses were swept away. The present owner is enthusiastically gathering together another collection of old roses. Apart from its beauty, the Double Yellow Banksia, had other uses. In some parts of China fishermen toughened their nets, and made them less visible to fish, by soaking them in a brew made from the roots of R. *banksiae*; while in Europe old-rose growers found it a fine stock on which to bud the tender Tea and Noisette Roses. Our plant of the Yellow Banksia was a gift to my husband from a Fielding rosarian: and our White Banksia was grown from cuttings given to me by a keen Auckland rosarian.

While in Rome, we admired a glorious white climber, Purezza. It has not arrived in New Zealand yet, as far as we know; but is sure to be a popular rose in time. This is a new break in rose breeding: it is a continuous-flowering hybrid from R. *banksiae*.

R. *fortuneana*, a perfect cross between the white Cherokee Rose and the Double White Banksia, is another treasure that was discovered by Robert Fortune on one of his expeditions to China. Our plant came to us from a very old garden in Whangarei. Once, on our way home from a trip to the Bay of Islands, we called in to see the owner of this garden, a charming and cultured grower of old roses. Later we paid other visits to her garden, and learnt from her a great deal about old roses and their introduction into New Zealand. Her uncle, who started the Mont Pellier Nursery in Auckland many years ago, was responsible for bringing a number of roses into the country. These were sent to him as cuttings, packed in dry moss, and enclosed in metal surveyor's tubes. Sealed hermetically, they survived the long sea voyage, and practically all rooted well when planted in this new country. Amongst their number was R. *fortuneana*. The transportation of living plants used to be the old collector's greatest problem, long before the days of air travel and polythene bags. It was Robert Fortune who was the first to try out an a big scale a new idea invented by a Londoner, Dr Ward. Dr Ward noticed that seeds germinated readily when the soil was covered with a glass jar; and from this small beginning, he made what came to be known as a Wardian case. Plants were put into soil inside an air-tight glass case, where they were seen to grow and thrive. In this way, the Tea plant, *Camellia sinensis*, was introduced into India: and other plants of commercial value found their way to the New and the Old Worlds. The rose world was enriched, also, by the safe introduction of R. *fortuneana* and R. *pseudindica* or Fortune's Yellow, two fine climbers.

When we saw R. *fortuneana* in this Whangarei garden it had travelled over thirty feet through trees in the company of a Yellow Banksia and the white Noisette Lamarque. Its persistent foliage is a glossy green with three to five leaflets similar to, though larger than, that of one parent, R. *banksiae*. From its other parent it inherits the habit of producing one flower only in each leaf axil, instead of a cluster. These fairly large double white blooms are sweetly scented, and rather globular in shape before they open fully; they look charming nodding down from a tree as we saw them that day at Pa Mairie This Northland garden, which adjoins a reserve of native bush, acquired its name from the fact that in the early days, when the Maoris were on the war-path, it was heavily palisaded with trunks of black mairie, a native tree. At the side of the garden is a path down which the warriors used to carry their canoes to the water's edge, and many Maori artifacts have been unearthed in this vicinity.

As we strolled round this garden, we were shown many roses which, until then, we had only read about; and were told how, in the owner's young days, she used to gather a basketful of snow white blooms of R. *fortuneana* whenever there was a local wedding, and cover a bell with these ruffled flowers, to hang over the bride's table. This is a charming custom which appears to be drying out. Our rampant plant, which flowered well in three years from a tiny cutting, has climbed up ten feet and attached itself, with its sharp little thorns, to the trellised panels at the end of the carport; from this elevated position it showers down on thin graceful stems, producing flowers intermittently through the winter. Robert Fortune found it cultivated in gardens round Shanghai and Ning-po, where it was held in high esteem by the Chinese. He considered it one of the best white roses he saw in China, especially when it was trained on garden walls, and used to cover arbours and trellis-work. Later, on the

Riviera, it was used as an under-stock and in some parts of Australia it is still used for that purpose. There is a beautiful painting of it by Alfred Parsons in the *Genus Rosa*; we saw the original of this picture, lately, in London.

The same celebrated botanical collector, Robert Fortune, discovered a rose that was new to him in a mandarin's garden at Ningpo. A rampant climber growing against a tall wall, it was a mass of unusual yellow, buff, and reddish blooms. Discovering that it came from Northern China, and realising that it would therefore be hardy in Britain, Fortune sent plants of this rose to England in 1845; there it was named Fortune's Double Yellow, or R. *pseudindica*. In time it acquired two further names, Beauty of Glazenwood, and Gold of Ophir. At first this vigorous rose was not a success in England, as it resented pruning, only flowering well on the previous year's wood. Also, it required a sunny spot with plenty of space in which to develop and show off its true beauty. We realised this when we were taken to see a tremendous plant of Fortune's Yellow growing at The Glen in Akaroa, a hundred-year-old, white, gabled house, with wide verandahs looking out over this historic habrour. The owner kindly showed us a grand old specimen of R. *pseudindica* climbing through trees to a great height in company with an equally old wisteria. It had been left to itself for many years, and was undoubtedly the largest climbing rose of any kind we had ever seen. The rose and wisteria bloom at the same time and create a breathtaking picture. Many years ago, an Akaroa friend sent us cuttings from this old rose; we rooted them with difficulty only to lose them when they had to be lifted in mid-summer. Now we have a budded plant coming on which we hope to train into a tree. The flowering season of Fortune's Yellow is early and short; but the loose flowers have such a flaunting, though fleeting beauty, and the rose is so distinctive, that we feel it should be included amongst the wild climbers that we grow.

Boursault Roses are little known or grown today, but several in our garden give us a great deal of pleasure each season. They come into flower early, soon after the Banksias: and, for this reason, are a valuable addition to our collection. They were bred from the Alpine Rose of Europe and R. *chinensis*. The first introduction was called the Old Red Boursault: it is a rose we have not, so far, found in New Zealand, but it was growing vigorously in the Roseta Communale in Rome, and we have good colour slides of it. The ancient R. *alpina* is known, also, as the Drop-hip Rose and the Thornless Rose. This latter peculiarity is interesting because of the saying of the followers of Zoroaster, that roses had no thorns until the arrival of evil in the world.

There is one plant of the double form of this low-growing Thornless Rose—the Alpine Rose—suckering on an old grave, dated 1879, in the Grafton cemetery. Another is in the early Bolton Street cemetery in Wellington. The thin stems are smooth, shiny, and dark reddish-brown; the flowers, which generally come singly or in very small clusters, are purple-crimson and of poor texture. However, the leaves make up for this by colouring brilliantly in the autumn. The first hybrid was bred in a Paris nursery about 1810: and a plant was sent to a Monsieur Henri Boursault, a keen amateur rose grower, who had at that time one of the finest collections in Paris. In 1820 it was given the authentic botanical name of R. *boursaultiana* in honour of this gardener; but Thory, who wrote the text for Redouté's *Roses*, named it differently. He called it R. *l'heritieranea*, after Charles Louis l'Héritier, the French botanist to whom Redouté credited much of his success as a painter of flowers. However, Boursault is the common name by which these roses are still known. Until recently, no doubts had been cast on their origin for a hundred years; but Dr Rowley, of the Bayfordbury Research Station is now experimenting with the theory that it was the American rose, *blanda*, not *alpina*, which was its wild parent. It will take time before the results of his work are made known; but we were interested to see R. *alpina* in one bed at the Research Station, and the rose Amadis in the next bed—Amadis being another crimson-purple Boursault.

We do not grow Amadis, but have got a close relative, Elegans, which was sent to us from Akaroa. It grew on an early farm on Banks Peninsula, where many French families settled. Elegans is to be found also in the old Bolton cemetery in Wellington, near one parent, the Alpine Rose of Europe. We find it a tremendous grower and a wonderfully free-flowering plant. The large trusses of cheerful rosy-purple, loosely double flowers, on flexible canes, continue in bloom for a long time, as they bear buds in varying stages of development. Some of the petals show a white stripe down the centre—an inheritance from the China parent, though its smooth stems and well-spaced clear green leaves resemble the other side of the family. We find Elegans an excellent cut flower, the long sprays lasting well in water. Soon after it has finished blooming, all old wood is removed, and fine new shoots quickly appear to bear next season's flowers. Gracilis, the first plant of this rose family to be grown in our garden, came to us from Mt Possession, in the foothills of the Southern Alps. One boundary of this large sheep station runs up to the snowline, and in the large garden, with glorious trees and spacious lawns, we discovered several early roses, amongst them this Boursault.

There were also two graceful and free-growing bushes of Gracilis growing in the shade of a large copper beech—these roses being equally happy in sun or shade, a very accommodating trait. They were smothered along the full length of the branches with hundreds of loose, lavender-pink, flothery blooms as Dean Hole described them in *A Book about Roses*. Each leaf has seven leaflets, well spaced on flexible canes, rather thorny on the older wood. When fully developed, the heps are pendulous, as are those of the Alpine Rose. Gracilis is not recommended in England, and we did not come across it in any garden we visited; but out here it blooms delightfully and is always admired. It grows by the roadsides as well as in early gardens, but improves tremendously when well cultivated and pruned at the right time.

On a trip down through the sparsely settled country bordering the Wanganui River, we came across another of these Boursault roses. After passing through Pipiriki, where tremendous bushes of Félicité et Perpétue were tumbling down from trees and banks, we came to Jerusalem, the site of a very early mission settlement. We visited the lovingly cared for church, and then the convent; and in the convent grounds we found many old roses—the rosy-purple Gallica, Anaïs Ségales, China and Moss Roses, old Hybrid Perpetuals and Gracilis, the rosy-pink Boursault. Further over in the hedges were the more modern roses, Silver Morn and New Dawn; while great stands of Félicité were growing across the river on the original site. Gracilis also flowers well in full shade on the coldest side of one of the early stone houses built in the days of Bishop Selwyn. Being descended from the hardy Alpine Rose, Boursaults flourish in spite of hard conditions. Nowhere can we find parentage of the old stock rose, Manettii, bred in Italy about the same time as the Boursault Roses were raised in France; but there is a resemblance between the blooms of some of these roses.

Our plants of this Boursault Rose are growing against a strong trellis panel let into the side of the carport, the lower branches being tied in and

▲ 33. Lamarque

▼ 34. Desprez à Fleur Jaune

35. Donna Maria

36. Mme. Sancy de Parabére and Gracilis

the upper ones being allowed to hang down gracefully. For the smaller garden this is a useful way of training the plant, as it does not take up too much space, yet looks attractive. When the flowers first open from the long-sepalled buds, they are a vivid rose, and are quite globular in shape, being rather reminiscent of the blooms of that lovely Macrantha Hybrid, Raubritter. They quickly become cup-shaped, before paling and opening quite flat, each flower lasting well in the soft, faded state. Further along this wall we grow the variegated variety of that fine climber, *Rhynchospermum jasminoides*, which flowers when the roses are over and scents the garden in the summer evenings. Originally, we grew the magnificent blue *Thunbergia grandiflora* from Nepal on the wall as well, but it proved far too rampant for this position and had to be removed.

Amongst the Boursault Roses that we know and grow, none have leaves that do as well as those of the double from of *R. pendulina*—the Alpine Brier. Even in the spring this foliage is attractive as there is a purple bloom to be seen over the green. Though this is not a spectacular garden rose, it is interesting botanically because of its thornless stems, which are noticeable in the following rose. Madame Sancy de Parabère we imported from England, to grow alongside our other Boursaults. It is the only one that is well-known today in Europe and North America; but, so far, ours is the only plant we have seen in New Zealand, though recently we heard of this Boursault growing in an old cemetery. Its flowers are not unlike those of Gracilis, though in colour they are a warmer shade of rose. In fact, we arranged blooms of both roses together and then photographed them. When the slides were shown on a screen it was quite difficult to distinguish one from the other, but there is a decided difference in the stems and leaves. In Madame Sancy de Parebère, the branches are completely thornless and quite brownish in colour, the leaves also being of a slightly darker hue than those of Gracilis or Elegans. There is a good illustration of this rose in *The Old Shrub Roses* and the author calls it the finest of the Boursault Roses.

A climber which we shall include here for convenience is an old stock rose, *R. indica major* which is still used as such in Europe and parts of Australia. Dr A. S. Thomas in his book *Better Roses* writes that it is known by several names in Australia; Boursault, Blushing Bride, and Maiden's Blush being some of them. In the first editions of William Paul's *The Rose Garden*, published in 1848, he describes the Blush Boursault, a hybrid between a Boursault and R. *chinensis*, as "an excellent climbing rose when planted in a good aspect. It holds its leaves well, it is pendulous and has very double, blush flowers with deeper pink centres". This is an excellent description of our stock rose but whether the two roses are one and the same, we cannot find out, because so far, neither here nor overseas, have we been able to discover the exact parentage of this old rose. Many years ago, the United States Department of Agriculture imported a cultivated climbing rose from China to try out as a stock plant. This was known as R. *indica major* in the United States, and as Fun Jwan Lo in China. Its use was discontinued later, as it proved not sufficiently hardy for the United States' colder districts. It is strange that there should be so much confusion over the origin of this rose when it has been, and still is being used as a stock rose in warmer climates.

It is an extremely healthy, early-flowering rose, but so far growers in this country have not given it a serious trial, though it should be good in the North. Large bushes of it grow semi-wild in the centre of the North Island and in the Gisborne district, so there is plenty of it available. Our climber came from cuttings collected from a roadside plant which grew in the shade of one of the highest railway viaducts in New Zealand. It grew, also, in the cemetery at Waimate North, site of one of our earliest mission settlements. We were interested to see lovely bushes of R. *indica major* hanging over high garden walls in the Labanon, as we drove from Beirut to Baalbek; and, later again, to see it in the village outside the site of the ancient city of Corinth. It grew also in the courtyard of the Corinth Museum, amongst broken columns and old statuary—having been planted there, of course, no later than the early part of the last century. This rose as well as China Roses, is also used for hedges in the south of France.

When John Champneys, a lover of roses and a rice grower from South Carolina, decided to cross the Musk Rose, R. *moschata* from the Mediterranean area, with the perpetual-flowering Old Blush China, a form of R. *chinensis* he did not realise that he was starting an entirely new rose family which was destined to add great charm and beauty to gardens all over the world. This group of climbing roses later became known as Noisettes. A neighbour of John Champneys, Philip Noisette, a Charleston florist, was given cuttings of the first of these new roses which was to be called Champneys' Pink Cluster. About 1817 he sent seeds of this plant to his brother Louis in Paris and, about a year later another Charleston man, John Fraser, raised a new rose by the same cross, plants of which were sent to England about 1820 and distributed under the name of Fraser's Pink Musk. Along with the first seeds sent to France, went a plant that had been raised by Philip Noisette—this proved to be a dwarfer form than the original cross, though it had the same large clusters of flowers and strong musk scent.

Redouté's fine painting of R. *noisettiana* gives an excellent idea of this plant. We collected a bush from an old garden in the Hunterville district; the climbing form is to be found in another old garden not far away. We grow a number of Noisette Roses, some collected in the country and others imported from overseas. The flowers are always produced in clusters at the ends of the branches and the laterals, as many as hundred at a time being seen on one spray of the earliest varieties. There are generally seven leaflets to each leaf stalk. The flowers are pale in colour, ranging from small double white blooms, to deep yellow. The oldest Noisette Hybrid we grow here is Aimée Vibert or Bouquet de la Mariée which was raised in France in 1828 by Vibert, who also bred several other roses in this garden, including Blanchefleur, a white Centifolia, and the Comtesse de Murinais, a Moss Rose.

The fragrant white flowers of Aimée Vibert are pink tinted in the bud, and hang in large sprays at the ends of the branches, which are flexible and clothed with dark-green, long, narrow leaflets like those of the Musk Rose. It never flowers with us before the late summer; and then not as freely as we would wish. We grow it up a ten-foot wall with several other roses; but Gertrude Jekyll wrote that, if this rose was allowed to grow through a tall tree, it would increase quickly in size, and bloom much more freely. One illustration shows it as a veritable fountain of flowers cascading down from a dark tree. Unfortunately, it has not been our privilege to see such a specimen. Next to Aimée Vibert in age comes Lamarque—a rare, lovely Noisette that was bred in France by Maréchal in 1830. In Mrs Earle's *Pot-Pourri from a Surrey Garden* she says that no garden was perfect without a Lamarque rose in it; and Canon Ellacombe also mentioned it when he wrote *In a Gloucestershire Garden*. He said that if he was limited to growing one white rose, it would have to be Lamarque That was written towards the end of the last century; now there are other fine new white climbers to choose from.

The blooms of Lamarque, several to each spray, are not up to exhibition standard; but their charm and decorative value are undeniable. The slightly serrated petals are lemon-yellow at their base and the fragrance of the flowers is clean and delicious. The whole plant has a young, fresh look, with its pale green leaves, and slightly pendant flowers clustered on the ends of the long, swaying laterals. Our winters are not severe, so Lamarque blooms for the greater part of the year. We had no success whatever in growing this rose from cuttings sent to us from the country, but found out later that it generally had to be budded. Mr Hunter, at the Mt Albert Research Station, did succeed in enticing one cutting to grow under glass; it is this plant, on its own roots, that is now doing better than the budded one. A keen gardener of Ohaupo, and another in Whangarei gave us cuttings of Lamarque, which has proved a valuable addition to our collection. Apparently, this was a popular rose in the old gold-mining settlement in California; and also in Madeira, where it grew rampantly.

When a Yellow Tea-scented China Rose was introduced into England from the Far East in 1824, French breeders were quick to assess its worth. They acquired plants and hoped by crossing this new acquisition with the original Blush Noisette, to produce a pure yellow Noisette. Two charming roses were bred, though neither were yellow. One was the white Lamarque; and the other was Desprez à Fleur Jaune, or Jaune Desprez. This is a lovely rose which we grow on a fence next to the lavender-blue, large-flowered clematis Mrs Hope. The buff-coloured flowers are shaded with warm yellow, peach, and apricot, and have a rich fragrance. Early and late in the season, these blooms are really lovely; but the midsummer ones are poor in comparison as they fade out quickly in the hot sun. It is grown on the Riviera, and so is Lamarque, though Jaune Desprez is good there only early in the season. It only arrived from England four years ago and has made wonderfully quick growth.

Madame Plantier has been listed for years amongst the Noisettes; but there seems to be some doubt about which family it really belongs to. Some class it as an *alba* × *moschata*, others as *damask* × *moschata*, and still others as *noisette* × *moschata*. It has always been summer-flowering only, unlike other Noisettes; but this year one of our plants produced autumn flowers, as has another summer-flowering rose, the lovely Alba, Madame Legras de Saint Germain. Many well-known writers of the last century, and Edward A. Bunyard in this century, list Madame Plantier as a Noisette. Whatever its ancestry, it is a glorious rose, healthy, non-thorny, with attractive, soft, lettuce-green leaves, and pink-tinted buds, the beauty of which is enhanced by the long, leafy calyx-lobes. The clusters of medium-sized, double, white flowers have a green eye, the outer petals reflexing back in a most attractive manner. When the bushes flanking either side of one entrance to our white garden are in full bloom, the thin, whippy branches are weighted down with the multitude of flowers.

Given the support of a trellis or a tree, Madam Plantier will climb and cascade down in a graceful manner. An illustration of this can be seen in Graham Thomas' book, *The Old Shrub Roses*. This photograph was taken at Sissinghurst Castle; and we were fortunate when we visited this famous garden, to see the same plants climbing through trees in the orchard. Although the rose is not perpetual-blooming, the flowers do appear in profusion over a period of at least eight weeks, filling the garden with scent and admired by all who see them. Madame Plantier was recommended as a hedge plant by the American writer, A. B. Ellwanger in his book *The Rose;* and since its introduction in 1835 it has received a warm welcome in many countries. Out here in New Zealand it is to be found in the earliest cemeteries, by the roadsides, and in old gardens; and in one country district, where there are great frothing bushes of it growing wild, it is referred to as the Bride's Rose. We heard also of Madame Plantier in Poverty Bay, growing on the site of an early homestead which had been destroyed by fire. It had been grazed over and trampled down by horses for fifteen years—and still survived. More recently a Nelson old-rose collector found it growing beneath tall pines in a neglected hillside cemetery at Collingwood, near the mouth of the Aorere River, where the third New Zealand gold-field was opened up.

From Lamarque and Desprez à Fleur Jaune came Céline Forestier, Cloth of Gold and Solfaterre—yellow Tea Noisettes, the first being paler in tone, but having petals folded and quartered in a delightful manner. Solfaterre, with its fully, fragrant, suphur-yellow flowers, is a superb Tea Noisette for a warm climate and a sunny wall. At one time, it was found to be an excellent stock on which to bud less hardy Tea Roses. However, the best known of this trio was undoubtedly Cloth of Gold which was being sold out here by 1860. Thomas River, an English rose grower, said of it "Fashion may change, but beauty never," when he saw Cloth of Gold in 1880, climbing up through a tree at Villa Cessoles, near Nice. The flowers, like golden bells, showed here, there, and everywhere amidst the branches. It caused a sensation when it was exhibited at the Third

National Rose Show held in England at the Crystal Palace.

Given a rich soil and a warm, sunny position, Cloth of Gold, with its full, golden yellow flowers, will cover a huge area, as it is long-lived, particularly on its own roots. Quite a few of our oldest gardens and settlements all over the country boast immense plants of this yellow Tea-Noisette. In Akaroa there are fine specimens with stems as thick as a man's arm; and cuttings of it sent to me some years ago from Rangiora, came from a plant that had been brought across from Banks Peninsula. Cloth of Gold flourished in sunny Nelson too. There was a huge specimen growing up to the attic on the front of the old Motueka Vicarage: it was planted there by the Rev. Samuel Poole, who came out to New Zealand as an army chaplain in 1853 and finally settled in Nelson. This same rose we saw growing vigorously at Lethenty, a lovely old homestead at Bulls; and we were told it did tremendously well near the Kaipara Harbour, in the north, where early settlers to that district grew it in their garden.

Several years ago we made a special trip to Rawene to visit Mrs Miller, a daughter of the late Mr J. R. Clendon who came from historic Okiato and settled at Herd's Point soon after the Treaty of Waitangi was signed. We had hoped to hear from her a first-hand account of the roses that grew in her mother's rose garden, which was shown in early maps as being situated on the sunny, northern slope of Okiato Point. The spot was purchased in 1840 to be the site of the first New Zealand Government, a plan which was quickly abandoned when Auckland was founded. Unfortunately, we missed meeting Mrs Miller, who was in her hundredth year, as she had just had a fall which necessitated her removal to hospital; but her son kindly showed us old papers and also the roses they grew at Rawene, which had been brought across to their new home on Hokianga Harbour. From the information which we gathered there, and our own findings in the Okiato district, we were able to build up a picture of one of the earliest recorded rose gardens in the country which was situated on a beautiful headland overlooking the Bay of Islands. Now no sign of this rose garden remains, the original site having been cleared by bulldozers and turned into grazing land for farm animals.

It is probable that Mrs Clendon grew Gallica Roses, Damask Roses, the old Cabbage Rose, white, pink and red Moss Roses, red and pink China Roses, the Dog Rose, and two forms of the Sweet Brier, one of which was checked for us botanically and found to be the low growing variety,

R. *eglanteria glutinosa*, the other being the taller common variety. The Chestnut Rose, a double form of R. *roxburghii* was also there, as well as the rampant, double pink R. *multiflora carnea*, the Double White Banksia, and Félicité et Perpétue. Most of these roses were grown, also, at the Kemp home in Kerikeri. Mrs Pyecroft, renowned for her paintings of New Zealand flora, lived in Opau, near Okiato, many years ago; she told me of visits to that historic spot, and one of the things she mentioned was the fact that large patches of a dwarf blue bearded iris and the white *Iris florentina* grew in the vicinity of the old garden as well as that fascinating perennial, Marvel of Peru, which had flowers of several colours, and opened only in the late afternoon. When Mr Clendon left to settle at Rawene he took cuttings from his bay-tree to plant at this new home and one of these grew and was still flourishing. Apparently, Sir George Grey used to stay with the Clendons after they moved to the Hokianga district; and, on one occasion, the children of the family persuaded him to plant their date stones and orange pips in the garden. The date palms are still there; but the orange trees had just been removed because of old age. Until recently, a Cloth of Gold rose had covered the entire front of the house; but a tremendous storm blew across that district a few years ago, and so damaged the front of the old, two-storied, gabled house, that this hoary rose had to be sacrificed in order that successful repairs could be made. The family were very sad about this, as it always flowered so well.

From a country friend we received a most interesting rose. It had been given to her by an old lady who called it Le Pactole. Many old roses introduced into New Zealand were given local or personal names such as The Bride's Rose, Aunt Mary's Rose or just Grandma's Rose. Now such titles are no guide towards helping to find out the correct name of a rose; but anything as unusual as Le Pactole could hardly have been imagined, so we shall presume that the rose which grew near Pirongia Mountain—an ancient volcano and a stronghold of the Waikato Maoris—was correctly named. If so, the only reference to it in any of our large collection of books on the rose is to be found in the first edition of William Paul's *The Rose Garden* published in 1848. We find this rose was known, also, as Pactolus and Madame de Challonge, and was listed as a Noisette. However, it was singled out as bearing a strong resemblance to the Tea Rose family; and this we found to be so, as the young foliage was reddish in colour and the growth not as vigorous as that of the Noisettes. It was described as a creamy rose with a yellow centre; but we found the blooms to be almost yolk-yellow in the centre of the tightly packed petals; and they more closely resembled the flowers of some of the old Noisettes. This was an interesting find, and though we may never be absolutely sure that this name is correct, we are grateful to the kind rosarian who gave Le Pactole and caused us to spend many happy hours searching through early books.

Up to the introduction of Gloire de Dijon in 1853 it was affectionately called Old Glory—all the Noisettes had revelled in warmth and sunshine; but this new rose was not affected adversely by a rigorous climate. Though Lamarque and Cloth of Gold grew magnificently in parts of the South of Europe, Madeira and the Azores, where they climbed to the top of tall trees, they were not as happy in the damp and cold of England. This was probably why we saw numerous plants of Gloire de Dijon in England and seldom came across Lamarque or Cloth of Gold. Unfortunately, Gloire de Dijon, in spite of its hardiness and free-flowering habit, can become bare and leggy at the base, as we saw it at Hidcote, a famous National Trust Garden in Gloucestershire, where it climbed to the eaves of a charming home built in mellow Cotswold stone. All the blooms on this particular rose were produced high up on the wall. We saw Gloire de Dijon, Madame Caroline Testout, and Paul's Scarlet growing against the brick and stone walls of many English homes. All have been popular roses in New Zealand, though they are seen less seldom against buildings. The finest blooms of Gloire de Dijon we saw overseas were on a plant growing against an old stone school in the grounds of a fourteenth-century church in Cheshire. The fragrant flattish flowers of this fine old Tea-Noisette are creamy-buff with salmon tintings deepening to a coppery-pink at the base of the petals. Good specimens are to be seen in old gardens in various parts of New Zealand. Our own plants grows against a wall in the company of large-flowered clematis—the lovely blue Mrs Cholmondeley, and the rosy-purple Sir Garnet Wolseley. Being a prolific seed-bearer, Gloire de Dijon—which itself was bred from a strong-growing Tea Rose and the Bourbon, Souvenir de la Malmaison—became the parents of many yellow-toned roses.

Maréchal Niel appeared about ten years later than Gloire de Dijon. It was a Tea-Noisette, and was highly esteemed overseas though it was considered to have a delicate constitution and was generally grown in glasshouses. When it was produced, it was hailed as the finest yellow climber of that time; but our experience with this rose was disappointing. It did not seem to thrive, so we were forced to discard it. We have never grown Rêve d'Or though we did come across plants of it in the South Island, where it appears to do well; and later saw it trained on a wall and cascading down beneath an enormous pedestal urn, in the fabulous garden of the Prince of Borromea, on Isola Bella, Lake Maggiore.

Madame Alfred Carrière, 1879, was given to us by a friend who collected it from an old garden in the Waikato district. This rose has been a constant source of joy to us. It covers one wall of a brick out-building; but we often wish we could find the space to grow it in the manner recommended by Gertrude Jekyll, in one of her many gardening books. She trained it as a hedge along wires supported by stout posts, so that its flowers, which appear at the ends of long, flexible shoots, were very easy to gather. The large loose blooms are delicately lovely, of a warm white tinted with blush at the base of the slightly indented petals. A bowl, filled entirely with the buds and fully opened flowers of Madame Alfred Carrière, is a sheer delight indoors. At Sissinghurst Castle we admired this rose growing against the wall of a two-storied, brick cottage with latticed windows, where it was carefully trained to show off an amazing display of flowers. There is a fine coloured illustration of this climber in the first edition of *House and Garden's Garden Book*, which gives a clear picture of one method of growing this lovely Noisette; but we saw it grown freely, and most attractively, in the Irish Free State, when we visited Mt Usher, the lovely home and garden of Mr E. H. Walpole. Situated in the heart of the heavily wooded Wicklow Mountains, alongside the River Vartry, this restful garden is famous amongst other things for the manner in which New Zealand and Chilian native shrubs and trees are grown. Here, along one side of the house, which is built on the site of an early Tuck Mill, where homespun and home-woven cloths were brought to be finished, runs the old mill race; and planted to top of its retaining wall was a flourishing plant of Madame Alfred Carrière. Branches of this rose hung down freely over the water in association with hardy fuchsias and other climbers.

There are two more Noisettes which are favourites in many old gardens, though lack of space precludes us from growing them here. One is Alister Stella Gray. Travelling from Little River to Akaroa one autumn, we saw a roadside plant of this rose which was producing stout, new, basal growths, and at the top of these, were tremendous sprays of smallish, tightly-packed, deep yellow blooms. It is a definite characteristic of Alister Stella Gray to throw such shoots late in the season. The other rose William Allen Richardson, with the richest coloured blooms in this family, ranging from deep yolk-yellow to orange. A splendid plant of this rose is growing in an Auckland garden. About fifty years ago, there was a great deal of speculation about William Allen Richardson. Many questions were asked in an English Rose Annual of that time; and varied were the answers. He was a florist, an Irish-American, and a keen rosarian. Finally, a letter came from the United States giving the true story. The rose grower who gave Mr W. A. Richardson immortality was a Frenchman, Monsieur Ducher. It was unusual for a French grower to honour a foreigner: what was William Allen Richardson's special claim upon him? Mr Richardson lived in America, and became much interested in the cultivation and propagation of roses. He imported many; and so made the acquaintance, by letter, of Madame Ducher, of Lyons. She was especially interested in a pale yellow rose he had sent her, which had thrown a deeper-coloured sport. Madame Ducher said that if this sport propagated successfully, she would name it after him. Successful this experiment must have proved; for the beautiful, copperish-yellow rose William Allen Richardson is well-known and still frequently seen.

Towards the end of the eighteenth century a member of Lord Macartney's embassy staff in China, Sir George Staunton, was given permission to search some of the coastal provinces for new plants—a signal favour, as at that time no foreigners were allowed into the interior of China. On this trip he found a fine evergreen rose which he introduced into England as the Macartney Rose. It became known, botanically, as R. *bracteata* – since each bud was enfolded in a number of wide, silken, silver-green bracts. This rampant, disease-resistant rose, with its glossy dark green foliage, was a slow starter in our garden; but when it finally became established, tremendous, thick new shoots, up to twenty feet in length, were produced each season. Though some rosarians advise no pruning, if we did not partially cut some of it out it would soon take charge of a large area.

When R. *bracteata* was naturalised in the United States of America, it became a menace, as it spread into fields from the hedgerows where it had been planted, and was extremely difficult to eradicate. However, the Americans have now found a use for it, as its underground stems help to prevent soil erosion—the bugbear of many countries. Most authorities mention that R. *bracteata* has a strong scent of ripe apricots. Next apricot season we tried to compare the two scents. The rich fruity fragrance was there, certainly; but we were unable to name it, perhaps because, in the middle of a particularly hot and dry summer, it was less strong than in a moister climate, and therefore more elusive. Bees swarm round this rose with its wide, flat flowers and ring of bright yellow stamens. These persist, and still look attractive, when the thick, milk-white petals have fallen.

In a National Trust garden, Nymans, situated in the south of England, many plants survived a great fire when one wing of the house was destroyed; they not only survived, but appeared to be taking advantage of all the windowless spaces, for they were climbing in and out in a spectacular manner. A *Magnolia grandiflora* and a Double Yellow Banksia Rose reached up to the tallest gable; while wisteria, winter sweet, bignonia, and the Macartney Rose, *bracteata*, seemed to be equally happy in these surroundings.

In 1854 Thomas Rivers, writing about R. *bracteata* and its good qualities, said he hoped that, ultimately, gardeners would not be satisfied unless all roses, even Moss Roses, had evergreen foliage, brilliant and fragrant flowers, and a long season of flowering: this might seem, he said, an extravagant anticipation, but perseverance in breeding would yet achieve wonders. His wish was partly realised, though of course long after his time, when the lovely climber, Mermaid, was bred from R. *bracteata*. This fine plant with its shining, bronze-green leaves and evergreen habit, flowers over a very long period, the extra large, single, butter-yellow blooms appearing in sprays at the ends of short laterals. Mermaid is a tremendous grower, like its parent; in the smaller garden it needs to be kept in check from time to time. Otherwise it requires little attention and has only one fault, if fault you could call it; this is, that it carries wicked thorns lavishly on all its branches.

Our plant is trained along, not across, a wooden pergola; and completely clothes it with rich, abundant foliage. The numerous large blooms open well in a sunny position and add necessary colour when two companion climbers are over for the season. At Government House, Auckland, there is a magnificent specimen of Mermaid trained along the full length of a stone balustrade in front of a wide terrace. This vies in size with plants we have seen overseas, such as the one growing on the front wall of the lovely laboratory building at the Royal Horticultural Society's Trial Grounds at Wisley in Surrey; and the one adorning a mellow brick wall surrounding the Tower Courtyard at Sissinghurst Castle. In the Dublin Botanical Gardens, Mermaid was growing in quite a different way, and very effective it looked too. The River Tolka runs through this park before it joins the River Liffey; and, as it is inclined to flood, its banks are contained within six-foot concrete walls, For a considerable distance on either side of an attractive swing bridge, the tops of the walls have been planted with Mermaid, which completely hides the ugly retaining work. These bushes, after only a few seasons, hang down almost to the water's edge, and look very charming in such a position. They also make a pleasant approach to the new rose garden that is being established across the river from Addison's Walk. R. *bracteata* seldom sets seed—in fact in many years we have not seen any on our plant—so that hybrids from it are very few indeed. Mermaid, the most important, came from a cross between a yellow Tea Rose and R. *bracteata* in 1918; but there is the earlier, semi-double Marie Léonida which was bred in France in 1832. We have not found this variety out here, though we did see it in Europe. However, both its parents, R. *bracteata* and R. *laevigata* are well-known in New Zealand.

When in England recently, we were delighted to see R. *arvensis*, the Field Rose, trailing along the roadsides through grass and hedges, and growing upwards too, if there was sufficient support. One of our lovely climbers, Dundee Rambler, was bred from it. This wild rose, with its strong musk scent, has been considered by some writers to be the one described by Shakespeare in *A Midsummer Night's Dream*

> I know a bank whereon the wild thyme blows,
> Where oxlips and the nodding violet grows,
> Quite over-canopied with luscious woodbine,
> With sweet musk-roses and with eglantine,

—rather than the Persian Musk, which was introduced from the Middle East. We sat on such a bank on the lovely downs above South Harting, amidst wild thyme, herb Robert, milkwort, lady finger, pink plantain, snowberry, quaking grass, and several colours of orchids; while in the hedges nearby were bushes of Sweet Brier, Dog Rose, and the trailing Field Rose. We gathered a small posy to photograph, and later, to help identify wild plants with which we were unfamiliar. R. *arvensis* has cup-shaped, pure white flowers, which generally appear singly on wiry, upright stems. It is a charming little rose, quite common in the southern countries; but not seen so frequently further north. It has still another claim to fame, in that it was thought by some to have been the emblem of the House of York rather than R. *alba*, an early introduction.

The Dundee Rambler is extremely vigorous and hardy, and will thrive under very trying conditions while keeping completely healthy. Our plant came to us from a friend, a keen and very knowledgeable gardener, who had been sent cuttings from an old New Zealand garden. It was scarcely rooted, and we were amazed when it not only survived but flourished. Within two or three seasons it had covered a vast area and climbed up over a high slatted, wooden shelter which protects a stone seat, halfway along one side of the pergola. The whole of the structure is smothered in early summer with sprays of the double milk-white blooms, which are faintly tinged with blush-pink in the bud and opening stages. As soon as the flowers fade, new shoots start to appear. At this stage we cut out all old wood, right back to where new growth is appearing. This develops at an amazing rate; and we find it necessary to guide and train the long shoots as soon as they are firm enough to handle.

Excellent black and white photographs in *Roses for English Gardens*, show the Dundee Rambler trained in an umbrella shape over a tall standard, clothing pergola and wall, and growing free through trees. Gertrude Jekyll mentions planting a *Clematis montana* and a Dundee Rambler together; and describes how the clematis raced away at first, but was eventually overtaken by the rose, which hooked its way up through a shining holly and a sombre yew, and came tumbling down from the top. We saw a fine specimen growing in New Zealand through one of our native trees and through tall camellias and rhododendrons. It had branches at the base as thick as a man's arm, having been left unpruned for nearly a hundred years; it made a most impressive sight as it cascaded down, in a shower of milky-white, from a height of thirty feet. The flowers somewhat resemble those of R. *noisettiana*; and this is not surprising, as the plant was bred in Scotland from a cross between an early Noisette and the Field Rose. This truly magnificent Dundee Rambler was growing at Pakaraka, in the Bay of Islands district, where Archdeacon Henry Williams built The Retreat in 1853. The present owner kindly took us round both gardens, where we came across a number of old ramblers that had spread over large areas.

We have sent her other roses of a suitable vintage to train over her trees: and we hear that they are happy in their new surroundings.

On this same journey we went from Archdeacon Williams' old home to nearby Waimate North—site of the third Anglican Mission Station to be established and the first to be built inland—to see if any old roses grew on this churchyard. Only two were there—the Old Blush China and R. *indica major* but we did see in a nearby garden, the first oak tree to be planted in New Zealand. The acorn from which this giant grew was brought from Goathill in Dorset by Richard Davis and planted by him, in the first place, at Pahia. Later, when his house was burnt down, he asked willing helpers to save his tree rather than the building. Mr Davis was an agriculturalist who came out to New Zealand to work for the Church Missionary Society, and later, about 1830, settled on a farm at Waimate. When he left Pahia, the oak tree went with him and is a magnificent specimen today.

In the Lisbon Botanical Garden, Portugal, in 1898, several crosses were made between R. *odorata gigantea* – a Burmese rose – and certain old Tea Roses. One of these, Belle Portugaise or Belle of Portugal, is well-known in Auckland. It is vigorous, has the healthy large foliage of its wild parent, and long, pointed buds which open to flesh-pink, tea-scented flowers. The rather large blooms are inclined to be weak in the neck, and resemble very closely, except in size, the illustration by Redouté of R. *indica fragrans* or *odorata* – another rose related to the Burmese climber – and the parent of many Tea Roses. Belle of Portugal is a better garden plant than an exhibition rose, as the weak stems would debar it from doing well on a show bench. La Follette, a rich-toned edition of Belle of Portugal, has the same parentage; and both are a glorious sight on the French and Italian Rivieras early in the season, as they love a warm climate. This is perhaps why Belle of Portugal thrives splendidly in Auckland's semi-tropical climate. Souvenir de Madame Léonie Viennot is the other parent of this climber; and it, also, is to be seen in many parts of the country.

The hardy Prairie Rose, R. *setigera*, is the last of our wild American roses to come into flower each season; and, because of this, we value it highly as it gives us a gay splash of colour in the garden during the hot and trying month of January, when so many climbers and ramblers have finished flowering. Its leaves, a fresh green at first and downy underneath, resemble those of the common blackberry—hence its other name, the

Bramble-leaved Rose. Generally, there are only three deeply serrated and tapering leaflets to each stalk, and the lovely flowers come as sprays from short side growths. The five indented petals open round a wonderful bunch of yellow stamens—their colour at first being a gay cerise which fades to a lavender-rose. A French botanist, sent out by his government to collect wild American roses, was so impressed with R. *setigera* that he felt it ought to be called the Rose of America. Actually, this is the only one of their wild roses that will climb, though it does make a fine showy bush also. A number of early climbers, well-known in the United States but not in New Zealand, were bred from this rose: the only one we saw overseas was Baltimore Belle. However, American Pillar, the best-known and most universally grown of the hybrids from the Prairie Rose, is to be found by our roadsides, in the mining and milling settlements, as well as in many gardens and parks. On one trip we saw a vivid splash of colour behind a Maori pa in the centre of the North Island, and found a marvellous specimen of this rose rambling over an old and decrepit shack. American Pillar resulted from a cross between R. *setigera*, R. *wichuriana* and an unknown old red Hybrid Perpetual, and is a particularly showy plant, the white centre of the petals making the rosy-cerise of the flowers gay and eye-catching. It is a strong, rampant grower, and suckers freely when on its own roots; but, unlike its prairie relative, is rather subject to mildew when conditions are too dry. For this reason, we have now discarded American Pillar and given its place in the garden to R. *setigera*, its trouble-free and attractive relative.

Modern climbers produce an abundance of bloom over a long season, and can moreover be cut for the house. In a garden devoted for the most part to the growing of older roses, there is insufficient space for us to plant many of these flaunting beauties, though we do appreciate their worth. In the past, before we changed our garden scheme, we grew the climbing forms of Étoile de Hollande, Mrs A. C. James, General McArthur, Dainty Bess, and Picture, as well as the true climber, Lady Waterlow. We loved Madame Abel Chatenay, and were sad when it had to be removed in mid-summer to make way for the erection of a new fence; and sadder still when we could not replace it. Parade, Peace, Blossomtime, and the winter-flowering Nancy Hayward give us many lovely blooms for the house. The late Sir Alister Clark of Melbourne bred many free-flowering climbers from the wild R. *gigantea* of Upper Burma. Nancy Hayward was one of them and it inherits from this parent its prodigous growth, ever-green foliage and large single flowers – in fact, R. *gigantea* has the largest flowers and heps of any rose. This cheerful plant blooms in the depth of winter when its cherry-coloured flowers positively glow in the garden, and are luminous and long-lasting in the house. A double pink sister plant, Lorraine Lee, we now grow only as a shrub; and a valuable one it is too, when the cold weather sets in. As a climber we found it too rampant for its allotted space; so reluctantly gave it away.

Climbing roses can be found in infinite variety to grace many positions in our gardens. It only remains for individual gardeners to choose those roses that will suit them best and that will give them the bloom and the colour they admire.

37. Seven Sisters
(R. *multiflora platyphylla*)

38. Albertine

▲ 39. Honorine de Brabant and fuchsias

▼ 40. R. *francofurtana* and fuchsias

A rosebud by my early walk,
Adown a corn-enclosed bawk,
Sae gently bent its thorny stalk,
All on a dewy morning.

Burns

A NUMBER OF RAMBLING ROSES GROWING IN THIS GAR-
den have been collected over a period of many years from country
roadsides in many parts of New Zealand. All roses had to be introduced
into this country, there being no roses growing wild in the southern
hemisphere – so it is amazing to find such diverse types happily thriving
in a semi-wild state. At certain times of the year, particularly during the
holiday season, from late November till well on in January, gay ramblers
laden with bloom brighten the countryside.

The largest-growing and most striking looking of these roses belong
to three main families, R. *sempervirens*, R. *multiflora*, and R. *wichuriana*.
But other types such as Noisette, Musk, Boursault, Tea, Dog and Brier
Roses can all be found in sparsely populated areas. Hedges of Old Blush
China are quite common; and there are even some of the rosy-purple
Anaïs Ségales, a Gallica Rose. These hedge roses are often twined through
other low-growing shrubs and can look very attractive at certain seasons.
We noticed China Roses used deliberately for this purpose in Australia,
Honolulu, Canada, on the Continent and in the British Isles, probably
because such hedge roses are perpetual-flowering and easily trimmed. Many
roadside roses have been garden escapes, though settlers frequently planted
cuttings along their fences, while others just threw rose prunings on to

the grassy verges. There, every piece that touched the ground rooted, particularly if they were Wichurianas. Open storm-water drains were dug at the sides of many older roads; as these were always moist, roses in their vicinity seemed to do particularly well and be free of mildew. This bears out what we have always thought: that roses require an abundance of water if they are to keep glossy and healthy. It is obvious in some places that new roads have been cut through the centre of early cottage gardens; and here ramblers, as well as many other interesting types of old roses, are to be found. With the advent of fast motor vehicles and the necessary widening and straightening of roads, many beautiful stands of roses are fast disappearing and our roadsides losing some of their charm. It has been our habit to take colour photographs of these ramblers as we travel through the country; these, in time, may prove to be a valuable record of early plantings in New Zealand.

Of the three main varieties of rambler roses adorning our roadsides the hybrids of R. *sempervirens* are the first to flower. The type itself, the Evergreen Rose, intermediate between the Field Rose of England and the Musk Rose of Persia, is to be found in a number of countries bordering the Mediterranean. At the beginning of the nineteenth century, it aroused the interest of Monsieur Jacques, head gardener to Louis Philippe, afterwards King of France. From it this breeder raised a number of rambling roses, several of which were introduced into New Zealand at a very early date. The best known is Félicité et Perpétue, which Jacques called after his two daughters, whose names were derived from those of the two saints and martyrs, Felicitas and Perpetua. This rose has practically evergreen foliage of a dark, reddish-green colour, and huge sprays of small creamy flowers, blush-tinted on the outside. Each bloom has masses of tiny, closely-packed petals, very similar to those of its small relative, Belle of Teheran. Félicité et Perpétue is, without doubt, the most rampant and indestructible rose in the country. At the entrance to the Treaty House at Waitangi there is a huge mass of it growing up through a high hedge.

It was here that the first British Resident to New Zealand, Mr Busby, lived. Not far from here, a little way up the Waitangi River, are the beautiful Haruru Falls, below which, in the early days, small sea-going vessels used to anchor alongside the bank, in deep water, to unload their cargoes. When Charles Darwin visited the Bay of Islands in H.M.S. *Beagle* in 1835, he was rowed up to see these Falls, by Mr Busby. Above them is the site of the **vanished** Haruru Hotel. The property is surrounded by tall, over-grown hedges and, along the entire length of this large block of land, Félicité et Perpétue is rampant. It climbs right up into adjacent trees, nearly smothering the hedge, as well as extending out over the grass verges and even in places appearing up through the hard metalled surface of the road itself. Across from the hotel site, an old and derelict cottage is now nearly smothered with roses and other climbing plants. Félicité et Perpétue was growing through the trees and shrubs and a Double White Banksia was almost covering the house; while at the side, in a veritable tangle of jasmine, ipomea, honeysuckle, periwinkle, and ginger plant, was a mass of the rosy-purple Gallica seen throughout the country.

All through the Bay of Islands district, wherever there are old settle-ments, Félicité et Perpétue can be found—generally covering a large area. At Matauwhi Bay, near Russell, it is growing through hedges and along roadsides in a most tenacious manner. At Whahapu, between Russell and Okiato, where Captain Gilbert Mair, in 1828, established the first trading station in New Zealand is another old garden where this rose, and many others grow. It is so indestructible that, when a big bush of it was chopped out on the hillside behind Pompallier House to make room for a memorial border of the Pink China Rose, it quickly appeared again, springing up from odd pieces of root left in the ground. Before long this tenacious rambler, and a white form of R. *multiflora* which had been similarly treated, were in danger of smothering the China Roses.

Further south we saw a deserted miner's cottage on Coromandel Peninsula sagging under the weight of a huge bush of Félicité et Perpétue; while the field in front of it was covered with frothy white mounds of the same rose. Nearer the tip of this peninsula, which bounds the Firth of Thames in the east, lies Kikowhakarere Bay, three miles north of Corom-andel township. Here we visited a house built 125 years ago for Judge Manning's brother, Alfred Manning. His little son died there and was buried across the road on a hillside, underneath some fir trees. Four bushes of the dwarf Red China Rose, one of the earliest roses to be introduced into this country, were planted on the child's grave. Later this early home, built out of wide, solid kauri planks was sold to John Callaway, who arrived in New Zealand in 1842. His granddaughter asked me to visit her old home, and to name for her some of the old roses growing there. We found a cottage behind the house, built about the same time. An old

Maori had lived there who must have been fond of flowers, for along the fence line she had planted the rambler, Félicité et Perpétue, and the Gallica, Anaïs Ségales. Both roses had spread and suckered freely, as is their habit. A granddaughter of the old Maori had asked the owner to spare these plants, when there was talk of the hedge being removed, as her grandmother treasured them so.

Across the road, in a field where eight people are buried in a tiny cemetery, are large box trees, over and around which ramble purple and green grapevines. These bear fruit amazingly, in spite of neglect, and the pear-shaped green variety is particularly delicious. On the banks of a clear stream more roses were growing. Old Blush China was very tall, as it had to struggle up through native scrub to reach the sun. Nearby were the Double Yellow Banksia and R. *multiflora carnea*, which has sprays of very small, full, pink flowers; while further over were huge bushes of the Crimson Rambler and Veilchenblau.

Félicité et Perpétue abounds also in the mining districts of Westland, and in most early settled parts of the South Island. Our plant grew from a roadside cutting; but we have to treat it drastically as it is such a vigorous grower and would soon take charge of our garden. Immediately it has flowered we cut out all the old wood at ground level, and then train no more than six strong new shoots along a wire fence. The next season we get particularly fine flower sprays which cascade down over a rock wall, making a delightful picture.

More lovely than Félicité et Perpétue is a sister plant, Adelaide d'Orléans, called after one of Louis Phillippe's daughters. The creamy flowers are loosely double and show the stamens, the outer petals being rose-tinted, as are the fat buds. These blooms are described by one writer as hanging in clusters like those of a Japanese cherry, and this was how they appeared to us at Sissinghurst Castle, falling from the top of an old fruit tree. We have planted cuttings from an old cemetery where two bushes of this rose cover early graves with a soft cream carpet of flowers. On one of these graves is a wild American rose, R. *carolina plena*, which Mr Wilson Lynes, an expert on the roses of his country, tells us is quite rare. It flowers at the same time as Adelaide d'Orléans; and the two roses look charming together. A low-growing, suckering, semi-double, crimson Gallica, the Red Rose of Lancaster, pushes its way up through the rambler which, lacking any support, lies on the ground. The horizontal position appears to make this plant flower more freely, the full length of each branch being covered with lovely sprays of bloom. This red and cream combination was very effective against the old grey headstone and the dark iron railing.

We grow Flora, another Sempervirens Hybrid, against a grey totara fence beside *Fuchsia arborescens* from Mexico. The full rosy blooms of Flora, larger than those of Adelaide d'Orléans, fade to a creamy-lavender. These flowers, drooping over the fuchsia, contrast pleasantly with the rosy-purple, lilac-like sprays. A perfect way to train this rose is up through a tree—the way it is often grown in England, where the moist atmosphere suits it well. With us, when the weather is hot and dry, the imported Flora must be sprayed and well watered if it is to be kept in a healthy condition. Fortunately it is the only one of this family that causes us any worry.

Two more Sempervirens hybrids have come to us from old gardens. A lovely white, with clusters of double blooms faintly tinged with yellow at the base, is being trained up a tree alongside the white garden. From studying early nineteenth century rose books we decided it must be either Rampant or Donna Maria. As the former produces some autumn flower, and we waited in vain for our plant to do so, we feel our lovely climber must be Donna Maria—a rose with the noticeable pale green foliage mentioned by William Paul in *The Rose Garden*. The other one was sent to us by a country friend, who collected it in the Raglan district. This uncommon rose, Banksiaeflora was recommended by William Paul, in 1848, as a good pillar rose. In our climate it would be too rampant for such a position, so we have trained it through a tree, a situation which it enjoys in the company of the winter-flowering *Clematis puberula*, which has green flowers and lovely seed heads. Banksiaeflora has bright, glossy green leaves, especially in the early growth; and clusters of cup-shaped blooms which open a pale yellow, with a deeper shade in the centre round the lovely stamens. If the weather is hot, the flowers pale quickly but still remain attractive. In size, these blooms are midway between those of Félicité et Perpétue and Flora.

We were charmed with another variety we saw in a beautiful English garden, Lyegrove, near Badminton. This was the blush-pink, rosy-budded Princess Louise, called after another daughter of the Duke of Orleans. It had very soft pink blooms larger than those of Félicité et Perpétue and was draped over a low stone wall surrounding a sunken garden, with tall purple spikes of *Campanula grandis* var. *highcliffe* behind it. This large-flowered, strong perennial was very popular overseas; and we noticed it was most effective when grown in association with old-fashioned roses. So far we have not seen it in New Zealand. In all, we have found six varieties of these very early roses out here, and possibly there may be others still to be discovered. Unexpected finds are always a thrill: recently, we were sent still another one to try out. This rose has small, compact, flattish blooms of creamy-blush, evergreen, smooth foliage, and thin, thorny stems. We wonder whether it could be *R. sempervirens minor?*

Coming into bloom a little later than the various types of the Evergreen Roses are two forms of the wild white Multiflora. They abound in many districts and one is much more prickly than the other. *R. multiflora* was first recorded in the Auckland district in 1869, by Kirk, who considered that it had arrived here at a much earlier date but later than the Sweet Brier and Dog Rose. These roses became naturalised here just as *R. alba*, from the Middle East, and *R. rugosa* from the Far East, became naturalised in England. With their vigorous growth, Multifloras make wonderful hedges for country districts. They are very beautiful when in bloom, and stock cannot penetrate through them. They have been used, also, to act as wind or snow breaks. In fact, for several decades Hungarians planted parallel hedges of such roses, in very open and exposed positions, to stop snow drifting across lines and roads. Today, in North America, similar use is made of them; and they are also grown, in quantity, alongside dangerous roads in an endeavour to prevent serious motor accidents. When planted closely they soon form an impenetrable barrier, strong and resilient enough to prevent a fast moving vehicle from careering off a roadway.

In the Bay of Islands, near Kawakawa, the roadsides for nearly a mile are covered with huge bushes of the extra prickly form of *R. multiflora*. They have spread also, up side roads and over the hillsides. In full flower, with the sea on one side and the green hills on the other, these plants are strikingly beautiful; and they also catch the motorist's eye during the autumn, when the bushes are covered with myriads of tiny, bright red heps. Our plant was grown from a small seedling we found on the roadside beneath one of these bushes; but later, owing to lack of space, we had to discard it. This was just as well, since this rose needs to be unrestricted to show its full beauty. In the centre of the North Island, alongside the main road between Taumarunui and National Park, there are many large plants of an even lovelier and almost thornless form of the white Multiflora growing free and wild. When they are smothered with bloom hardly any green is visible; and the bushes stand out beautifully against the background of native bush. Tremendous plants of R. *multiflora* were seen in a secluded valley, by the Maungatarata Stream, in very hilly country running parallel to the Wanganui River. These bushes were growing round the remains of an early, and what must have been a very lonely, cottage, with Crimson Rambler poking up here and there amongst the snow-white blooms. In the same country are numerous plants of R. *multiflora calva*, mentioned earlier, which is a parent of R. *multiflora carnea*. This is similar in every respect to the white form except that the flowers are faintly tinged with pink. It is surprising in such a young and small country, far away from Europe and Asia, to find so many types of Multifloras, both species and cultivated forms, growing in gardens or semi-wild.

At the far end of the long lawn bordering the Heath Garden at Wisley, the Royal Horticultural Society's Trial Gardens, are some tall trees; when we saw them in June they were smothered with the double white blooms of R. *multiflora alba* – one of the few members of this family not seen in New Zealand. The huge sprays of this rose open a pale flesh colour but fade quickly; the two tones on the plant at the same time create a soft and pretty picture. Even we were amazed when we counted up the number of Multiflora ramblers in New Zealand. Of course there are some not represented, such as the fine double type at Wisley and the glorious orange-yellow, Ghislaine de Féligonde which we admired on the pergola at Roseraie de L'Hay near Paris; but there is no doubt that we have a good varied collection. Even the feathery, freakish R. *watsoniana*, the Bamboo Rose, is well-known in New Zealand gardens. Lack of space is the determining factor when it comes to planting ramblers. That they are hardy and will stand long periods of neglect is obvious; it then remains to choose roses whose colour will harmonise with the general garden scheme, or those that have a sentimental or historical interest.

In *multiflora platyphylla* we have an old and seldom seen plant, better known as the Seven Sisters or Grevillia Rose. The name Seven Sisters has been wrongly applied in this country to Félicité et Perpétue: the two roses are really not alike. We discovered this vigorous but tender rambler

R. multiflora platyphylla, growing on the steep bank of a stream in the Kaeo district in the far north of New Zealand, where one of the early mission stations was established. It was growing over fallen willow trees, through a tangle of the ever-present ginger plant, and a tall white eupatorium, which we also grow in our garden. Most of the roses we found in this area were growing alongside the river and its tributaries. Of necessity, people lived close to the waterways in those days, since there were no roads, and all stores had to be brought by boat. Flood waters had passed over this Multiflora and left the plant rather muddied; but we were excited to see, and for the first time, the varied coloured sprays of bloom for which it was famous, and from which it acquired its common name. Up to seven shades, from pale pink, through rose, to mauve, cerise, and rosy-purple, can be seen on a cluster at the same time, but the colour is only really good when the bush gets plenty of water.

Plants were sent from China to Charles Greville of London in 1815, and cuttings were taken to France by Louis Noisette in 1819. *R. multiflora platyphylla* was thought to have been a natural hybrid between the double pink *R. multiflora carnea* and *R. rugosa*. The extra large leaves have a definite rugosa look, though they still show the heavily fringed stipules of the multiflora parent. We took cuttings home with us and also leaves and flowers, to show Dr Cooper, head of the Botany Department of the Auckland War Memorial Museum, in case he could help to confirm our identification of this rose. We had seen no other plants of it, neither could we find an illustration of it in any of our many books on the rose. He kindly searched through old volumes at the Museum; and finally unearthed a copy of one of Loudon's books, in which there was a clear black and white illustration of the Seven Sisters Rose. This showed the blooms to be larger and fuller than those of the true Multifloras, the petal edges being slightly serrated. The leaves, also, were identical with those we had brought down from Kaeo. However instead of rushing to a hasty conclusion, Dr Cooper suggested we speak about it to Miss Dingley, another Auckland botanist, in case she had seen the rose in England. We were overjoyed to find that she knew it well; it had grown in her grandfather's English garden. So far, this is the only stand of it we have come across in New Zealand: it must have been there for a long time, as it had spread for quite a distance along the bank of the stream. Up behind Kaeo, we found another member of this family with open cerise-magenta flowers that faded out to a uniform lavender-grey. Nowhere, neither here nor overseas, have we seen another rose that resembled this: the size and colour of the flowers and leaves suggested a relationship to the Rugosa family. Geschwind, an early Hungarian breeder, did produce a number of interesting crosses by using types of R. *multiflora* and R. *rugosa;* we wondered if it was possible that a settler, coming here from the Continent, could have brought out one of these with him.

A parent of the Seven Sisters Rose, R. *multiflora carnea*, was growing a little north of Kaeo, between the river and the roadway on a swampy piece of ground, its only support being the bulrushes amongst which it threaded its way over soft green mosses. The very double, pale pink blooms, so well illustrated by Redouté, looked charming against such a background. We were not successful here with this Multiflora until we moved it to a damp position: it did not appreciate a rather dry situation, after all the moisture it had been used to up in the north. On a later trip, we saw R. *multiflora carnea* growing in a swamp, and climbing up burnt-out tea-trees, in Oronga Bay, not far from Russell. It had survived both flood and fire; in fact the floodwaters had receded not long before we saw it. This was another Chinese Rose introduced into England at the beginning of the nineteenth century; and was considered to have been a natural hybrid between R. *chinensis* and R. *multiflora cathayensis*. A single, pale pink form, has smaller flower sprays than the common white type. There is not much of this latter plant, R. *multiflora cathayensis*, in the country; though we did find one notable plant in a very old garden at Mangonui, in the far north near Doubtless Bay. But R. *multiflora calva*, the plant from which this last rose was derived, grows along the roadsides in the centre of the North Island. Except that its flowers are tinged with pink, it is almost identical with the wild white form.

Many have been the hybrids bred from R. *multiflora*, and they abound in New Zealand. Owing to lack of space, we have now discarded some we used to grow, in favour of better varieties. Those now in our garden are Tausendschön, Veilchenblau, Kathleen and Blush Rambler—all hybrids from Crimson Rambler – and the old R. *multiflora platyphylla*. But the New Zealand countryside is amazingly rich in Multiflora types and hybrids— even the famous French garden, Roseraie de l'Hay has no more. These roses are very easy to identify: their habit of throwing up stiff, thick, basal shoots after flowering is quite distinctive; and their very large leaves have heavily lacinated stipules, a characteristic they impart to their descendants, even to the miniatures, Anna Marie de Montravel and Mignonette. Sufficient water, and the cutting out of all old wood after flowering are the only attentions these hardy roses require to produce thousands upon thousands of lovely blooms each season.

We purchased Tausendschön, or Thousand Beauties, in this country and quite accidentally, planted it in a perfect position. It is by a corner of the house in a narrow bed below a brick wall topped with a wrought-iron railing. It has now climbed up the wall to the eaves of the house where it is firmly anchored, so that all the graceful, light stems can hang freely from the top. When the long branches are heavily laden with clusters of small flowers in several tones of pink, it is one of the loveliest sights in the garden, being greatly admired and much photographed. If the spent blooms are removed it does flower again, though not with the same gay abandon. It requires very little attention and is not difficult to handle, as its stems are almost thornless. Nowhere on our travels did we see this lovely rose, which was derived from various crosses between Crimson Rambler and Tea and Polyantha Roses.

Crimson Rambler, thought to be a natural hybrid between R. *multiflora* and R. *chinensis*, produced quite a stir when it was introduced into England in 1893. An engineer on board a trading vessel brought it from Japan for an Edinburgh friend, who called it the Engineer Rose, and it eventually came into the possession of an English rose grower, Mr Charles Turner. Afterwards it became known as Turner's Crimson Rambler. Many tremendous bushes of this rose are to be found growing semi-wild throughout the country; and very lovely they look when in full bloom during the Christmas holidays. The colour of the flowers out here is richer than any we noticed in England.

One evening, as we were returning from a fishing expedition in the heart of the King Country in the glow from the setting sun we saw an old unpainted milling shack, grey with age, surrounded by huge bushes of Crimson Rambler in full bloom, with the Red Dorothy Perkins, Excelsa, nearby. At a distance it is difficult, sometimes, to decide which rose is which; but there are definite ways of identifying these two groups. Multifloras have fairly erect, heavy canes, whereas the Wichurianas have thinner, flexible stems which tend to trail over the ground. The leaves also are quite dissimilar. In the former family they are very large, of a light green and hairy underneath, the stipules being heavily fringed. In the latter they are smaller, darker, and glossy on both sides, with wide but less heavily fringed stipules. While the Multifloras have enormous panicles of small flowers, the Wichuriana blooms are larger, with very prominent stamens, and come in smaller clusters. At close quarters there is no trouble at all in identifying Crimson Rambler, a very popular rose in the King Country. We found, also in the far north, a bush of what must have been its autumn-flowering sport—Flower of Fairfield. This rose was flowering at Easter time when the original plant would show no blooms whatever.

We grew its relative, Veilchenblau, from cuttings collected many years ago from a roadside plant in the centre of the North Island. This rose is not highly spoken of in overseas books, but we find it most attractive when grown in association with tall, modern fuchsias, the flowers of which harmonise perfectly with its unusual smoky, rosy, mauve blooms. The foliage is a healthy bright green: and looks well against the wall when the flowers are over. We train it horizontally, since the large sprays of bloom are produced from nearly every leaf axil. Individually, the flowers have more colour in them than would appear at a casual glance, odd stripes of cerise and white adding life to each bloom. In the Opotiki district there is one hedge, nearly a quarter of a mile long, composed entirely of bushes of Veilchenblau alternated with those of the ubiquitous Dorothy Perkins and, when the two are out together, they make a charming picture. We were so impressed that we stopped to take colour slides.

An interesting point about Tausendschön and Veilchenblau is that they were once crossed, and produced the stock rose I.X.L. which was well-known in New Zealand many years ago, and which is once again being tried out at the Department of Agriculture's Testing Ground at Avondale. The large sprays of reddish-purple blooms are unusual, the individual flowers being larger than those of Veilchenblau. We photographed these flowers and also those of the semi-double, rosy, New Zealand raised Lippiat's Manettii—a stock rose which has not been used by nurserymen for many years though at one time it was very popular. Violette, a Hybrid Multiflora, was bred later than Veilchenblau. It also grows in the Avondale district. The small, double, dark smoky-violet blooms, when they change to a rich maroon, often remind us of the larger flowers of the subtly toned Cardinal Richelieu, a Gallica Rose.

In Rose Kingsley's useful book, *Roses and Rose Growing* there are two fine coloured reproductions of the Multiflora hybrid, Blush Rambler. This is the last of these roses to come into flower; and one of the loveliest. The clear rose of its huge sprays of bloom is refreshing, and looks well against the rather light green of the extra large leaves. Our plant was grown from cuttings taken from a big bush in the grounds of an historic house in Auckland; but, like Veilchenblau, it can be seen along our country roadsides. On one occasion it made a perfect photographic study as it grew up through a clump of tall bamboos on the side of a stream and cascaded down from the top in a rosy shower. Huge gunnera leaves dominated the foreground, and contrasted well with the long, thin leaves of the bamboo. Another time, on a fishing expedition, we saw Blush Rambler in a sparsely settled area by a dismantled milling site near the upper reaches of the Wanganui River. In spite of its beauty it is seldom seen in gardens or parks; probably because it has only one flowering season, and that is comparatively short.

William Paul of England brought out a remarkably fine book *The Rose Garden* in 1848, which we find a most valuable aid in checking up on old roses. His firm bred many roses, including a number of showy climbers, from the wild ramblers R. *moschata*, R. *multiflora* and R. *wichuriana*. One of these, Kathleen, was sent to us from Thames. It is a charming plant with the typical, strong, upright growth and good healthy foliage of the Multiflora family. The individual, single blooms of rose-pink with a white eye, are a little larger than those of the Blush Rambler and are held well spaced on firm stems. Kathleen and Blush Rambler are the last of this group to come into flower, but their fresh, rosy blooms are always worth waiting for. Kathleen not only sprays out over the high tennis court wall, but has climbed up and through a large, upright crab apple. This acts as an anchor; and holds the swaying branches gracefully.

An interesting rose, though it is far removed from the wild Asian parent, is Multiflora de la Grifferaie, an old stock rose. Through its mixed parentage its get a rich scent from the Damask. Its full and sometimes malformed flowers and suckering habit from the Gallicas—and its large leaves from the Multifloras. As long as the plant gets plenty of moisture, flowers can be lovely: the colour is a rich cherry-magenta which pales to pink on the outer petals. Practically every old settlement, garden, or cemetery in the country boasts plants of this rose, many of them covering quite an area. It is obvious in some gardens that more tender roses have been budded on to this stock, and later died out, leaving the stock rose to take charge. This rose seems to be variable in colour; one plant we saw had crimson-purple colouring, and another rose-pink. We grow this as a bush, and also trained it as a climber; and we are able to cut long sprays from both plants.

As well as the roses already mentioned we have found many more ramblers by our roadsides, some old and not very attractive, such as Ranunculus and Royal Cluster, which grow in the Opotiki district; but we have seen many others of outstanding merit. The Dawson Rose and Laure Davoust are very old pink roses; while Queen Alexandra, Euphrosyne, Waltham Rambler, and Leuchtstern, all in pink and reddish tones, were not bred till very much later. The yellow-flowered Multiflora ramblers are beautiful. Goldfinch and Phyllis Bide are very popular varieties in Great Britain and on the Continent; we have seen them in gardens here, though not by the roadside. But the Golden Rambler—Aglaia, and Claire Jacquier, both showy roses, with lovely buds—can often be found growing semi-wild. One extra fine specimen of Claire Jacquier was growing over and through an old and rusty corrugated-iron tank near the seashore in the Bay of Plenty, with Félicité et Perpétue hanging in graceful festoons from a tree overhead, and American Pillar making a gay foreground to an attractive picture—the whole backed by golden sands, white breakers, and a vivid blue sea. Free-growing ramblers such as these can be really lovely; and the best plants are found on really moist sites.

One of the largest and most important groups of ramblers, the Wichuriana Roses, produce a splendid profusion of flowers all along their arching stems, and have fine, glossy, almost evergreen foliage. They are astonishingly hardy and quick-growing and will thrive in almost any soil or situation. Most varieties produce a spectacular display of bloom for a period of four to six weeks; but, as there are early and late types, these Wichurianas make a gay show for a long time. All were bred from two closely allied wild roses which grew in Japan, Korea, and Eastern China—R. *wichuriana* or the Memorial Rose, and R. *luciae*, a smaller, more glossy leaved and more upright-growing variety of the former. Although R. *wichuriana* was not introduced into Europe till the latter part of the nineteenth century, and no hybrids were created before 1890, over eighty varieties were available to the public within ten years of this time. These hybrids were hailed as valuable new garden plants; and, before long, were being grown in a number of attractive ways.

As a ground cover for unsightly banks they soon form a dense, weed-destroying screen—the flexible stems rooting wherever they touch the ground. However, not many of our gardens are spacious enough to warrant treating banks in this manner. We saw Wichurianas carpeting the ground in parks and large gardens overseas and covering the steep banks leading down to airport tunnels; but we have often found them neglected and left to grow wild. Thus, they have spread themselves round old milling and mining settlements. In the upper reaches of the Wanganui some steep banks were smothered right to the water's edge with the gay pink and red blooms of small-flowered Wichuriana Roses. The river at this spot was bridged with huge rimu trees which had been felled and thrown across from bank to bank, then packed with pumice, after being chipped level, and boarded with heavy timber. The roses growing along the banks of this clear blue river made a delightful picture, seen from the improvised bridge with a background of native bush. Wichurianas are often seen camouflaging old stumps, or unsightly outbuildings, and they can be trained to make tall hedges, providing there is a rigid, permanent support to carry the weight of their long stems. Pergolas, arches, and summerhouses can be clothed, most decoratively, with these useful roses: and they look lovely festooned along chains or ropes hanging between stout uprights. Wichurianas planted in giant urns on top of balustrades or pedestals make a spectacular display during the flowering season—the same effect being achieved, but more cheaply, when they are grown as tall standards. It is no wonder, then, that these versatile plants should have become so universally popular in so short a time. A great number can be found in New Zealand, particularly in older gardens, along the roadsides in less populated areas, and in parks: though many are now being discarded by growers in favour of the more pereptual-flowering modern climbers and pillar roses.

One of our most valued ramblers for a spectacular display over a period of several weeks is R. *wichuriana grandiflora*, a more vigorous form of the wild plant which was discovered in an English nursery. The fine flower sprays are similar to those painted by Alfred Parsons, for Ellen Willmott's *The Genus Rosa*. While in England, I visited the Bayfordbury Research Station where Dr G. Rowley pointed out to me an interesting prostrate form, with very shiny leaves and smaller flowers that appeared either singly or in tiny clusters. Ours is a larger-flowered and more vigorous plant, the thorny, trailing stems growing up to twenty feet each season. It was given to us by a Manurewa rosarian who had trained it up over a large tree stump in a driveway of huge old macrocarpa trees. Now the land has been cut up; and the rose has disappeared, though its descendant still lives on in our garden and gives us endless pleasure each year. Several white climbers and ramblers grow along a tall green trellis that divides our white garden from the tennis court, and this Wichuriana is the last of them to come into flower. The earliest is R. *laevigata*, then comes the Double White Banksia, to be followed by Madame Plantier, R. *bracteata*, and R. *brunonii*, the Himalayan Musk. They make an interesting collection and, of them all, the one that produces the greatest amount of bloom is R. *wichuriana*—and how the bees swarm round those lovely flowers with their prominent yellow stamens! Great sprays are delightful when arranged in a tall pedestal vase. Owing to its wicked thorns R. *wichuriana* is a treacherous rose to train; but this can be done without too much difficulty if a long bamboo pole with a notch at one end is used to lift the training stems and hook them on to wire above the trellis. These branches do not need tying, as the shape of the thorns guarantees that they will stay where they are placed.

We grow two other white varieties, Lady Blanche and Albéric Barbier, the former bred in America and the latter in France. Lady Blanche is a delightful rose, fragrant, with shining bright green foliage and open, ruffled flowers showing yellow stamens. When we saw it first growing on a steep hillside in the Thames district in association with several forms of R. *moschata*, it looked a picture. The masses of pure white flowers on the low training stems made the ground appear, at a distance, as if it had been liberally sprinkled with snow. In autumn Lady Blanche produces a fine crop of bright red heps. Three years ago we put in cuttings of this rose at the foot of a twelve-foot fence; it is now a large, healthy plant, well clothed with foliage from the base upwards, and it flowers almost as well as it did on that rocky hillside.

There are three other varieties of small-flowered Wichurianas—all bred by Walsh of America, who created some lovely ramblers by crossing this wild rose with one of the earliest Dwarf Polyanthas, Paquerette. They can often be seen by our roadsides. The least spectacular, in this country, is Mrs H. M. Walsh, with its clusters of tight, very double flowers;

but Maid Marion and Milky Way are really beautiful plants. The former has single, medium-sized flowers with good petals and pronounced stamens, the foliage being rich, glossy, and very healthy. We saw it first growing through roadside grasses, on our way out to South Head on the Kaipara Harbour. Later we found it trailing down a clay bank near Nukuhau in the Bay of Plenty. Milky Way, with semi-double blooms faintly tinged with pink in the bud, fully justified its name when we saw it as a great frothing bush near a Maori pa in the thermal area of Tokaanu. So far, this is the only bush of this Wichuriana we have found; but the White Dorothy grows in many parts of the North Island. This rose, and the exquisite pale pink Dorothy Dennison, both sports of the harsher pink Dorothy Perkins, are frequently found together.

More often than not all three, and even the deeper toned Red Dorothy or Excelsa, have been planted in the same area. White Dorothy is not a pure white like the lovely Lady Blanche, since the blooms are often tinged with pink: nor is its flower as finely formed; but when all four roses, white, pink, deep rose, and red, are seen growing together through grass and bracken, as in the old milling settlement of Waituhi in the lovely Taringamotu Valley, they make a delightful tapestry of colour. In the Thames area they grow to tremendous heights through high old hedges, and ripple down like coloured waterfalls. As their feet are generally near moist ditches these ramblers keep fairly healthy, the grass covering their roots giving them a cool root-run. Sander's White, a fine, small-flowered Wichuriana of a slightly later vintage, is the only one of these white roses sold today in New Zealand. It makes an excellent weeping standard, being used for this prupose overseas as well as in this country. We saw it trained in various ways in England and there were also big bushes of it in the rose section of the Edinburgh Botanic Gardens.

Probably the most widely distributed and best-known of the larger-flowered Wichurianas, Albéric Barbier was bred in France from a cross between the Tea Rose, Shirley Hibberd and the wild Japanese rose. The flower sprays are small but appear in great profusion, each creamy-white bloom being fully double, quartered, and of good form. Pale yellow buds, rich, dark, almost evergreen foliage, and a refreshing scent of green apples, all add to the attractiveness of this old favourite, which we grow on a high fence near Lady Blanche. Its main display is in early summer, but odd flowers appear later in the autumn. It smothers clay banks at

▲ 41. Raubritter

▼ 42. R. *roxburghii plena*

▲ 43. R. *francofurtana*

▼ 44. R. *carolina plena*

Mangonui in the far north—climbs up through trees in the vicinity of Auckland—and clothes the old wall round an early stone house built in Bishop Selwyn's time. In fact, it is everywhere; and never is it anything but free-flowering and healthy. Another rose in the same class, La Perle, with even finer flowers and a clean, astringent scent, makes an excellent ground cover along quiet roads in the King Country.

Two early American ramblers, with large creamy-yellow flowers, were raised from a cross between R. *wichuriana* and the straw-yellow Tea Rose, Perle des Jardins—a favourite in some of our older gardens. Unfortunately, we do not grow either of these beautiful roses. Jersey Beauty has superb single flowers with fine stamens; and its double counterpart, Gardenia, was known in the United States as a hardy Maréchal Niel. Both these plants thrive in the sulphur-laden air of Rotorua, in the heart of one of our thermal districts, where they are growing in a garden once owned by a man who used to drive the old mail coaches. This rather derelict house is surrounded with roses and other plants he collected he as travelled round the country.

Still a favourite in present day gardens, Silver Moon is a semi-double creamy-white Wichuriana hybrid with flowers as large as its other parent, the Cherokee Rose. In one sparsely settled area down the Wanganui River we were amazed to come across this striking rose, and the pale pink New Dawn, growing side by side through a tall hedge on a hillside.

Single roses are always fresh and charming; and a quartette frequently seen growing alongside our quieter roads, all pink-toned and with a white eye, are Evangeline, Paradise, Delight, and America. Paradise, which we train up a tree, is a vigorous, fragrant rose with notched white petals deeply tinged with rose. This was grown from cuttings collected in the Albany district; while we found Evangeline near Te Kuiti. The other two we photographed in the Bay of Plenty, where they were thriving by the roadside amongst a varied group of Wichurianas. On a hillside near Thames we came across a rose new to us. This, also, had single white flowers with a pink edge to the petals; but the blooms, instead of being cupped, were flat, and the growth of the plant was noticeably upright. As it was growing wild between R. *moschata* and the double white Lady Blanche, we wondered whether it was a natural hybrid. A semi-double rose of unusual colouring, which we discovered growing up through a tree in the Opotiki district, has puzzled us, since we looked for it in vain overseas.

The cupped flowers of carmine-rose shaded with lilac are larger than those of most small-flowered Wichurianas and very beautiful. In fact, the bloom looked like a small edition of that of the Boursault Rose, Elegans. In the same area, another rambler had rather similar colouring, but produced larger sprays of smaller flowers, carmine at first but fading to rosy-mauve. This could be Paul's Rowena; but we have no definite confirmation.

Double pink small-flowered Wichurianas were very popular plants during the early part of this century and many are still to be found throughout the country—all flowering later than the large-flowered varieties. The cheerful Lady Gay, which produces a few of its bright rose flowers in the autumn; Minnehaha, with paler blooms; and Lady Godiva, a very double and pale pink sport of Dorothy Perkins, are quite commonly seen. Pink Roamer we have seen only once, and that was in a field amongst a tangle of blackberry. We admired the delicate shaded Lady Godiva climbing thirty feet up through a tree, in a bushclad area not far from the Wanganui River. From this height, it fell down in a pink shower and made a charming picture in this remote and rather lonely district. It is so difficult to find out just who planted all these treasures, now that the early settlers are fast dying out; that in itself would make an interesting story, if all the material were available.

Most of the small-flowered, red Wichurianas were bred in America—one parent being the well-known China Rose, Cramoisi Supérieur; but R. *wichuriana rubra*, a single rose listed here many years ago, and one we have never seen, was bred from a cross between Crimson Rambler and the wild Japanese rose. Many of these rich red roses grace our old gardens and roadsides, though we grow none of them here; it is interesting to recall their attractive names. Troubador and Arcadia are both doubles; but Diabolo is a glowing semi-double, the flowers being produced on distinctive, stiff, upright stems. The single, very dark red blooms of Bloomfield Courage have a white eye. This Wichuriana grows well as a standard; and we saw it again at Beccles, an old-world garden near Bulls, where it trailed over a large pergola in the company of Crimson Glow, Coronation, Albertine, and Joseph Billiard. This last is most distinctive, having brilliant red flowers with a bright yellow centre. Ethel, Dorothy Perkins, La Perle, Albéric Barbier, and François Juranville grew in other parts of this large garden, at the far end of which we saw the remains of an old block-house with earth fortifications where roses were growing happily.

While staying with friends at Picket Ridge, which is charmingly situated on a plateau above the Taringamotu River, near Taumarunui, we were delighted to find several fine ramblers in full bloom, festooned along the whole length of a glossy green laurel hedge. Excelsa and Crimson Rambler, both mentioned previously, were there, and between them we found Hiawatha. This rose was smothered with sprays of single, crimson flowers, with a white eye. The golden stamens were most pronounced, and shed a warm glow over the small, cupped blooms, giving them a luminous look. Hiawatha must be very attractive to bees, as there were literally hundreds of them busy at work, extracting the honey to take to their hives just over the fence. Both this rose and the larger-flowered, vivid American Pillar we have now discarded, in spite of the fact that they give so much joy as we motor through the country at Christmastime. In our garden American Pillar was rather too prone to mildew, though one of its parents, R. *setigera* – the Prairie Rose, which grew nearby, was always healthy and trouble free. Another red Wichuriana, with medium-sized, semi-double flowers (the only plant of its type we have seen) was growing on a lonely farm alongside two rampant bushes of the Himalayan Musk. Comparing our slides of this rose with a coloured illustration of Chaplin's Royal Scarlet Hybrid in *Climbing Roses* by G. A. Stevens, we found them to be almost identical; and have since discovered that Royal Scarlet was introduced here.

Paul's Scarlet is the red rose most frequently seen in Europe and the British Isles, where it is trained up buildings and fences, over archways and pergolas, twined round trees and columns, and cascades down from tiny balconies on tall blocks of flats. We grow this in front of a totara fence which has weathered to a pleasant shade of grey. Crimson Conquest and Chaplin's Crimson Glow are further along, and between each rose is a tall-growing fuchsia to give colour when the flowers of the climbers are over. All these are well-known plants in New Zealand, as is Blaze, which is thought to have been bred from Paul's Scarlet and Gruss an Teplitz, another well-known rose. At the Villa Taranto, on the shores of Lake Maggiore, Blaze was trained up to the eaves of a white walled building in the grounds. These gay flowers, their green leaves and huge bushes of *Philadelphus virginale* nearby, made an unforgettable study in white, green and red.

A real gem amongst the larger-flowered Wichurianas is François

Juranville, which was bred in France. Its other parent, the pink-toned China Rose Laurette Méssimy, we grow on a rock trough. It is difficult to imagine this thin-petalled, semi-double rose having produced such a magnificent offspring. We discovered François Juranville happily growing near an old mill site, with its feet in a very wet swamp. The bronze-green foliage was rich and glossy; and the rather upright-growing bush was smothered with small clusters of very large flowers, with a strong scent of green apples. Later we saw a magnificent hedge of François Juranville near Russell, with perfect glossy foliage to set off the lovely mass of blooms. The flat, full, and quartered blooms are rosy in the centre but pale to salmon at the edges. The colour varies from garden to garden, as we noticed overseas, looking at one of the finest specimens in the beautiful garden, Lyegrove, near Badminton. Our plant revels in a wet season; dry weather produces poor flowers with less colour, so it is no wonder that it flourished well in a swamp, even though it was surrounded with bracken, tea-tree, ferns and rushes. It this garden, François Juranville has climbed into a dark-leaved prunus, which makes a wonderful background for the rosy-salmon flowers.

Unfortunately we do not grow Albertine, a universal favourite, and one of the most beautiful of the large-flowered Wichurianas, though it does so well here. In a wonderful Auckland hillside garden this rose extends round two sides of a high fence enclosing a small intimate garden, and it flowers profusely for several weeks. On the other hand, it appears to do equally well when quite neglected. On the site of an old saw-mill on the western heights overlooking Lake Taupo, we saw Albertine growing alongside stumps, through tea-trees, and tall bracken. The warm, coppery-salmon flowers with a yellow base were really fine, and the foliage was without blemish. It made a perfect picture against the deep blue of the lake, the low-lying thermal area round Tokaanu, and the high bush-clad range in the background. Albertine is seen frequently overseas, where it climbs to the eaves of many an English home. At Sissinghurst Castle it was truly magnificent trained along a high, mellow brick wall. On a raised border in front of the rose was a shapely tree of our native *Gaya lyallii*. Scarcely any foliage was visible through the mass of large, white, cherry-like blossoms. For contrast, there was an unusual planting of rosy-mauve *Indigofera gerardiana*. The white, the mauve, and the salmon colours along this border stood out effectively against a tall, dark, clipped yew hedge which ran at right angles to the brick wall. Several feet in front of this was a lower box hedge, behind which alstromerias had been planted in mass to match the coral-salmon tones of Albertine. The whole made a breathtaking picture we shall never forget.

At one time, before we made major alterations to the garden, we grew Emily Gray as a standard and trained it, umbrella fashion, over a wire frame. This buff-yellow, large-flowered Wichuriana was bred from the single Jersey Beauty and the coral-flame China, Comtesse du Cayla, both lovely roses. Pearly White, a beautiful American rose, had to be sacrificed about the same time when a new boundary fence was erected and also the pale-pink Dr Van Fleet but we can still enjoy New Dawn, as it is trained right along a neighbour's fence. This rose is very well-known to New Zealanders and is always in great demand, as is its near relative, the deeper-toned Dream Girl. Along the entire length of the fence in front of our hotel at Stresa, on Lake Maggiore, we saw bushes of New Dawn. It was early summer and the bushes were laden with the soft pink flowers. In this same garden, tall palms bordered a wide pathway running down to the lake; and either New Dawn or Paul's Scarlet had been twined up each palm. When we saw them they were in full flower and looked very gay against the blue waters of the lake.

Paul Transon, which grew over an arbour in the Parnell (Auckland) Rose Gardens till recently: August Barbier; Léontine Gervais; and Chaplin's Pink Climber, all grow in New Zealand; but so far we have not found one plant of either Alexandre Girault or Honoré Barruet, two Wichurianas which we admired tremendously in the internationally famous Roseraie de l'Hay, near Paris. Neither have we come across Wichmoss, with its double, pale-pink flowers and mossy buds, though we grow and love both its parents, the wild white Wichuriana and the rose-pink Damask Moss, Salet. This attractive plant, Wichmoss, was growing on a pergola at the Roseta Communale in Rome. It is listed in overseas catalogues with the warning that it is very subject to mildew, a sad fate which often befalls mossy roses. The variegated Achievement is a decorative Wichuriana for either house or garden. It is not a vigorous grower; so we were able to plant it by a low, white trellis next to pink fuchsias which tone with the small double flowers of the rose. We watch it carefully, as it is inclined to sport back to the green-leaved Dorcas from which it came. Thelma and Easlea's Golden Rambler we admired in English gardens; but so far we have not seen them out here in New Zealand.

The great majority of these ramblers can be found by our roadsides in various parts of the country; though from trip to trip, with the widening and straightening of roads, we sometimes find our old favourites are missing. In time many more will suffer the same fate; and, gradually, their numbers will be thinned out. As town gardens tend to become smaller, it is only in the country, in parks, and the larger gardens that there will be room for these vigorous, floriferous, once-blooming roses. Of necessity, and wisely so, people now favour the fine perpetual-flowering climbing roses which are becoming available in ever increasing numbers. But each new trip we take creates fresh interest, and gives us plenty to do in the wintertime, when there is the leisure to search through old-rose books and check up on our many colour slides.

The Flowers,
Early as well as late,
Rise with the sun and set in the same bowers.

Henry Vaughan

FUCHSIAS AND OLD ROSES, BOTH POPULAR FLOWERS OF the Victorian era, have come into favour again. Their colours harmonise perfectly, and make a charming picture in the garden. Both these plants look their best when grown quite informally, either as shrubs or semi-climbers—the fuchsias providing the necessary colour when the old roses are not in flower. We have planted dwarf azaleas in some of the borders to give colour in early spring, when the roses and fuchsias are cut back; a carpeting of low-growing perennials and bulbs also helps to keep such spots attractive throughout the year. Both roses and fuchsias, as long as they are of suitable growth, are equally at home in the small garden, but we keep to soft shades as much as possible; so fuchsias in the orange to flame shades, though most striking, have to be barred, as the majority of our roses are in shades of white, pink, rose, red, and purple. This creates a restful effect which visitors to the garden appear to appreciate.

The wild roses all came from the northern hemisphere; but the original fuchsias came either from New Zealand and Tahiti, or from the West Indies, and Central or South America. Right down from Mexico in the north to the Mountains of Magellan and Tierra del Fuego in the far south, wild fuchsias abound—the hardier varieties coming from Peru,

Chile, and Magellan. There are beautiful fuchsias growing in the equatorial countries of Venezuela, Colombia, and Ecuador; but these are tender, with softer, larger leaves, and would not thrive out-of-doors in districts were there are heavy frosts. On the other hand there are many fuchsias, growing in the American countries near the Tropics of Cancer and Capricorn, which will grow in colder districts if planted in warm, sheltered spots. There are over ninety fuchsia species; of these, Tahiti produced one and New Zealand four—all the rest coming from the countries previously mentioned. Though our native fuchsias have not been used for hybridising, New Zealand did produce the tallest, as well as the lowest-growing forms: but the beautiful garden varieties available today were all bred from wild American types. We are very favoured in Auckland, as we can grow both tender and hardy fuchsias out of doors all year, and have them in flower for very many months. Species, as well as the delightful new importations, do equally well: and we count them amongst those valuable plants that really do pay dividends in a garden.

One of the most satisfying species to plant near old roses is *Fuchsia aborescens* from Mexico. It is found also in Guatemala, Panama, and Costa Rica. This shrub has large sprays of lilac-like, tiny, rosy-purple flowers—hence its other name, *Fuchsia syringaeflora*. The healthy, glossy green foliage is always attractive in the garden, and for months on end the bush is covered with bloom, blue-purple berries following the flowers. *Fuchsia arborescens* harmonises splendidly with Japanese Rugosas. There is one lush bush of it at the rear of a bed of these large-flowered and attractive-leaved roses—roses such as the fragrant, crimson-purple Roseraie de l'Hay, which is now used in the making of attar of roses; the mauve-pink Belle Poitevine with its loosely double flowers; the single rosy-magenta R. *scabrosa*, with petals like crumpled silk; and the delicate, flesh-pink R. *fimbriata* or Phoebe's Frilled Pink, with its smallish, picotee-edged blooms.

With so much perimeter planting, many of our roses are grown alongside walls or fences. Certain types of old roses, such as the Chinas, Portlands, Teas, Bourbons, and Rugosas, are perpetual-flowering; but a great number are not; so, to make up for lack of colour over many months, tall-growing fuchsias have been established between the roses. These generous plants produce a mass of bloom for the greater part of the year. The slaty-mauve, multiflora rambler, Veilchenblau, planted against a tall grey totara fence has, as its companion fuchsias the lovely Boudoir, with its double blooms of blue and cream; and Aunt Juliana with huge flowers of muted lavender and carmine. The rosy-toned, *sempevirens* rambler, Flora, an Evergreen Cluster Rose, which was grown in so many attractive ways at Munstead in Surrey, sprays out over a bush of *Fuchsia arborescens:* the double blooms of the rose, extra large for this family, look charming against the dainty rose-mauve flowers of the wild fuchsia.

Further along this wall the handsome, crimson-purple Bourbon, Great Western tones beautifully with two richly hued fuchsias, the deep violet and carmine Violet Gem, and Wave of Life, a golden-leaved beauty with double flowers of crimson and blue-purple. On this same wall Kathleen, a Multiflora rambler, blooms profusely, producing masses of fairly large, single pink flowers with a white centre. Here the supporting fuchsias are the tall-growing Ecstacy, with double flowers of hyacinth-blue, veined with pink, and having rosy sepals; the lovely Queen Mary, white-tipped, pink sepals, and large corolla of rosy-mauve; and Potentate, which makes an excellent climber or tall standard, the blooms of rose-madder being very large and full. All these plants complement one another perfectly, and make a happy background for a border of the winter-flowering camellias, Phil Doak, Barbara Clark, Bernice Body, Debutante, Elegant Beauty, and Golden Temple. Low-growing ericas, azaleas, dianthus, and pulmonarias help to cover the rock edging to this long bed and give added interest throughout the year.

At one time, we grew the tall, hardy *Fuchsia magellanica alba* with its myriads of small blush, lavender-tinted flowers – not white as the name would imply. This plant comes from Magellan as well as Tierra del Fuego, Chile, and Peru. It will stand cold and frost which the larger-leaved forms from the north will not tolerate. Apparently fuchsias growing near the Equator are to be found at higher altitudes than many of the southern ones but, even so, they will not stand up to extreme cold. We used to grow this extra vigorous form of *magellanica* where its roots kept cool and moist amongst rocks, but it grew so tall and lush that it was repeatedly damaged in stormy weather, the growth being sappy in our warm semi-tropical climate. In the end, we reluctantly discarded it in favour of its lovely hybrid, Mrs W. P. Wood. The flowers of this shrub are larger than those of the wild type, their pink and mauve tones blending in well with the semi-double blooms of the tall, greyish-leaved, R. *pomifera duplex*, or Wolley Dod's Rose. The single form of this rose, which is known as the Apple Rose of England on account of its large, red heps, develops into a small tree; and our semi-double bush has grown very tall also, and is rivalling in size an upright-growing, pink-flowering cherry nearby.

Round our original plant of Wolley Dod's Rose, which came from England, a number of suckers appeared which flowered the following season. The rosy blooms and large, downy, grey-green leaves are particularly fine on this short, new growth. The fuchsia, the cherry, the rose, and *Rhododendron* Pink Pearl which grows nearby, all flower together in one corner of an intimate fuchsia and old-rose garden; but only the fuchsia continues to bloom right through the season. A rank-growing and coarser form of *Fuchsia magellanica* grows in a neighbour's garden, and hangs over our fence; but we have not spared it a place in our garden, though its red and purple flowers looked quite effective when we saw them against white-washed cottages in Ireland, or growing up through hedges. The lighter-looking *Fuchsia magellanica gracilis* is much used for hedges in the British Isles as well as in New Zealand, but we grow only the variegated form which thrives in sun or shade, and highlights some of the larger rock pockets. In one of these *R. francofurtana* or the Empress Josephine's Rose – a natural hybrid of the Cinnamon Rose of Northern Europe—throws its arching branches over the variegated leaves of this useful fuchsia. The full, ranunculus-shaped blooms of rose, veined with a deeper shade of unusual grey-green foliage, look most attractive when spread out in this manner. This same graceful form of *Fuchsia magellanica* and another variegated fuchsia Meteor, are trained against a low, white trellis on the western wall of the house near the tall, red, China Rose, Cramoisi Supérieur and the ferny-foliaged, pink-flowered, sweetly-scented Stanwell Perpetual. This is a valuable rose which is thought to have originated as a natural hybrid between *R. spinosissima* and a perpetual-flowering pink Damask. Further along this trellis Achievement, a pink-flowered Wichuriana with dainty, variegated leaves, rambles through Keystone, Flirtation, and Pastel, all lovely pink to rosy-toned fuchsias. This year we are adding another imported rose, Général Schablikine to this long narrow border under the trellis—a rose with fine shapely foliage of a clear blue-green shade and full, rosy-salmon flowers. It has been settling in for two years in our vegetable garden; we are delighted with its healthy, vigorous growth and free-flowering character, these excellent qualities having been inherited from its China and Tea Rose ancestors. It was a worry at first to know what to plant in this spot, which lies away from the morning sun, but becomes very hot in summer afternoons. Fortunately, with regular water-spraying from below, the roses and fuchsias have both done well and are quite a feature alongside the grassy pathway that leads down to the formal garden.

Lately a number of exquisite white fuchsias have been brought into New Zealand and though often more delicate than the deeper-toned varieties, they thrive splendidly out-of-doors in Auckland. They are a decided acquisition and have filled a need for extra perpetual-flowering plants in our white garden. We find that the pale-coloured fuchsias and camellias do better in semi-shade, richly toned ones tolerating more sun. The vigorous and very beautiful Sleigh Bells has large, bell-shaped, single white flowers, the upturned sepals being attractively tipped with green. Sleigh Bells flowers consistently for many months, as do its two companion roses, the white Hybrid Musk, Prosperity, and the modern Floribunda, Irene of Denmark. Ave Marie, a pretty but less vigorous fuchsia with double flowers faintly tinged with pink and green, is planted across a narrow pathway between another bush of Irene of Denmark and the Floribunda, White Wonder, which has flat blooms like some of the old roses. The partial shade of a tall grey stone wall, topped by the trellis on the carport, helps these fuchsias and protects the blooms from the morning sun. To clothe this wall, and to help with the general green-and-white effect, we planted two fine white-flowered climbers, as well as the rampant R. dupontii and R. fortuneana, in a narrow bed at its base. One of the climbers, is the lovely clematis Madame le Coultre, with huge flowers of great substance; and the other is the fragrant *Ryhncospermum jasminoides*, which grew on so many walls in Florence and was rampant in the Prince of Barromea's garden in Isola Bella, Lake Maggiore. Later, we saw it throughout the British Isles; in fact the whole front of Lord Aberconway's house, Bodnant, in North Wales, was covered with it. In none of these gardens was this climber allowed to grow as freely as it does here. Continual clipping kept it hugging the walls, and prevented the wonderful display of flowers this *rhycospermum* produces each summer with us. Across the oval lawn of our white garden a curving border is sheltered from the afternoon sun by a tall green trellis which supports the rampant roses R. *bracteata*, the Double White Banksia, and the less vigorous Madame Plantier, Boule de Neige, and Moonlight. A rose and a fuchsia, both with the same name,

Summer Snow, flourish in this border, behind an edging of the large-leaved *Bergenia cordifolia*, and the unusual hosta, Thomas Hogg, the leaves of which are edged with a narrow band of white.

Alba Roses thrive and flower extremely well in semi-shade; so a number are planted at the rear of the house in association with several white-flowered camellias – the single Amabilis, and two beautiful doubles, Shira-Botan and Yuki-Botan or Pride of Descanso. These are interplanted with white fuchsias, the hardiest and most floriferous being Barbara Mathews and Lydia Bignall, which are named after two New Zealanders whose gardening articles are very popular. Barbara Mathews, a sport of the graceful White Spider—a fuchsia we have trained up a rock wall behind the trough garden—has semi-double flowers faintly tinged with pink; while Lydia Bignall is a sport of another fuchsia growing by the camellias. This is a useful and free-flowering one called Flying Cloud. It was the first of these pale-coloured ones we purchased, and it still ranks as an excellent plant though many newer varieties are now on the market.

Its neighbour, the charming Lace Petticoats has been more temperamental with us, though it does very well in other Auckland gardens. When grown to perfection, its outspread sepals and ruffled corolla are a sheer delight. Joan of Arc is not a tall plant, but we love its white, green-tipped flowers. All these fuchsias, a smaller form of *Lilium philippinense*, and pure white, large-flowered polyanthus, add interest to this part of the garden when the camellias and the roses are not in flower. One of the loveliest of the Alba Roses, the white, lemon-flushed, Madame Legras de Saint Germain grows in this spot, and further round are the pink-flowered Albas, Félicité Parmentier, and Koenigen von Danemarck. These roses are planted in front of a tall chimney round which we have trained on spaced wires, to a height of ten feet, the strong-growing fuchsia Whitemost, whose pink and white tones harmonise delightfully with those of the Alba Roses. We prune these white fuchsias with discretion and take care to strike a few cuttings from time to time, in case replacements are necessary. By using sprinkler hoses beneath the fuchsias to stop the undersides of the leaves being attacked by thrip and red spider we maintain these delightful plants in a healthy condition with the minimum of trouble. The hardier ones we cut for the house as the need arises, the graceful sprays being useful at the base of mixed flower arrangements. This cutting acts as a light summer pruning and is quite beneficial to the plants.

French Roses, in all their subtle tones of pink, lavender, slaty-grey, crimson, and purple, look best when interplanted with moderate-growing, bushy types of fuchsias in similar muted colours. Harmony must be the keynote, a harmony of softly blended shades. Near-pink Gallicas, such as the exquisite Duchesse de Montebello, the Duchesse d'Angoulême, and Antonia d'Ormois, the low-growing double fuchsias Crinoline, Cameo, Shy Lady, and Moonlight are perfect, since their pink and white tones complement those of the roses. The tall fuchsia Whitemost, trained on a wall behind these other fuchsias and roses, makes a splendid background. It is difficult to make a choice of suitable fuchsias to tone with rosy-mauve and purple Gallicas such as Belle de Crécy, Jenny Duval, Cardinal Richelieu and Charles de Mills, as there is such a variety in these soft tonings; but fuchsias that we find particularly useful are New Horizon, Frenchi, Treasure, Mona Lisa, Vie en Rose, Winston Churchill and Fritz Kreisler. There is even a striped fuchsia, Lucky Strike, to go with striped roses such as the white-striped, smoky-pink and lavender, Camaieux. In fact, there are suitable fuchsias to go with every old rose in the garden. Shrubs and small trees, interplanted with tall strong-coloured fuchsias look most effective as a background to these lower-growing Gallica Roses and fuchsias. Uncle Jules, Victor Hugo, and Othello all fit in well with such a scheme and are vigorous enough to make a decided feature.

In the pink and rose shades, there are some wonderful fuchsias of moderate height to plant among such roses as the Portland Rose, Jacques Cartier, the Bourbon Rose, Honorine de Brabant, and the China Rose, Mrs Bosanquet. Even their names are appealing—Easter Bonnet, Marie Louise, Pink Quartette, Colonial Dame, Azalea, and Bon Accord. All make a continuous and lovely show in the garden though, at certain seasons, the fallen blooms of the fuchsias are so numerous that it is quite a problem to get them gathered up each week, before they smother the low-growing primroses, forget-me-nots, and polemoniums used as carpeters.

Many fuchsias naturally trail, or weep, and are invaluable for clothing rock banks, especially if the position is partly shaded. The trailing *Fuchsia procumbens*, a native of New Zealand, is an excellent plant. The tiny flowers, tinted yellow, green, and blue-purple, are held erect; this is an unusual feature, as are the distinctive bright blue stamens. Apparently at one time the pollen from these blooms was used as a dusting powder by Maori maidens. Large, cherry-coloured fruit adds to the attractiveness of this wiry, useful plant which, if left unchecked in our warm climate will soon cover quite an area. A low rock wall alongside the tennis court is completely covered by the hardy, old red Marinka. Twice a year it is cut back but, in a very short time it is full of leaf and flower again. On a nearby wall, the golden-leaved form of Marinka is growing near Meteor, Pinto, and Mayflower, in association with the variegated periwinkle and tradescantias, and a blue-flowered trailing convolvulus. Such a planting helps to soften rock work, with pleasing effect.

A lax shrub, the tall-growing Peruvian species *Fuchsia serratifolia*, appreciates the backing of a wall and the close promiximity of other plants such as the mauve *Lantana selloviana*, the blue *Ceratastigma willmottianum*, and the grey-leaved *Senecio greyii*. The leaves of *Fuchsia serratifolia*, as well as the flowers, are long and narrow, the blooms springing from the upper leaf axils. These have slender, pinkish tubes ending in green-tipped sepals, which almost cover the short, red petals. Two young Cornish brothers, William and Thomas Lobb, found this plant in Peru and introduced it into England in 1843. Not far away from *Fuchsia serratifolia* is the tallest and most vigorous of our Moss Roses, the rosy-smoky-purple William Lobb, which was called after one of these Cornish plant explorers. We find *Fuchsia splendens*, which grows wild in Mexico and Guatemala, a difficult plant to place, as it has vivid scarlet flowers; but, because of a sentimental association, it has been given a home in a shady corner near the old yellow rambler, Banksiaeflora, and the creamy Hybrid Musk, Pax. There the large, light-green leaves of the fuchsia help to soften the rather bare base of the roses. These leaves are pubescent, rounded at the base, but pointed at the tip; while the flowers are rather unusual, being finished off with short, vivid green sepals and petals, The varied nature of wild fuchsias is fascinating, and always stimulates our interest. Some have minute leaves—others long, narrow ones—and still others, large, wide, downy ones; while the blooms are just as diverse in type.

On one boundary fence the strong climbers Paul's Scarlet, Crimson Conquest, and Chaplin's Crimson Glow are interplanted with two vigorous, hardy fuchsias, Beauty of Exeter and Star of the East, both in tones of rosy-red, and both requiring hard pruning at the end of each season. We generally cut back the roses and the fuchsias at the same time: and then re-tie them on to the wires that run along this wall. Thus the whole wall is amply covered with foliage, never bare and unsightly. These roses and their companion fuchsias thrive together, and make a grand splash of colour in the garden.

Small-growing wild fuchsias make wonderful rock garden plants, flowering for months, and absolutely trouble free. The dwarf, tiny-leaved *Fuchsia pumila*, a form of *Fuchsia magellanica*, and the wiry red China Roses, have flowers of the same tone; both flower continuously. If cut back hard each year and kept compact, *Fuchsia pumila* can be grown alongside even smaller roses such as Zwergkonïg, Perla d'Alcanada, Perla de Montserrat, Granada, Oakington Ruby and Midget, without looking out of place. As cuttings strike readily, we often discard a bush altogether and replace it with a freshly rooted plant which will not grow beyond one foot in a year. These small bushy fuchsias can be very attractive amongst other rock plants of similar size. The fuchsia Tom Thumb, a little beauty, with fatter, larger blooms of red and lavender, can be treated and used in the same way as *F. pumila*, being more showy in the garden because of its colourful and fuller flowers. A small Mexican species, *Fuchsia thymifolia*, with very fine foliage grows into a dainty shrub, taller than either *F. pumila* or Tom Thumb; but it is not quite so showy, as its blooms are tucked into little whorls of leaves. It flourishes—and throws up plenty of fresh, basal growth each year—at the rear of a raised, rock garden which is backed by a creeper-clad wall. In this same bed is an unusual Hybrid Rugosa, with lovely foliage, and maroon-coloured flowers. Both the rose and the fuchsia flower continuously and are underplanted with the autumn-flowering crocus, Salzmanni and the sweetly-scented dianthus Waithman Beauty, whose ruby-red flowers have a white flash on each petal. All these are hardy, trouble-free plants that appear to enjoy their close neighbours. Still another fuchsia growing nearby—in appearance more like a perennial, as it keeps throwing up fresh two-foot stems from ground level—is a wild type from Bolivia which we saw exhibited in London. This is *Fuchsia triphylla sanctae-rosae*, an unusual and useful plant for associating with some of the lower-growing rose species.

In recent years we have introduced some unusual modern roses into certain parts of the garden. These are all in soft tones of lavender and rosy-mauve, with underlying shades of grey and buff. Planted amongst old roses and fuchsias of similar colouring, they give us a greater profusion of flower in this area, and generally stimulate our interest as well as that of our garden visitors. Sterling Silver, which was so popular in England; Magenta, one of Kordes' very successful roses; Prelude, Lavender Lady, Lavender Pinocchio, and Royal Tan are all lovely, the first two being particularly useful as cut flowers. This season the Spanish-bred Intermezzo is to be added to our subtly-toned group. Roses in these shades are still not universally popular but we noticed that more and more people are coming to appreciate their decorative worth, as well as their value in selected parts of a garden.

When Canon Ellacombe wrote *In a Gloucestershire Garden* in 1895, he said he was amused to see that fuchsias were coming into fashion again because of their general hardiness and rich autumn blooming. He would have been amazed to see the wonderful modern fuchsias which have revolutionised the plantings in present day gardens. Though we grow many other fuchsias, those described in this chapter have all stood the test of time; they do well in our hot climate and on our heavy clay soil.

▲ 45. Stanwell Perpetual

46. R. *rugosa alba*

▲ 47. Frau Dagmar Hastrupp

▼ 48. R. *scabrosa*

SHRUB ROSES

Richest odours the soft air perfume,
While now mild Zephyrs blow and rose trees bloom

Rapin

THE MID-TWENTIETH CENTURY HAS BROUGHT US MANY
wonderful things, amongst them labour saving devices for the house
and the garden; but in spite of all these aids, with the rush and bustle of
modern life a gardener is faced with many problems if he wishes to ensure
some time for relaxation, so that he can enjoy the delights of his garden.
If he does all his own work, or even if he employs some labour, it is
necessary to choose plants with care, and to group them in such a manner
that unnecessary work will be avoided. Shrubs (and this includes shrub
roses) are now one of the mainstays of present-day gardens, as they create
few problems, need no annual replanting, and are cared for with the mimi-
mum of labour, and add character to the general scheme.

Unfortunately, space does not permit us to grow many trees in this
garden. Those we have are mostly deciduous, and enough of the shrubs
are evergreen to provide solid colour in the winter. Where a long lawn
bordered with mixed shrubs and roses runs down from the house terrace
towards the rock gardens and the lower white garden, we have planted,
at strategic spots on either side of the curving steps and pathway, two
trees—*Liquidambar styraciflua*, which turns a delightful colour in the
autumn and sheds its leaves so that any winter sun can reach the rock
plants below; and a graceful purple birch, *Betula pendula purpurea*. This,

as the result of major injuries received when a lorry crashed down on it has now decided to weep more than usual—the shock, and a year's doctoring, having caused it to alter its habits. Beneath these trees some of our shrub roses are thriving, in spite of the semi-shaded position. We give them a good dressing of a general fertiliser once a year, and mulch them well in the summer: besides keeping them moist with the sprinklers used on the rock gardens. The ground beneath is carpeted with pink and dark-blue forget-me-nots, the clear blue hybrid *Aquilegia alpina* var. Hensol Harebell, dwarf bearded irises, the variegated anthericum, and bulbs.

Underneath the liquidambar, and on top of a low rock wall above the bed of Rugosas we placed an unusual rose, R. *micrugsoa*. It is known also as R. *vilmorinii*, being called after an imaginative French rose-breeder who was interested in the lesser known species. One parent is our hardy Rugosa; and the other is a Chinese Rose we admired tremendously in Rome, R. *roxburghii* or R. *microphylla*. The beautiful healthy foliage and thorny stems of R. *micrugosa* make a good background for the wide, single blooms of silvery-pink, faintly lined with a deeper shade, and the pale cream stamens. These flowers generally appear singly on the branches and are followed by large bristly heps of orange-red, which stay on the bush for a long time, as the birds to not appear to eat them. This rather rare rose, which originated as a spontaneous hybrid in the Botanical Garden at Strasbourg, provides a valuable touch of colour beneath the tree. Recently, several seedlings have appeared beneath it: they will be grown on, in case an interesting natural hybrid should appear.

Not far away is a close relative of R. *micrugosa*, the double Chestnut Rose, R. *roxburghii plena*, so called because its extra large, bristly fruits resemble those of a low-growing form of the American Chestnut. The first time we saw this unusual rose growing, unnamed, in the Christchurch Botanical Gardens, we were most impressed—and very delighted on arriving home to find a beautiful and faithful painting of it in *The Genus Rosa* by Ellen Willmott. From this fine illustration by Alfred Parsons we were able to name it without further trouble. Early Spanish settlers in the New World called it the Chilcote Rose; the French named it Rose Châtaigne; and the English referred to it as the Burr Rose. Mr. Roy E. Shepherd, an American authority who wrote the *History of the Rose*, said that "this more generally cultivated double form was discovered in a Canton garden in China by Dr Roxburgh, and sent by him to the Calcutta Botanic Gardens, where other Chinese Roses were rested before being sent on to Europe". It reached England in 1820, and America in 1828, but we saw no plant of this early-introduced rose in any of the gardens we visited in the British Isles, and only in one Continental garden did we come across a large stand of it, and that was at the Villa Taranto, in Northern Italy. The single form, however, which has been found in Japan as well as Northern China, was magnificent in Rome.

This parent of R. *micrugosa* must have been the rose Reginald Farrer referred to when writing of his travels in China in *The Rainbow Bridge*:

"We traversed gorges and a pass and gorges again; each day on this track takes you through and across a chain of hills, and brings you out to rest in the intervening valley. The only incident of this stage was a low-growing rose, conspicuous with very large, thick, rounded fruits, like young pomegranates, of flushed golden amber, beset with rare, dark bristles."

From what we have seen of it in New Zealand the Chestnut Rose must have arrived out here in the early days of the colony, because it still grows wild near many of our earliest settlements in the north. One large stand was growing on a hillside between Opua and Kawakawa, just opposite a country garden in which we found many well-loved old roses; and not far away in Oronga Bay, on the site of the first American Consulate in New Zealand, and close to Okiato Point, which also knew this rose—we found plants of the double Burr Rose as well as many half-wild turkeys, in a field near the old home. But the biggest colony of R. *roxburghii plena* we have ever seen was growing in a field, along with many smaller bushes of the same rose, on a farm near Silverdale. When the owner's grandfather came from Australia in 1860 he settled on this riverside property, which has been owned by the same family ever since. Many tall Australia acacia and eucalyptus trees surround the spot where the first home was built, the seed having been brought across the Tasman and planted by the original owner. The old, thatched, sod cottage was later destroyed by fire; but one rose survived—R. *multiflora carnea*, growing on its own roots.

In the same field, we found a stand of R. *roxburghii plena* thirty feet in diameter, through the centre of which came a cascading bush of the lovely white Noisette, Madame Plantier, known in that district as the Bride's Rose. The hundreds of full, rather flattish blooms of the double form of the Chestnut Rose found in this spot made a striking picture, each flower being packed with uneven-edged, rosy-magenta petals, the outer ones paling to pink, while the sepals of the extra large buds, unlike those of any other rose, were alternately smooth and very bristly. At one time we grew this rose next to *Robinia kelseyi*, a form of the False Acacia; and we were most forcibly struck by the strong resemblance between the leaves of these plants, each leaf-stalk boasting eleven to fifteen leaflets of similar shape; and also by the fact that the rose and the acacia each had a pair of thin straight thorns at the base of the leaves. The older wood on the Chestnut Rose is angular, and the grey-brown bark, has a tendency to peel off as it ages. Blooms of this distinctive rose were sent to us for identification from a farm between the Raglan and the Kawhia Harbours on the west coast of the North Island, in the district where the Maori chief, Te Rauparaha, was born and brought up.

The bush from which these flowers came grew on the bank of an oft-flooded stream alongside the remains of an old water wheel. In spite of the fact that it was sometimes submerged, this Chinese Rose had flourished there for a very long time and was still blooming well. Older gardens, particularly in the north, boast many plants of this justly renowned rose—and we saw a lovely planting of it in Wanganui. An Auckland old-rose enthusiast has a fine specimen on her rock wall and we find in our own garden that visitors always stop to enquire its name. Our plant has never produced any fruit; so we were delighted to find bushes of it in a Kerekeri garden with large, bristly, yellowish heps topped by persistent leathery sepals. The owner of this fine seaside garden in the Bay of Islands has trained her low, spreading plants of the Chestnut Rose on either side of wide, grey, stone steps, as we saw R. *laevigata* grown in Italy; in the same way *Cotoneaster horizontalis* is used to clothe the sides of steps in England. We find it difficult now to remember from which old garden our first plant of the double R. *roxburghii* came; but it certainly came from an early established colony; and we treasure it for this, as well as for its unusual beauty. A long narrow shrubbery situated above our tennis court, and bordering a lawn that curves in towards the rock garden, accommodates not only unusual roses, but low-growing shrubs and some taller ones up which roses can climb. Between these again, to add character and interest, are plants with strap-like leaves. All are decorative, easy, and trouble free. Variegated and plain forms of anthericums, irises, and our own New

Zealand flax are used here, as well as two Australian plants of unusual charm—the unusual kangaroo paw, and a stiff-leaved, blue-flowered member of the Irid family, *Orthrosanthus multiflorus*.

Further along the same shrub border is the comparatively modern shrub rose, Nevada a great favourite in gardens and parks in the British Isles. Some of the finest and most floriferous bushes were growing on Chester's lovely rock garden, outside the Roman Wall, and looking down on the River Dee not far from the small and historic Garden of Re-erected Roman Columns. After seeing this rose in Chester and elsewhere, we realise that though some of our shrub roses do well in semi-shade, Nevada is certainly more free-flowering and beautiful when grown in the open in full sun. Its country of origin, Spain, may have something to do with this; it was bred there by Pedro Dot from a form of R. *moyesii* and La Giralda, offspring of two of our much loved roses, the white Frau Karl Druschki and the flame-coloured Madame Edouard Herriot. This winter we intend to move Nevada to a sunny corner of the garden and so give it more space in which to develop its true beauty. This shrub does flower off and on all season; but never as well as in early summer, when the whole length of the arching branches is smothered in the lovely creamy blooms, some of which have small curled petaloids round the yellow stamens, others being faintly tinged with pink. We were interested to hear that a pink sport of Nevada was now being sold overseas as Marguerite Hilling, because a Dutch friend—who has created a lovely garden during her few years in New Zealand—found that one part of her bush had sported pink flowers; we were able to get good colour slides of the pink and the cream flowers side by side on the same plant. Since then we have heard of Nevada doing the same thing elsewhere.

One of the finest of the species, and a rose that makes an excellent garden shrub, is the R. *moyesii*, already mentioned, a native of south-west China. It was discovered near the Tibetan frontier, between Mount Omi—home of the lovely four-petalled R. *omeiensis*, with its broad-based thorns and ferny foliage, a rose we know well, but do not grow—and Tatien-lu, at heights of between six and ten thousand feet; and was named after the Rev. J. Moyes, of the China Inland Mission who, while stationed at Tatien-lu, greatly helped E. H. Wilson with his exploration in that area.

China has given us many lovely roses, not the least of these being the tall R. *moyesii*, with its disease-free, ferny foliage and richly-coloured flowers of an unusual shade of smoky-red. The petals often look as though they had been dusted with pure gold, from the pollen scattered by the central ring of stamens. So far the finest bush of this rose we have seen was in the rose species section of the Christchurch Botanical Gardens. It was growing in full sun, not overshadowed as we saw it sometimes in England. It was a magnificent sight with the vivid blue sky as a background for the ferny foliage and subtly-coloured flowers. Later in the autumn, when orange-red, pitcher-shaped heps are produced in profusion, R. *moyesii* justifies A. T. Johnson's description of it in *The Mill Garden*, as "one of the most valuable introductions of the present century." Seedlings are produced freely, though the flowers are often of poorer colour than those of the wild type. *Moyesii rosea*, also a native of China, has lighter, though still very showy, blooms.

A form of R. *moyesii*, Sealing Wax, grows in New Zealand gardens, as well as R. *hillieri* or *pruhoniciana*, the darkest-flowered of the rose species. Though the blooms are very lovely with their rich and velvety petals and dark gold stamens, R. *hillieri* needs sunshine for the flowers to be fully appreciated, as we have found to our cost. This is another *moyesii* seedling: its other parent is the Chinese R. *wilmottiae*. A truly spectacular shrub which even overshadowed its handsome parent R. *moyesii* in many English gardens and parks, was R. *highdownensis*, with its larger cerise-crimson flowers and decorative foliage and heps. It is a rose we have not seen in this country, and was named after a famous Sussex garden, Highdown, where it was bred by Sir Frederick Stern. Many species besides this, grew splendidly there, even on the chalky soil of that district. One of our colour slides of the late Major Lawrence Johnston's garden, Hidcote, shows a narrow grass pathway bordered on either side, for its entire length, with the delightful single Balkan *Paeony peregrina* or Sunbeam, as it is sometimes called. Spaced at intervals behind these glowing red paeonies are tall, dark clipped cupressus, cut flat across the top to a uniform height. Slightly further back are enormous bushes of R. *highdownensis*, the arching branches of which spray out between these dark trees, and over the borders of paeonies—creating a picture in several shades of green and glowing red. In another part of the same garden we admired a further colour harmony: here, plants of the crimson-purple Rugosa, Roseraie de l'Hay, and an unusual yellowish-green spurge, were backed by bushes of the cherry-crimson R. *highdownensis*. It is glimpses such as these that remain as satisfying memories, long after a visit to any particular garden is over.

Our loveliest pink-flowered shrub rose, *Gallica complicata*, has very large, single flowers of a vivid rose-pink, with a white zone round the yellow stamens. We are never surprised when people pause by this tall, arching bush, which has large, healthy, deeply-serrated leaves and good heps. *Gallica complicata* blooms splendidly in semi-shade; and is now starting to climb up a tree and through a high wire fence above the tennis court. From this vantage point the flexible branches spray down, literally smothered in early summer with glorious pink blooms, which stand out from the foliage, and last well on the plant. Large orange heps topped by firm sepals follow the flowers, so that the bush is attractive for a considerable period. The only attention it receives is the removal, once a year, of the oldest branches, and plenty of watering during the hottest weather.

North American wild roses may not be as spectacular as some of our beautiful European and Asiatic species, but they are all shrubs that give endless pleasure with a minimum of trouble. We imported some plants from England; others we grew from cuttings that came from the Christchurch Botanical Garden; and one we found in an early cemetery. Most of these roses sucker freely, have good foliage that colours vividly in the autumn, fragrant flowers, long elegant buds, and persistent, bright red heps. All are healthy, require no spraying, and thrive in poor positions with little attention, thus turning awkward spots into something useful and attractive. Most of these American roses bloom late in the season. In fact, the Prairie Rose, *R. setigera*, is the last of our species to come into flower and, because of this, is an admirable garden plant during the hot month of January.

The oldest cemetery in Auckland, where New Zealand's first Governor, Captain William Hobson, was buried in 1842, lies along the side of Grafton Gully. Many old roses, some of historic significance, are to be found in this area; amongst them is the only bush of a wild American rose we have found, either in an old garden, or an early cemetery, though a number are now grown in Botanical Gardens and in newer private ones. According to American authorities this delightful rose is *R. carolina plena*. This Pasture Rose, its single form, grows from New Brunswick down to Florida and as far west as Texas and Wisconsin; it is also the state flower of Iowa. As we were not sure at first of the name of our cemetery rose, we made a note to check up on it in Europe. We took our colour slides with

us; but neither in Italy, France, nor England did we find it. While in
London we studied a copy of H. C. Andrew's *Roses*, at the Royal Horticultural Society's Library and this helped us considerably. In it were three
delightful coloured reproductions of the bloom of R. *carolina plena* in different stages of development.

As soon as we saw these illustrations we felt fairly certain that we had
at last identified our rose. The double, soft pink, fragrant flowers open in
a distinctive manner, some of the central petals remaining tightly folded
like the bud—rather reminiscent of the blooms of the old pink camellia,
Lady St Clair. Others open wide, showing the yellow stamens. These
characteristics were most noticeable in the fine paintings of Andrew's
valuable book. Mr Graham Thomas advised us to send slides of the rose
to an American expert, Mr Wilson Lynes, in order to check up on it more
fully; so we took a comprehensive set of colour slides on our return, and
posted them off to the United States along with a page of pressed specimens.

Mr Lynes was most interested, particularly when he heard it had been
planted on a grave in New Zealand in 1881; and he was able to confirm
our identification. This American authority has recently published an interesting brochure which proves that R. *rapa*, so long believed to have
been a double form of R. *virginiana* was, in fact, R. *carolina plena*. Apparently, this double form of *carolina* is now quite rare, even in its native
haunts; and this is borne out by the fact that Richard Thomson, in his book
Old Roses for Modern Gardens, calls R. *carolina* his pet amongst the wild
roses, but does not mention the double form. The late Mr Will Tillotson
of California, who was an old-rose grower and enthusiast, considered the
single form of the Pasture Rose the most interesting plant in Mr Thomson's
collection. Both these authorities confirm that it hybridises freely with
other American species; and that many varieties are to be found. In 1955
Mr and Mrs Wilson Lynes rediscovered R. *carolina plena* on an early farm
in New York State. It was growing in a tangle of lilac and snowberry; only
the shrubs, Gallica Roses, and this lovely wild American rose marking the
site of an old homestead. The same thing occurs in New Zealand, where
valuable and rare roses are often discovered in overgrown and neglected
gardens, and round early settlements.

How this double rose first came to New Zealand from the United
States, and how the only bush of it we have seen out here should be grow-

ing in this early cemetery, is quite a mystery. So far we have not been able
to find out anything concerning its arrival in the country. This bush is growing side by side with Adelaide d'Orléans, that delightful trailing cluster
rose with creamy pink flowers, the blooms of which tone so well with the
warm pink blooms of R. *carolina plena*. These two make an attractive picture
in the old cemetery. It was a thrill when we were able to add this enchanting rose to our own collection of American species. On a visit to the
Edinburgh Botanic Gardens, we were most impressed with a hybrid form
of our much-loved R. *carolina*, the other parent being R. *rugosa*. A large
circular bed had been planted with this tall rose, which had perfect foliage,
handsome sprays of large rosy-red, single flowers, and slender elegant buds.
The label read simply *Carolina x Rugosa;* so we hope in the future to hear
more of it, as it will certainly become popular when well known.

A close relative, which suckers up around R. *carolina plena* in our
garden, is the shiny-leaved R. *lucida* or *virginiana*. It is a real treasure, one
of the easiest and most amiable plants; and the first American species to be
introduced into Europe. It was mentioned by Parkinson in 1640 as the
Virginian Bryer Rose; it had shining green leaves, bright cyclamen-pink
single flowers, and was later painted by Redouté. Gertrude Jekyll grew it
at Munstead and considered it one of the most delightful plants in her
garden. Our original plant came from Ilam, in Christchurch, and quickly
settled down in Auckland. Quite accidentally we planted it in semi-shade;
it prefers this position, thrives splendidly, and completely clothes an awkward corner. The glossy, deeply-toothed leaves—shiny, thin, reddish-
brown stems—and clusters of single, cyclamen-pink flowers with long
sepals and creamy-yellow stamens, combine to make a charming plant.
Add to this the beauty of the vividly coloured autumn foliage, the shining
round red heps, and the fact that these remain on the reddish stems when
the leaves have fallen; and you have a rose that is well worth the space in
this corner of the garden.

Very popular in England, both in bush and standard form, was R.
virginiana plena, or Rose-button, as it was called by William Paul—the small
elegant buds making excellent buttonholes. It grew much taller than the
single form in our garden; and the bushes were covered with delightful
double blooms of rosy-lilac. At Mount Stewart, in Northern Ireland, it was
doing splendidly on rather tall standards. Until we saw this rose in England,
we had wondered why the flowers on our plant of the double Virginian

Rose, which had been sent to us from an English nursery, differed in colour from those of our single form. When we saw these roses overseas, it was obvious at a glance that, though closely related, this double form and our rose were not identical. After our return to New Zealand, we sent pressed specimens and colour slides of this, as well as of the rose we found in the cemetery, to Mr Wilson Lynes in the United States; he had no hesitation in saying that the rose we had imported from England was a hybrid of *R. virginiana* and *R. carolina plena*—the rosy flowers and lower-growing and earlier-flowering habit being an inheritance from *R. carolina plena*.

As Rose d'Amour is considered now to have been a hybrid between these two fine American roses, not the double form of *R. virginiana* as had previously been supposed, this was a happy mistake as far as we were concerned. This charming hybrid has given us endless pleasure in a corner of the rock garden beneath a tall purple birch, three other wild American roses—*foliolosa*, *virginiana* and *carolina*—suckering freely nearby. The shiny fresh green foliage of this double rose colours well in the autumn and is always attractive, as are the fully open medium-sized flowers of a delicious shade of rosy-pink; but it is the bud, with its long, reflexing, curled sepals which has made it famous.

Count d'Orsay, a distinguished man of letters and a Director of Fine Arts during the Third Empire, was a great dandy—in fact, by the cut of his coats, he set the fashion for the men of his day. He generally wore a rose in his buttonhole, his favourite one being Rose d'Amour, which came to be known, also, as Count d'Orsay's Button-hole Rose. After the introduction of this charming rose into Europe, it quickly became popular. In Venice, it was called St Mark's Rose, as its flowers were said to open first on that saint's day. Edward Bunyard in *Old Roses*, A. T. Johnston in *The Mill Garden*, and Gertrude Jekyll in *Roses for English Gardens* all praise the beauty of the low-growing Rose d'Amour and speak of its rarity: while Sacheverell Sitwell, in *Old Garden Roses*, mentions being sent a plant of an Oleander Rose which he discovered afterwards to be the lovely fragrant Rose d'Amour, a real garden treasure.

The American Swamp Rose, *R. palustris*, grows into a tall, upright shrub with smooth, shiny, red-brown stems, and the usual fine, healthy foliage of these New World species. It is not supposed to grow tall in a dry situation; but in our garden it has reached a height of nearly eight feet and is delightful both in flower and fruit. The single, deep-rose blooms come in sprays at the ends of upright branches—a ring of slender buds, with long, elegant sepals, encircling the first flowers to open. We keep all sprays away from this rose so as to avoid damaging the leaves: and the shiny, red heps are a gay sight in the autumn. It hybridises freely with R. *carolina* and R. *virginiana*, as it is to be found in the same swampy localities. Our plants of this, and R. *foliolosa*, were grown from cuttings sent to us from Christchurch. R. *foliolosa* comes from further west—from Arkansas, Texas, and Oklahoma—and is a lower-growing shrub suitable for a large pocket at the rear of a rock garden. Its foliage, with narrow leaflets, also colours splendidly; but the plant is not as free-flowering as some of the other North American species. However, as it suckers well, it soon makes a pleasant thicket of thin, non-thorny stems well clothed with attractive, healthy foliage. At the same time, we received cuttings of R. *nitida*, which unfortunately failed to strike. We were sorry, as this low-growing rose is useful for the odd pocket or corner and is hardy, having had to stand up to tough conditions in the eastern part of Northern Canada. It was discovered there in 1776 by Sir Joseph Banks; and by him named the Bristly Rose. There was an excellent specimen of this species in the garden of the Villa Taranto in Northern Italy. It is a distinctive little rose, with erect stems covered in slender prickles and brown bristles. The very narrow, shining, dark green leaves become red and purple in the autumn: and the prickly fruit colours well, also, but we saw it in the spring when it was covered with small rosy-red flowers: we could well understand why North Indian maidens use these blooms to garland their hair.

A wild rose found from Alaska down to northern California is the tall brown-stemmed R. *nutkana*, which has been used as a stock for tree roses. It is an attractive plant, with pale-pink flowers that appear singly on the stems. Our cuttings come from the Wanganui district, where it does very well in several gardens. We were sent cuttings also of what was supposed to be R. *blanda*, or the Labrador or Hudson's Bay Rose; but, when they grew, we found them to be incorrectly named. This was a disappointment; we had seen the bushes of this Meadow Rose in Canada on the Island of Orleans, in the St Lawrence Waterway, and later near Toronto; and they were most attractive, with extra large, fine leaves. The Gooseberry-leaved Rose, a native of Mexico, has unusual leaves, very prickly heps, and cistus-like flowers with thin, crumpled petals of rosy-lilac. We saw this rose, R. *stellata mirifica*, for the first time in an old-rose garden near Woking, and were so attracted by it that we are now trying to grow it from seed. It should make an excellent rock garden shrub, if we are lucky enough to raise it.

On a recent visit to the Rocky Mountains we were amazed at the vast areas covered with wild roses. They grow densely right up to the snowline amongst rocks, larches, and spruces. Here their companion plants on the lower slopes alongside the great, snow-fed Bow River were delphiniums, asters, artemesias, anaphalis, chickory, spireas, and epilobiums. There were two forms of R. *acicularis*, the Arctic Rose, one with charming lavender flowers; and also large stands of the low-growing R. *macounii*, which has been proved a valuable seed parent by Canadian rose breeders. Recently we received seeds of R. *acicularis* from the Wisley Trial Gardens, in England and are hopeful that a few of these may germinate. There is a vast difference between these small roses from the North, the trailing Prairie Rose, and the taller plants from the Eastern States; but all have their place in any collection of wild roses of the world.

Spring heralds in all the lovely yellow-flowered, wild shrub roses along with forsythias, daffodils, and primroses. The first to come into bloom here, and one of the earliest to be grown extensively in European gardens, has been a popular plant in New Zealand for a long time. It is the ferny-leaved R. *hugonis*, the Golden Rose of China, which was discovered by Father Hugh Scallan at the end of the last century. He sent seed to Kew, where it was raised and later distributed to nurserymen. Single, cup-shaped, yellow flowers are borne with great freedom along the thin, brown, arching stems; they look as though a host of golden butterflies had alighted on the branches. Dark, almost black, heps follow the flowers; they are somewhat similar to those of the *spinosissima* family. We were interested to see two modern hybrids of R. *hugonis* in England. One called Hidcote Gold was raised in the late Major Laurence Johnston's Gloucestershire garden from a cross between R. *hugonis* and R. *omeiensis pteracantha*—a white, four-petalled rose with translucent red thorns. This hybrid has the yellowish flowers of one parent, and the glowing red thorns of the other; but by far the most impressive hybrid was one raised in the Cambridge Botanic Gardens from a cross between R. *hugonis* and the creamy-white flowered Himalayan R. *sericea*, which was given the name R. *cantabrigiensis*. It is a tall, free-flowering shrub, with large, creamy-yellow flowers; you can see it growing freely in Kew Gardens, in roadside plantings along the route to

London Airport, and in many private gardens in the British Isles.

Slightly later-flowering, but a finer shrub in this garden, is R. *zanthina spontanea* var. Canary Bird, one of the easiest, as well as the finest, of the yellow shrub roses. The clean, fresh-looking, ferny foliage is splendid for months on end, even in a rather dry shrubbery, and we are always amazed that it stands the heat so well when, in its native habitat, it ranges the mountainous districts from Afghanistan across to Northern China. The single, sulphur-yellow flowers have petals of good substance which do not damage easily; and welcome odd blooms appear, from time to time, after the first flush of flower is over; but we never see many of the dull red heps on our bush. Until G. S. Thomas' new book, *Shrub Roses of Today* appeared, we had always understood that R. *zanthina* var. Canary Bird was an improved single form of R. *zanthina* (Syn R. *slingeri*)—a rose which was discovered in Chinese and Korean gardens, and which had been cultivated there for over a hundred years. This double rose, R. *slingeri*, which grew splendidly in Rome, was introduced into Europe before the single form, R. *zanthina spontanea*.

The better known and much finer rose which has been listed, until now, as R. *zanthina* var. Canary Bird, is apparently a hybrid, possibly between R. *hugonis* and either R. *zanthina* or R. *spinosissima*. Whatever its breeding, it is a splendid garden subject where a yellow-flowered shrub is desired; and in Auckland it blooms a little later than R. *hugonis*. The clear green, fresh-looking, ferny foliage is splendid right through the season; and contrasts well with the almost thornless, shiny, rich brown stems. The medium-sized, single yellow flowers appear along the length of the branches, which, when heavily laden, arch over gracefully. The individual blooms have more substance in the petals, open flatter, and have a richer colouring than those of R. *hugonis*. We see few of the very dark red heps on our specimen, so there is no autumn display: the shrub relies for its beauty on stems, leaves, and flowers. These alone make it an indispensable garden plant.

Just as a low-growing, suckering, purple Gallica Rose has found its way through all the early milling, mining, and mission settlements in New Zealand, so did a golden yellow rose travel, by covered waggon, along the gold rush trails in North America. This was Harison's Yellow, a double rose which was discovered, as a natural hybrid, in the garden of a New York lawyer. In this same garden grew many of the *spinosissima* family—

the tall Siberian R. *altaica; R. hispida,* an Icelandic form; and the lower-growing Double Yellow which we saw by the roadside in Cumberland. It was presumed that the Double Yellow must have crossed with the Persian Brier, R. *lutea,* which grew in the same garden. We have found R. *harisonii* making an excellent low hedge, also, in many old gardens; but never, semi-wild, by our roadsides. Our original plant came from the South Island, but others have been sent to us from various parts of the North Island as well. Now it is firmly established in a smallish triangular area, bounded on two sides by rock edgings, with a narrow paved pathway on the third. This confined spot, at one end of a curving yellow and white border, is to its liking: our specimen is extremely vigorous and free-flowering. Just below this pocket is a sunken garden planted with silver, blue, and yellow perennials; so the yellow rose acts as a good colour link between it and the white and yellow border on the higher level. We achieved a very happy plant association in this spot by planting what we mistakenly thought was a low-growing alstromeria in front of Harison's Yellow. This wonderful alstromeria—one we never saw in England, even amongst special exhibits of this perennial at a fortnightly Show in the New Hall, though we read of it being on view the following year—is the yellow and cream Walter Fleming, which has wider and rounder petals than those of most other alstromerias. Each flower resembles an orchid; and lasts extremely well both in the garden and in the house. It loved this sunny corner and its companion rose. It grew at a great rate, travelling up through the prickly brown stems and ferny foliage of the gay, double-yellow *spinosissima* hybrid: and a rose thicket made an excellent support for the long flowering stems of this new perennial. Both flowered for several months on end, and made a striking picture in tones of yellow and green and brown. Earlier in the year the ground beneath R. *harisonii* is carpeted with yellow *Narcissus bulbicodium* and an unusual, double, yellow-flowered camassia, with taller yellow bearded irises at the rear. Later, in the summer, the ramping, white-flowered *Nierembergia rivularis* springs up everywhere to make a cover over the fading bulbs.

A little further along the yellow and white border, in a warm, sunny position, is the famous rose Persian Yellow, which created such a sensation when it was brought back from Teheran in 1838 by Sir H. Willock, Envoy Extraordinary and Minister Plenipotentiary to Persia. Pure yellow roses were rare in those days, particularly double ones. There was the Sulphur

Rose, R. *hemispherica*, which was brought to England in the seventeenth century—a lovely thing, very similar to Persian Yellow, except that the foliage was grey-green, not bright green. However, it is not a hardy plant. The low-growing Double Yellow Spinosissima was another pure yellow rose: and the newly introduced R. *harisonii* made the third. So it was not surprising that this new double Persian Rose should prove such an attraction when it was shown in England and France, especially when it was found to be much hardier and easier to flower than the older Sulphur Rose. Our plant, which came from England several years ago, has settled in splendidly; and last season produced a mass of the large, deep golden-yellow, full cup-shaped blooms.

These appear singly along the shiny brown, thorny branches, amongst bright green, healthy foliage. The large fat buds, with long curling and reflexing sepals, are lime-green before they open to show the richly-coloured petals. Persian Yellow was the rose used in the breeding of many modern roses—particularly those of the Pernetiana strain and is said to have been responsible for that rose family's susceptibility to black spot. We find this hard to believe, as there has been only the slightest trace of this disease on our plant. The thing this lovely rose lacks is a pleasing fragrance—a sad lack, certainly, but somehow compensated for by the magnificence of the blooms. Star of Persia, a tall semi-double rose, and the single form of Persian Yellow, R. *lutea*, are both well known in New Zealand. We grow neither of them, as cuttings of Star of Persia failed to strike. Now we raise cuttings sent to us at difficult times by placing them under glass jars. In an issue of one of the Royal Horticultural Society's *Journals* there was an article on plant collecting in Persia, which described a trip from Teheran to the Elburg Mountains which lie between the Caspian Sea and the desert. In one attractive little village the explorers came suddenly on an oasis surrounded by trees; and round one of the houses were hedges and banks of the magnificent Golden Rose, R. *foetida* or *lutea*, five feet in height, and literally covered with brilliant yellow single flowers. The double Persian Yellow is a garden form, and has not been found in the wild. Its exact origin is not known: though the single yellow R. *lutea* and the double Sulphur Rose have been suggested as parents.

From Turkestan, where the old caravan routes from Persia ran through Samarkand and on to distant China and Mongolia, comes another of our shrub roses—this time one with light-looking, greenish-grey foliage, and single white flowers. It is R. *fedtschenkoana*, one of the few wild roses, apart from the Rugosa family, which blooms intermittently after the first flush of flowers is over. It was discovered by a Russian botanist, Olga Fedtschenko, in 1875; she sent it to the Botanic Garden of St Petersburg. From there it was sent to Warley, Ellen Willmott's garden, where it was painted by Alfred Parsons for *The Genus Rosa*. The brown stems of the rose are covered with thin prickles and fine bristles; the bright red heps are also covered with bristles, and have long persistent sepals. R. *fedtschenkoana* is not a showy, flaunting beauty, but it produces a quiet, restful effect in a garden. This rose and the Apple Rose have the same, useful greyish foliage. If the old wood is cut out after flowering, fine new shoots soon appear which will flower later in the season: and this fresh growth is particularly attractive in colour.

Herr Kordes, of Sparriestroop, Germany, an imaginative rose-breeder, crossed the tall Siberian *spinosissima altaica* with the grand old Hybrid Perpetual, Frau Karl Druschki, and produced a splendid shrub rose, Karl Foerster. The tall, upright growth, bristly stems, and healthy, ferny foliage are an inheritance from the Siberian parent; but the large double white flowers and free-flowering habit come from Frau Karl—also the lack of a rich scent, though we would not say that Karl Foerster was entirely scentless. This is a splendid acquisition in our white garden, since the tall stems, when laden with bloom along their entire length, arch over gracefully. After the first flowering is over we cut out a certain amount of older wood and, very soon after, new shoots appear which will produce bloom later in the season. No special attention is necessary to keep Karl Foerster healthy and happy right through the year—so it is a real asset in the modern garden. Herr Kordes has spent considerable time and thought in breeding from some of the lesser known species in order to produce hardy, vigorous and healthy shrub roses—a type in which he is particularly interested. From the Siberian parent of Karl Foerster came another splendid series, a number of which are grown in New Zealand, two of them being particularly beautiful. These are Frühlingsgold, which thrives well in one exposed coastal garden that we know: and Frühlingsmorgen, whose charming single pink blooms have cherry edges and red stamens. They hold their colour better in the south than in Auckland; and the best blooms we have ever seen on this shurb were in Edinburgh—so it obviously likes a cool, moist climate.

◄
49. R. *laevigata* or
    R. *sinica alba* —
    the Cherokee Rose.

▼ 50. R. *dupontii*

▲ 51. Madame Alfred Carrière-Noisette

▼ 52. Maiden's Blush

A lax-growing rose, which can be trained successfully on a wall or used as a shrub or a hedge, is the *spinosissima* hybrid, Stanwell Perpetual. It blooms early and late, bearing fairly large, flat, blush-pink flowers, richly scented and tinted with salmon at the base of the tightly curled central petals. While the flowers resemble those of the Autumn Damask, which was considered to have been one of its parents, the grey-green leaves—bearing nine leaflets—and the very prickly stems are an inheritance from *R. spinosissima*, the other parent. This shrub benefits from having the oldest wood cut out from the base each season, as the quickly formed new growth produces finer foliage and flowers. In *Roses and Rose Growing* by Rose Kingsley there is a splendid illustration of Stanwell Perpetual used as a hedge plant. Our own bush is trained on to a low white trellis against a brick wall, its companion plants on either side being the fuchsias Flirtation and Pastel.

R. *macrantha*, a natural hybrid between the low-growing R. *gallica* and the Dog Rose, R. *canina*, was discovered in a French garden in 1823. This is one of the really fine shrub roses, and our only regret is that we have not sufficient space to do it full justice. It has grown vigorously since its arrival from England. We noticed this shrub particularly in gardens on the Continent and in the British Isles: and have a photograph taken at the Villa Taranto, in Northern Italy, of the most impressive specimen of R. *macrantha* we saw anywhere. The tall bush was smothered with the large, single, peach-pink flowers; the colour of these blooms looked perfect against a background of the unusual beech, *Fagus sylvatica tricolor*, which has coppery, purple foliage, and leaves edged and blotched with rose and pinkish white. At Newby Hall in Yorkshire, at Highdown in Sussex, and in many other gardens and parks, R. *macrantha* was both a distinguished looking shrub and a decorative garden plant. We find that some of the softer-toned, peach-pink regal pelargoniums, such as the South African Mrs Gill, make excellent companion plants for such a tall shrub rose, and add colour for a long period. A very unusual rose, Raubritter, was raised by crossing a hybrid of R. *macrantha* with a rambler rose. This is a perfect plant for trailing over a raised bank. The globular, thin-petalled, rose-pink blooms—rather reminiscent of the flowers of the Shell Rose, La Reine Victoria—come in large sprays, and last unblemished on the sprawling bush for a remarkably long time. They also look splendid cascading over a low wall. The small, dark leaves are undistinguished and, later in the season, are subject to black spot; but even this fault, which can be remedied, does not detract from the pleasure Raubritter gives us each season. It is summer-flowering only but we always look forward to seeing it, backed by tall fuchsias, trailing over the grey-leaved plants that clothe the front of a low wall.

Another natural Gallica hybrid, the Frankfort Rose, or R. *franco-furtana*, was known early in the sixteenth century. It makes a lower spreading shrub, with excellent blue-green, shapely foliage, and large, double, ranunculus-like flowers. These have loose papery petals, deep rose at the base flushed with purple, but paling to near pink on the edges. Its rosy-purple tone is inherited from the other parent, R. *cinnamomea*, which grows wild right across northern Europe and Asia. Redouté painted this glorious rose at Malmaison and called it R. *turbinata*. It was a great favourite with the Empress; and has been given her name, also. We grow R. *francofurtana* in a large, raised, rock pocket, below *Rhododendron* Pink Pearl. The bed is edged with variegated fuchsias, low azaleas, and *Hypericum moserianum tricolor*, as well as being carpeted with dwarf bulbs and plants of *Primula obconica* in colours that tone with the rose.

Some of the finest flowering shrubs we saw throughout the British Isles were Hybrid Musk Roses. Great use was made of them in many different gardens. At Newby Hall they were planted in tremendous mixed borders; at Hidcote they were interplanted with paeonies and other interesting perennials in small, intimate, walled gardens; at Lyegrove they were featured at intervals on top of low walls surrounding sunken gardens; and at Mt Stewart, not far from Belfast, they were grown not only as bushes, but also as tall standards. Large-flowered clematis grew also on these standards: the mixture of pink roses and mauve clematis was very attractive. Hedges of the Hybrid Musks, Felicia, Penelope, and Cornelia were very popular and were used with great effect at Kew Gardens. We have also seen such hedges doing splendidly in New Zealand.

These roses were bred by the Rev. J. H. Pemberton who, when he retired from the ministry, devoted the remaining years of his life to the breeding and growing of roses, and bequeathed a legacy of wonderful plants to rose lovers throughout the world. Though these Musk hybrids are related only distantly to this interesting rose family, some of them have leaves and subtle scent very reminiscent of their famous ancestors. We find them quite indispensible, and really trouble-free. In full bloom they are an amazing sight, the whole bush being covered with flowers. Space does not permit us to grow many of them as shrubs, though this is the ideal way so we compromise by growing some of them on trellis frames against the walls of the house, where they quickly reach the eaves. Felicia and Penelope, both bred from the old favourite Ophelia, grow side by side on the eastern wall of our home and flower tremendously well. The former is a soft salmon-pink with full flowers; the latter has a creamy-yellow semi-double flower just flushed with salmon. The flowers of Penelope closely resemble those of the Hybrid Moschata, Princesse de Nassau, except that the blooms of the climbing rose are a little smaller.

Three creamy-white roses we also find extremely useful are Prosperity, which we grow as a shrub in the white garden; Moonlight, which climbs up a trellis nearby; and the larger-flowered Pax, which is trained on another wall. All flower perpetually, all are healthy and cause us no trouble; and all are useful for indoor decoration. Cornelia is a popular rose in New Zealand, but two Hybrid Musks we admired overseas do not appear to have reached this country so far. They are the lovely Buff Beauty, which grows into a splendid shrub; and Vanity, which was so effective at Hidcote and Newby Hall. Kathleen is a single-flowered member of this family with soft reddish-green foliage and sprays of white blooms, pink-tinted on the edges of the petals. We have now started to train this sweet rose up a tree. Not far away is another climber, also named Kathleen; but this is a Multi-flora Hybrid, with single pink, white-centred flowers, and a much more vigorous rose than the Musk Hybrid.

Long before the days of hybridisation the simple Sweet Brier—so lovely and so refreshing—was grown by roadsides, in hedges, and in cottage gardens, where it surrounded the windows, filling rooms with its sweet fragrance, particularly after rain.

> . . . It grows along the poor girl's pathway, by the poor man's
> door
> Such are the simple folk it dwells among.

No wonder, then, that our earliest settlers brought this much-loved, single rose with them when they sailed from their homeland to start life anew in far-off New Zealand. It established easily and quickly, and must soon have been like a breath of home to many lonely wives. The Sweet Brier and the willow were introduced into the country by the missionaries and their wives; and in one book on the early days in New Zealand are referred to as Children of the Church. When H.M.S. *Alligator* called at the Bay of Islands in 1834 the ship's surgeon, William Barrett Marshall, described a visit he paid to the Anglican Chapel of Paihia, which then stood back from the road in an enclosed square. Within the fence, on all sides, was a thick Sweet Brier hedge, which was mixing its perfume with the breeze, thus scenting the pure atmosphere breathed by those who assembled on this spot to worship God. A year later Charles Darwin arrived in H.M.S. *Beagle*, and visited this mission station established in 1823 by Henry Williams. Later Darwin wrote in *A Naturalist's Voyage* that "they went ashore at Paihia, to one of the large groups of houses, that hardly deserved the title of a village. It was the residence of missionaries, and all the cottages, many of which were white-washed and looked very neat, were the property of the English". He found it pleasing to see several kinds of roses, honeysuckle, jasmine, stocks, and hedges of Sweet Brier, in the front garden.

As well as the common form of R. *rubiginosa* (*eglanteria*) or the Sweet Eglantine of the poets – a rose from which Queen Elizabeth I had concocted an elixir to promote long life – three other types were introduced into New Zealand at an early date. From the spot where Mrs Clendon grew her roses, on historic Okiato Point, we were sent a bush of the very low-growing, thorny R. *eglanteria glutinosa*. Its bright pink, white-centred, flowers generally appear singly on the branches, not in clusters. In the heart of the King Country, and on the heights above the western side of Lake Taupo, we found many plants of the taller-growing but small-flowered, R. *eglanteria micrantha*. On several occasions we have photographed this rose when blooms, as well as heps, were on the bush together: we have not noticed this occurrence in the other varieties. The still taller, more upright R. *eglanteria agrestis* or the Grasslands Rose, grows in the old hillside cemetery above Tararu. This uncommon Sweet Brier has small flowers for its size; they are also paler than those of the other forms already mentioned. In spite of its beauty and its medicinal value, the Sweet Brier was declared a noxious weed in 1900, and now it is only on the waste spaces and along minor country roads that it is seen to any great extent. The sweet, single flowers and the gorgeous autumn heps are things we should be sad to lose; but we have noticed that, though these plants may grow and spread freely by the roadsides off the beaten track, they do not extend into the fields when the farms are well managed.

In our garden we now grow only hybrid forms of R. *rubiginosa* or *eglanteria*, old and modern; so it was interesting to see still other varieties in England—varieties that had only been names to us previously. From many parts of the country we have been sent one of the early hybrids to name. Comparing notes with other old-rose enthusiasts we wondered if this semi-double, medium-sized rose was the form of the Sweet Brier discovered long ago in a Cheshire lane, and named Janet's Pride; but the real Janet's Pride, when we saw it in England, had smaller flowers, with a very narrow carmine edging to the white petals. From information later received we think it possible that this rose grows on Banks Peninsula. Our rose, so often seen in early milling and mining settlements, and in old cemeteries, has slightly larger, fuller, semi-double flowers of twenty petals, with a much wider bank of rosy-carmine that fades down to white near the base of the petals. It is a sweet rose, with good stamens, and fine firm foliage on the tall arching stems. There is little of the lovely leaf fragrance of the true Sweet Brier; but, on the whole, this is typical of all these hybrids. The French breeder and nurseryman, Prévost, was producing hybrids of R. *rubiginosa* well over a hundred years ago, and catalogued fifteen of them at one time. The most important variety, Hessoise, with semi-double, rose-coloured flowers, was so popular in France at that time that its name was appropriated by growers and given to other hybrids. As the rose growing in New Zealand does not resemble any of the better known varieties we saw in England—varieties such as Manning's Blush, La Belle Distinguée, and the later Penzance hybrids—we feel that it may be one of these early varieties from France, brought by French families who settled out here in the early days of the colony.

In an old garden in the King Country we saw another rose, similar to the hybrid we grow here, but with flowers much paler in colour. This is Julia Mannering, an Eglanteria hybrid with semi-double, flesh-coloured flowers of medium size. Unfortunately this bush, along with other old roses, has now been destroyed; but we have several good slides of the whole plant, and individual blooms to which we can refer. The Penzance hybrids are quite well known in this country: we have grown Lord Penzance and Lady Penzance as well as Amy Robsart; and friends have Flora McIvor and Lucy Ashton in their gardens. When Lord Penzance became interested in using the Sweet Brier for breeding he created sixteen varieties within the short space of five years. Thirteen of these were given the names of characters in Sir Walter Scott's novels. Now new varieties are appearing: Wilhelm Kordes of Germany has bred some fine shrub roses from Magnifica, a seedling from a Hybrid Sweet Brier.

In a large rock pocket, edged with fuchsias, we grow Fritz Nobis, another of his lovely introductions. This plant has spread by means of suckers and now fills the whole bed. In early summer there are masses of the soft, salmon-pink, semi-double flowers but it does not bloom later in the season, though the foliage is always most attractive. However, we have underplanted this lovely rose with low-growing, perpetual-flowering fuchsias in soft shades of pink and cream, so when the rose is not in bloom, the fuchsias are still gay. We have parted with Prestige that has bright sprays of double, cherry-red flowers: and rather regret its going, as it flowers for a longer period than Fritz Nobis, and is an excellent garden plant.

The double form of the Tree Rose, R. *pomifera duplex*, was discovered in an English hedgerow and called Wolley Dod's Rose, after its finder. Edward Bunyard in *Old Garden Roses* said that this lovely plant was worthy of a place in any garden; and Dean Hole describes trees of the single form growing to a height of thirty feet. We grow Wolley Dod's Rose at the back of one of our wider shrubberies; already, in six years, it has grown very tall. A fairly upright flowering cherry blooms at the same time as the rose and quite close: the flowers of both tone delightfully. The large, handsome, grey-green leaves, semi-double, rich pink blooms encased in hairy calyx and sepals, and extra large and showy heps, are all most decorative.

The single form, known as the Apple Rose of England because of its enormous heps, is not only a true native of the British Isles but also of Europe. We heard of it growing especially well in the alpine valley of Romsdalen, in Norway: but were never fortunate enough to see it growing wild. Neither have we come across it in New Zealand, except in gardens, though its close relative the Dog Rose was introduced into the country at an early date and recorded by Hooker in 1864. This sweet, wild rose, with its creamy, pink-tinted flowers, has not spread far and wide like the Sweet Brier; it is still found mainly in the spots where it was first planted. One of these places is within half a mile of our home, on the hillsides round Orakei. The Leatherleaf Rose, or R. *canina coriifolia*, was the type introduced; at a distance the bushes could easily be mistaken for those of the hawthorn, especially when there are no flowers or heps on the plants. The dark red fruits are quickly devoured by birds, who instinctively recognise their extra high vitamin content. So the bushes are not as showy in the autumn as those of the Sweet Brier, which is a gay sight, particularly in the rays of the setting sun, when the whole shrub simply glows. However, we always enjoy seeing the modest Dog Rose as it climbs up into trees through our neighbour's hedge.

A member of the same family, R. *rubrifolia*, is a distinguished plant with unusual plum-coloured foliage overlaid with a bluish metallic sheen. It was one of those grown by the Empress Josephine at Malmaison. The mountains of Southern Europe are its native habitat, so it is hardy and well able to stand up to extremely cold weather. In England great use was made of R. *rubrifolia* as a foliage plant, particularly in red, brown, and purple borders, where its subtle-coloured leaves made a perfect foil for roses such as the spectacular new shrub rose, Scarlet Fire; or the older R. *moyesii*. It had been our intention to use R. *rubrifolia* in a similar manner; but this was not a success. Where it does well, R. *rubrifolia* makes a magnificent hedge, as it can be clipped freely, and it is also most attractive for use indoors. It flourishes in the Christchurch Botanical Gardens side by side with its hybrid, Carminetta. This was bred in Canada by Isabella Preston who is a renowned breeder of lilies, lilacs, and unusual roses. It is a cross between R. *rubrifolia* and R. *rugosa*, which grows so freely in that northern country, and both these roses are used with great effect on the Heights of Abraham, above Quebec. Carminetta has not such distinctive plum-coloured foliage as R. *rubrifolia*, though its single pink flowers are larger than those of this parent. Both plants were very fine in Rome, where old roses and rose species were thriving on a hillside above the Rose Trial Grounds for Italy.

One of the listed British wild flowers, R. *tomentosa*, another form of the Dog Rose, was quite the finest hedge rose we saw growng wild in England. It is not seen all over the British Isles; but only in certain localiities, notably North Wales. On a trip from Cheshire across to visit Bodnant, Lord Aberconway's famous garden on the hills opposite Snowdon, we passed by some rather desolate and lonely hill farms. Round one cluster of poor, whitewashed houses and outbuildings, we saw beautiful high hedges surrounding the farm. These were a smother of perfect pink blooms, each individual flower being larger and of richer colouring than those of most other forms of R. *canina*. We found out that this rose was *canina tomentosa*, a rose closely allied to the fine Apple Rose of England, and having similar grey-green foliage. We saw the owner surrounded by a miscellaneous collection of animals and birds, and asked whether we could photograph the roses. He laughed and told us, in his lilting, soft Welsh voice, to take the lot, if we wanted them, as they were only Dog Roses. But, to us, they were a thing of beauty; for they stretched along the road and well up into the hills. Nowhere else in the British Isles did we see bushes of this particular wild rose, with its slightly cup-shaped and rich pink blooms, and we have not seen it here, either. At Nymans, in Sussex, there were immense bushes of a fine hybrid Dog Rose, *canina andersonii*, with extra large, very bright pink flowers. Early this century, R. *canina mollis*—the Bloomystem Rose—was sold out here and is to be found in Nelson.

Shrub roses are coming more and more into prominence with the modern trend in gardening. Some magnificent roses have been put on the market in recent years, most of them bred in Germany; but there is one lovely rose that was produced in Denmark—Poulsen's Park Rose—a cross between two well known roses that we have in our garden, Great Western, a Bourbon, and Karen Poulsen, an older Floribunda. This shrub rose was given to us by an old-rose grower of Wanganui, who grew a magnificent bush of it in one of her wide borders. The raiser describes the colour of the loose blooms as Conrad-Meyer pink, and they are equally as lovely as the blooms of that handsome Rugosa hybrid, Berlin, dark red; Elmshorn, cherry red; Queen Elizabeth, rose; and Bonn, cinnamon-red, are all excellent shrub roses. The last is particularly handsome, with extra large, healthy leaves and loosely double flowers, whose unusual colour is inherited from Independence, the rose which caused a great stir when it was first shown. It grows to a tremendous height each season, though pruned fairly hard at the end of the winter. Bonn reaches to the eaves of our low house, in a very few months. The large, cinnamon-red blooms come at the ends of long swaying branches, appearing off and on all season and creating a fine spectacle alongside a double-flowered, peach-coloured hibiscus. The tall Queen Elizabeth is more vigorous than most of the Floribundas; and grows here to a height of eight feet. An Auckland friend has a splendid hedge of this fine rose growing alongside her driveway; the bushes are covered with loosely double, rose-coloured flowers for most of the year. Scarlet Fire, Sparrieshoop, and Nymphenburg, are some we admired in English gardens; all are available in New Zealand. Recently Sparrieshoop and Nymphenburg have been added to our collection.

The range of Shrub Roses is remarkable. There are tall ones and short ones, the colours ranging from white, through pinks and yellows, on to the darkest of reds. There are single and double species, with their natural hybrids, and modern ones. They come from all over the world, to help the modern gardener and to grace many a garden.

Said the rosebud "Ware the thorn;
Thou shalt rue it, scratched and torn,
In the sunny weather!"

Goethe

SOME OF THE MOST ADAPTABLE ROSES IN OUR GARDEN are the hardy healthy Rugosas which, in their wild state, are found in Japan, Kamchatka, Eastern Siberia and Northern China. R. *rugosa* has been called the Hedgehog Rose—and no wonder, as it is almost as difficult to handle as that small, well-armed animal; though both hedgehog and rose are the gardener's friends. However, once this rose has been firmly planted, it is possible to leave it entirely alone except for the occasional removal of spent blooms; but even this small service is not absolutely necessary, though autumn flowers appear more regularly if it is carried out.

The Japanese R. *rugosa thunbergiana* was discovered in a Kyoto garden in 1784. The plant was found by Carl Thunberg, a Swedish botanist, and, by 1786 an English nursery had imported two varieties discovered by the same collector. For nearly a hundred years these hardy plants were little appreciated; though we were amazed, when studying books at the Royal Horticultural Society's Library to find this Japanese rose listed as a British wild flower. And certainly, while in England, we saw almost as much of it growing in old gardens, and semi-wild, as we did of the Dog Rose and Sweet Brier, and far more of it than we did of the Field Rose, R. *arvensis*. Some of the bushes and hedges were very tall—ours, that has to put up with harder soil conditions, is only half as high—and all were covered with the single, cyclamen-pink blooms for which this rose is renowned. Both leaves and flowers on the Japanese Rugosas are smaller than those on the plants from the mainland; the foliage is less richly green, and the blooms paler in tone with long persistent sepals. The handsome, shining, orange-scarlet fruits on Rugosa Roses are enjoyed by the birds, being richer in health-giving vitamins than those of most other rose heps. All the human inhabitants of northern and rugged lands eat these fruits for medicinal purposes, and value the rose highly. In fact one Chinese, who had lived in New Zealand nearly all his life, made a pilgrimage to a Buddhist monastery in the far north of China in an endeavour to secure from the monks a local herb for the relief of asthma. As he walked round the monastery garden, he was interested to see that the monks were gathering and eating rose heps – one of the roses growing there being a form of the wild Rugosa.

Though this attractive species has to tolerate our heavy clay it thrives best in sandy soil; in parts of Japan, where it grows near the sea-shore *R. rugosa*, with its large fruits, is known as the Shore Bringal—*Bringal* being the Anglo-Indian name for the huge fruit of the egg-plant. Round the coast of Ayr, in Scotland, old established colonies of this wild Japanese rose are to be seen; and, in that interesting book *The Pageant of the Rose* are fine coloured illustrations of forms of *R. rugosa*, in full flower, growing semi-wild on the sand-hills round Cape Cod on the eastern seabord of the United States, where they have been established for a long time. Many plants of this hardy rose can be seen around Quebec, and we noticed huge beds of Rugosa Roses planted on the historic Heights of Abraham, not far from the spot where General Wolfe made his famous ascent. The two plants that impressed us most in Quebec were the hardy Rugosas and *Hydrangea paniculata*—another native of Japan and China—which was grown so extensively and flowered so magnificently that it could have been called the Flower of Quebec. On the way up to the Heights, we drove in an open, gaily-painted victoria past a large sunken garden, in the centre of which was an imposing statue of Jeanne d'Arc. The garden, dedicated to this saint, was surrounded by a hedge of the red Rugosa hybrid, F. J. Grooten-doorst. The mass of fringed, carnation-like blooms looked very effective, as there were a great number of red and white perennials planted in the long beds inside the hedges.

We were interested to see, in English nurseries, standard roses being budded on Hybrid Rugosa stock—a stock produced in Holland. It was amazing that the densely prickly stems could be handled at all, let alone budded so successfully. R. *rugosa* is not used for this purpose either in Australia or New Zealand; but at one time, nurserymen in the Wanganui district used both Rugosa and Canina as stock until Lippiat's *manettii* became popular. This stock also has been superseded, but it did flourish better in Wanganui than in most other districts of New Zealand.

A wide, raised, curved bed—backed by the tennis court fence, and bordered in front by the pathway leading up from our white garden up towards the rock garden—is planted with Rugosas, though the wilder types are relegated to a less obvious spot in the garden where they can be left to their own devices. The magnificent R. *rugosa scabrosa* is a marvellous plant with large showy heps and perfect foliage. A single bloom can measure nearly six inches across, in the early part of the year before the dry weather sets in. When the rosy-magenta flowers, with petals like crumpled silk, and the orange-red heps are on the bush together, they create an interesting discord of colour. The fruits of all Rugosas retain the typical, long, curled sepals of this family, many other roses losing their calyx lobes as soon as the fruit forms. Next to R. *scabrosa*, Belle Poitevine's semi-double flowers of soft rosy-mauve tone in beautifully, though with us it is not as free-flowering as its single neighbour, nor is its foliage as large and shiny. Twice we have been sent bushes of a double Rugosa with flowers of similar colouring to those of Belle Poitevine, though its central petals are not as neatly incurved. A huge stand of this rose grows in a very old Akaroa garden near a huge golden catalpa and hundred-year-old grape-vines that trail along a wide colonial verandah. Another piece of it came from Wanganui. We feel sure that this must be R. *rugosa plena*, which was first noticed in the St Petersburg Botanic Garden last century. This double Rugosa probably occurred as a sport from the Siberian type, which was discovered by a Russian botanist much later than the Japanese Rugosa. Further over in this same border, we enjoy the clear pink, single blooms of Frau Dagmar Hastrupp. This is a lovely rose, lower-growing and more spreading than R. *rugosa scabrosa*, the slightly smaller flowers showing no trace of the typical magenta colouring of this type of rose. Like all other true Rugosas, Frau Dagmar has the same rich green, healthy foliage.

Wild roses abound in the long narrow tongue of land that spreads down from northern Siberia towards Japan; and one of these, R. *davurica*, is thought to have crossed with a wild Rugosa to produce R. *kamchatica*—

a rose that was introduced into Chelsea Botanic Gardens as early as 1771. We photographed this hybrid, with its crumpled mallow-pink flowers, in the Christchurch Botanic Gardens, where many species and their hybrids are planted in one corner of a magnificent garden. Many years ago we were sent an unusual Rugosa, but unfortunately cannot remember now the district from which it came. Because of its low growth, smaller flowers of cyclamen-pink, softer leaves, and slightly pear-shaped heps—a characteristic of R. *acicularis*, the Circumpolar Rose, a form of which is to be found in Japan—we feel it is probably a natural hybrid of these two roses which grow in that country. It is charming, and suckers freely in an odd corner beyond the tennis court. The late Captain Kingdon Ward, who wrote many books on his plant hunting expeditions to India, Upper Burma, and China, brought back with him from one trip a single Rugosa which, when we saw it in a fine hillside garden in Wanganui, surprised us by the unusual shape of its rosy-magenta petals, each one being partly furled and rather pointed at the tip. The blooms, otherwise, were about the same size as those of the single Rugosa found further north.

Some years ago we were given another most unusual hybrid Rugosa that has turned out to be a real garden treasure. It came to us labelled as R. *foliolosa*. R. *foliolosa* is a low-growing, narrow-leaved, pink-flowered, wild rose from Texas, Arkansas, and Oklahoma, which we grow in a large pocket at the rear of a rock garden. Next to it, in a lower pocket, we have planted this interesting hybrid Rugosa, and there is a vast difference between the two plants. R. *rugosa* imparts its strong stems to its progeny: they are heavily clothed with large and small prickles, and bristles. On the other hand, its leaves are smaller, narrower, softer and of a less vivid green than those of many pure rugosas. The flowers, which come in spaced sprays, are a rich maroon-crimson, with long, elegant sepals which extend beyond the petals, and yellow not cream stamens. These blooms look delightful against the soft green foliage, and the bush flowers splendidly—much better than its small, pink-flowered neighbour R. *foliolosa*. Even the partial shade of a tall purple birch does not seem to affect its free-flowering habit.

In *Les Plus Belles Roses*, M. Maurice Vilmorin is mentioned as having produced an interesting and very remontant hybrid between R. *rugosa* and R. *foliolosa*. A black and white sketch of the bush shows it as being of low stature and having very dark blooms. We took slides of this rose with us to England and were able to compare the flowers and leaves of our rose with those of William Paul's hybrid R. *rugosa atropurpurea*. This we found to be a much taller plant; a very fine rose, but not our unusual one. On our return to New Zealand, we sent slides to Wilson Lynes, an authority on wild American roses. He confirmed our impression that it was a hybrid between an American and a Japanese rose, both types hybridising freely. In fact, Mr Lynes said that many of their own native roses are closely related. He was referring in particular to *foliolosa* and *humilis*, two low-growing roses from the same area, both of which have crossed with one another as well as with a form of R. *rugosa*. He considered that our rose, because of its low growth and fairly narrow leaves, was probably a hybrid from R. *foliolosa*. As we did not come across this rose either in Europe or North America, we hope its naming is correct; it certainly makes a very striking garden plant. *Fuchsia procumbens* and *Fuchsia thymifolia* trail over the front of this rock pocket, and dwarf blue aquilegias and campanulas carpet the area under the rose. We are now awaiting the first flowering of a self-sown Hybrid Rugosa, with unusual pink-tinted young foliage.

Wonderful hedges of R. *rugosa* and its hybrids were seen in many parts of Britian and Eire. At Mt Usher, in the Wicklow Hills, a tall hedge of the Japanese Rugosa was planted alongside the old mill race which separated the intimate house garden and lawn from the lovely parkland beyond. Then further north, near Belfast, two National Trust Gardens were situated not far from beautiful Strangford Lough—one at Mt Stewart and the other at Rowallane. In a walled garden at Rowallane, in the shade of one of the attractive towers seen so often in Ireland, were low hedges of the double-white Rugosa hybrid, Blanc double de Coubert—a favourite rose in our own garden. It is referred to, sometimes, as the Muslin Rose— the thin, almost transparent, chalk-white petals suggesting this name. Long-sepalled, tapering buds add to the beauty of this fine hybrid. In fact, the half-opened buds made a charming coronet for a very young bride. In Regent's Park, in Queen Mary's Rose Garden, there were large bushes of a sport from Blanc double de Coubert called Souvenir de Philémon Cochet. We had not seen this rose previously, with its blooms like those of a double white hollyhock, so we took some photographs of it to show to New Zealand rose lovers. Later we were able to purchase this rose out here, and have been pleased with its strong growth. Nearby grows R. *rugosa alba*, a lovely single rose with pale cream stamens nestling at the base of the pure white flowers, and the usual green, crinkly foliage and large shining heps of this family. On their own roots these roses sucker freely so, where possible, we use budded plants in our small, white garden. Rugosa Roses spread their scent on the air—a grand attraction when fragrant plants were being chosen for this area.

Another of our well-loved Rugosas, Roseraie de l'Hay—bred by M. Jules Gravereaux in the famous garden whose name it bears—was planted in narrow borders on either side of a long pool at Hidcote. This rose, with large, double, fragrant flowers resembling paeonies, and extra fine foliage, is worth a place in any garden. The fresh green leaves turn a clear yellow in the autumn, as do those of the Muslin Rose. We have now discarded the American bred hybrid Hansa in favour of the gorgeous Roseraie de l'Hay, as Hansa's smaller, harsher blooms could not compare with those of the latter rose.

One of our finest and most useful Noisette Roses, Madame Alfred Carrière is a parent of the dainty R. *rugosa fimbriata*, or Phoebe's Frilled Pink. The small, heavily fringed flowers of palest blush-pink are exquisite and suggest its other name, R. *rugosa dianthiflora*. With us it is not a tall grower, though we have heard of it making more height when planted against a wall. We grow another carnation-flowered rose, Pink Grootendoorst, a sport from the red F. J. Grootendoorst. This pink rose makes a useful and strong-growing hedge; but its flowers, though attractive, have not the subtle beauty of those of Phoebe's Frilled Pink.

Schneezwerg or Snow Dwarf, a Hybrid Rugosa of uncertain origin, has proved an excellent shrub in a white and yellow border. Its semi-double, medium-sized blooms, with rich yellow stamens, are reminiscent of the flowers of the autumn-flowering, all too invasive, *Anemone japonica*, which grows in the same area. Schneezwerg was planted overseas extensively and seemed to be happy in very diverse situations. Except for removing spent blooms, we leave this shrub severely alone, as it seems to be immune from all ills in this semi-tropical climate. Would that we could say the same of every rose in the garden!

While we were overseas we admired three dark red Hybrid Rugosas, some of which are in New Zealand, though none are in this garden. However we do grow their parents, so were very interested to see them all in England, France, and Italy. One of our oldest Hybrid Perpetuals, Général Jacqueminot, was used in the breeding of the dark red Mrs Anthony

Waterer, which filled a large circular bed at Kew. It was one parent, also, of Rose à Parfum de l'Hay, which grew well in the garden where it was bred. This rose acquired its rich fragrance from a Damask ancestor. Sanguinaire, a third dark red Hybrid Rugosa, was lovely in Rome; and we saw in this same garden two tremendous plants of the pink and white forms of R. *paulii*—a hybrid between R. *rugosa* and R. *arvensis*, the Field Rose of England. These roses had been spread out for quite a distance over a low frame and pegged down at regular intervals. This treatment, which is used also by a Nelson friend, produced a mass of single flowers, making an attractive carpet of pink and white on a green ground. Two roses from Japan, R. *rugosa* and the Memorial Rose, R. *wichuriana*, produced a trailing hybrid, Max Graf, which was trained in a similarly attractive manner. Limited space precludes us from growing these unusual, sprawling hybrids in our own garden.

Rugosa Roses generally retain the magenta tones of the original types, with the exception of a few white forms, and one or two pale pink ones. Yellow tones were unknown until this century; when first in France and later in Canada, yellow-flowered Rugosas appeared. M. Jules Graveraux bred Daniel Lesueur by using the old yellow Tea Rose, Safrano, as one parent: and produced a rose with nankeen-yellow blooms. Later, a Canadian grower successfully crossed Harison's Yellow and Persian Yellow with R. *rugosa*. Two more yellow-flowered Hybrid Rugosas resulted from these experiments: Grace and Agnes. The former is not known out here, but Agnes we grow in our own garden. Its clear green foliage and small leaflets are an inheritance from its Persian parent, and also its yellow-toned flowers, but whereas the blooms of Persian Yellow are a rich chrome-yellow, those of the hybrid Agnes are a much softer shade, though still very lovely. We grow this rose at one end of a blue and silver garden, near a yellow and white border.

As all true Rugosa Roses are perfectly healthy it is disappointing to find lovely hybrids causing trouble. The more the Rugosa characteristics are lost, the more susceptible to disease these plants become. Sarah van Fleet with its sprays of lovely, clear rose-pink blooms, and magnificent early summer foliage is a martyr to rust late in the year. We have watered and sprayed this bush regularly, removed and burnt all infected leaves—but still this dreaded disease persists. Now we are trying it on its own roots to see if that will help. We were therefore amazed to find Sarah van Fleet

▲ 53. Aspahan — Summer Damask of unusual beauty

▼ 54. Gracilis, a free-flowering pink boursault rose

▲ 55. Lamarque

▼ 56. A general garden view

planted by the roadside on the way out to London Airport. The plants were healthy, though rather wind-battered; but we would have been interested to see them again in the autumn, the season when our own plant suffers. Wild and semi-wild roses have been used with great effect in the vicinity of several modern airports, notably at Zurich; the clay banks often leading down to airport tunnels, are also closely planted with pegged-down, trailing roses, making a close and protective ground cover.

Roses that filled our hearts with envy when we saw them in Rome were Conrad Ferdinand Meyer—a large-flowered Rugosa hybrid—and its white sport, Nova Zembla. We discarded the former some years ago, on account of its susceptibility to rust, though it grew vigorously and flowered well. However, we still enjoy our colour slides of its large, full blooms of tender pink. Another prickly, tall and gaunt hybrid, Dr Eckener, with yellowish-pink flowers, grows well in some parts of New Zealand, though it is not to be compared with Sarah van Fleet or Conrad Ferdinand Meyer.

When we are asked to recommend just one or two species of old roses for small gardens, we unhesitatingly include at least one of the hardy, free-flowering, true Rugosas in our list—Blanc double de Coubert and the single R. *rugosa scarbrosa* being the ones most generally admired. As labour-saving plants the pure Rugosa roses are without peer and all are highly decorative, having magnificent foliage, beautiful flowers, and showy heps. Such garden treasures are a boon when time for leisured and gracious living is scarce and precious.

*'Tis the Rose of the Desert
So lovely and Wild!*

G. W. Francis

THIS POEM REFERS TO THE DOG ROSE, ONE OF THE FOUR
wild roses native to North West Africa—the others being the Sweet
Brier, the Musk Rose and the Evergreen Rose. As successive waves of
traders and fighting men moved westward by slow degrees from that home
of lovely roses, Asia Minor, more roses were carried with them, either as
seed or plants, and established along the coastal districts, and even south
of the Atlas Mountains in the Northern parts of the great Sahara Desert.
In this way, R. *damascena*, so famed in art, literature and poetry, must have
arrived in North Africa – probably having come by easy stages, as it was
grown in Egypt in Cleopatra's time. It not only arrived in Morocco, but
survived and flourished to become the main source of supply of rose petals
for the great modern perfume industry which has sprung up there since
the war. In Bulgaria, vast areas were planted with Damask and Alba Roses
suitable for the making of attar (or otto) of roses, for which this country
became famous. The beautiful Valley of Roses at Kazanlik is now out of
bounds to Western Europe; so a fresh source of supply was essential. This
was found in districts bordering the oases of the Sahara, where Damask
Roses have been grown for centuries. An English friend who is interested
in the perfume industry described these rosefields to us, and we were
delighted to find that some of the roses growing in our garden were iden-

tical with those growing round these desert oases. Through his kindness we were supplied with a very fine paper on the subject of the *Roses of the Dades*. It was so full of delightful information pertaining to the growing and the processing of these roses, that we felt that others besides ourselves would enjoy reading it.

"It is well known that the sedentary population of the Oases in the Sahara has, for a long time, been involved in the cultivation of roses. In fact, ever since the magnificent exploring of Father Charles de Foucald to the south of the High Atlas, we know that these cultivations are vast and sometimes very important, to the point of giving rise, in certain areas, to wide-scale commerce in dry roses.

Situated in the Algerian Sahara, six hundred miles south of Algiers, the Oasis of El Golea is renowned for its beautiful rose groves. In that central Sahara oasis, the fertile, sandy soil, the plentiful and soft artesian water, as well as the remarkably dry atmosphere, are all extremely favourable to rose cultivation. According to Jean Grattesfosse, the El Golea rose bush is an old variety of *R. damascena*, particularly well acclimatised to the Continental conditions of Algerian oases.

The El Golea rose bush, remarkably resistant to 'rust' is tall, with green, opaque foliage. The thorns and stems have the same shade of green. The flower is large, full and of a rosy-violet hue. Its development is prodigious and it is not unusual to find, in Nesabite gardens, some bushes of two or three years growth, having hundreds of stems.

The Moroccan rose, according to Jean Grattefosse, belongs to the variety, *Rosa centifolia*. It grows abundantly in certain areas where it has been known for some time, particularly in the oases and valleys of the south—Shoura, Dades, Todra, Ferkla, Draa, and Tafilalet.

There are two fairly typical species, that of the north, near Marrakech and Meknes, botanically identical to the Rose de Grasse; and that of the south, *Rosa damascena*, long adapted to harsh climatic conditions. The southern variety is very vigorous with abundant flowering. On a five-year-old bush, seven-foot high, thousands of blooms can be seen, as well as thirty or more offshoots. The foliage is dark green, hairy under the leaves, particularly on the veins. The flower is small and bright pink in colour, with a penetrating odour. Owing to its rustic origin, it is very resistant to extreme temperatures, extreme drought, and sand storms. Due to certain sterilising properties, it is free from rust, whilst the northern Centifolia, even at an altitude of four thousand feet, is regularly stricken with this same dreaded disease".

This portion of the article is of great interest to us, as the rose of the Southern oases is the same as our R. *damascena trigintipetala*, one of the Kazanlik Roses, a native of Persia. This is why it flourishes in the heat of Auckland and the greater heat of the Sahara. At first we managed this tall rose very badly by pruning it at the end of the winter instead of immediately after flowering. As *damascena trigintipetala* flowers only on well-ripened wood, this treatment was fatal—only a few blooms appeared on any growth left unpruned. This rose produces hundreds of highly fragrant, bright pink, semi-double flowers—the green thorny stems being weighed down with the mass of blooms. The large soft green leaves, typical of Damask Roses, are very handsome on the new shoots and suckers sent up from the base each year—these shoots corresponding to the offshoots mentioned in the article quoted.

The Rose de Grasse which grows in the northern part of Morocco is a form of R. *centifolia*, sometimes referred to as the Rose of Provence. This richly scented, full, globular rose is neither as tall nor as strong a grower as the Damask mentioned previously, and it is susceptible to rust in this garden, just as it is in North Africa.

The late Dr C. C. Hurst, in his work on *The Evolution of the Modern Rose*, writes that the Autumn Damask is still preferred to any other kind for the commercial production of rose-water, and attar of roses, as in the old days; and there are vast plantations of this variety of rose in Turkey, Bulgaria, Egypt, Persia, India, and Morocco. This is most interesting as R. *damascena bifera*, or the Pink Four Seasons Rose, also thrives in our garden, producing its smallish, rather muddled looking pink flowers off and on all year. The large soft green leaves and long elegant buds add to the attractiveness of a moderately sized bush. This rose came from Persia to Egypt, where it was called the Alexandrian Rose; and from there we hear of it arriving in Carthage, the Moors taking it thence to Spain where it became famous as the Rose of Castile.

The article goes on to describe how these roses are cultivated in semi-desert conditions.

"In the Southern Oasis, and notably in the Valley of the Dades, the rose bush is nearly always used as fencing for the small vegetable and cereal gardens. They are also grown as hedges along the watering canals and at the foot of partition walls. There never existed any form of systematic cultivation, apart from frequent watering which took place automatically whilst watering the vegetable and cereal gardens, and the elimination of dead stalks. The rose bushes evidently benefit, particularly after April, from extraordinary periods of sunshine and an abundant irrigation by silt – carrying water, which also creates precious artificial irrigation due to its deposits."

This is most interesting, as the secret of successful rose growing in any hot climate seems to be the ready availability of an ample water supply. This is borne out by the fact that so many roses, growing wild by ditches and swamps in New Zealand, are perfectly healthy and free from disease. Our soil is as heavy as the Algerian desert soil is light, but they both require ample water if roses are to thrive in them. With the heavy sub-soil so close to the surface, plant roots in our garden cannot go as deep as they would in a light sandy soil, so need plenty of water in dry seasons to prevent cracking of the underlying clay and the consequent damaging of roots. At the same time, we have found it necessary to put in field tile drains to carry off excess water in winter when the rainfall is very heavy. To continue:

"There is no definite information available on the introduction of perfume roses in the oases of the South, and notably those in South Morocco. One can assume that they were introduced very early in the Sahara Oasis, possibly even before the Arab invasion, and came from India and Persia, from where they were exported westwards by successive generations and civilisations."

R. *moschata*, which grows wild in North Africa is supposed to have found its way westward, centuries ago, from Persia through other countries bordering the Mediterranean; and this was one of the roses used for the distillation of rose-water and attar of roses in India, Persia and Turkey, though no mention is made of its having been used for such a purpose in North Africa.

"From time immemorial, and until recently, the quasi—totality of South Moroccan production was used for dried rose commerce. The dried buds—five and a half pounds of fresh buds giving one pound of dried ones—were called 'Pale Roses'. There are various qualities, the lesser appreciated being known as 'Fatifa' and 'Glacua'. The better ones are the 'Shoura' and especially the 'Dades'. Dried roses of good quality are hard, compact and retain the shape of the bud. Dark, purply-red in colour, they look velvety and taste rather harsh. Their sweet and powdery odour is a far cry from the exquisite scent of the fresh rose in full bloom.

Dry roses are used for the manufacture of an inferior quality of rose-water used in pastry cooking, confectionery and for eye treatment. The Arab Pharmacopoeia prescribes them for treatment of nasal and mouth infections. They are also used to perfume the laundry. The prices and qualities produced for the dried rose commerce vary considerably.

The very favourable agricultural and climatic conditions of South Morocco could not fail to attract the attention of the perfumery industry to the possibilities of Morocco as a new production centre for perfume roses."

Then the articles goes on to say that the first two attempts at establishing rose plantations for a modern perfume factory were a failure, owing to the humid conditions prevailing round the coast in the vicinity of Rabat and Casablanca, causing great losess amongst the crops from rust. Repeated set-backs then caused the industrialists to become interested in the drier, better conditions in the Dades Valley, in the interior, where the density of cultivation and the quality of the flowers could permit national industrial processing.

"The Valley of the Dades, situated south of the High Atlas, at the foot of the Sagho Mountains, stretches from El Kelaa des M'Gouna to Boumalne, for many miles, at an altitude of 4500 feet. After the last war, as soon as security conditions permitted, a first extraction factory was built by the Société Floral de l'Atlas at El Kelaa des M'Gouna. A few years later, the Société Aromag, in which our friends are interested, built a modern distillation and extraction plant in the heart of the Dades Valley, members of this Society having flown in many times to explore the possibilities thoroughly. These two factories, and their joint efforts, created great interest amongst the inhabitants of the Valley who increased the number of their rose bushes, and took more care with their cultivation. Later, when newer and better equipment was installed in the factories, growers were encouraged still further to increase their plantings of perfume roses. The total production of roses in this valley had risen from four hundred tons in 1949, to twelve hundred tons in recent years. There is a great solidarity between the growers and the manufacturers, the only contracts existing being moral ones. In 1952, when a devastating frost wiped out the whole crop, the manufacturers took the initiative in helping the whole body of growers: and granted them an important, interest-free loan. This spirit of enterprise and co-operation created at the very edge of the desert a flourishing and still expanding industry. So no longer are the roses '. . . born to blush unseen and waste their sweetness on the desert air. . . .'

The growers are entirely responsible for the production, for gathering and transport of the flowers to the centres of purchase—these being set up at intervals along the twenty miles of the Valley to enable the peasants to make deliveries near the areas of production. All purchases are paid for in cash, and it is amusing to note that the manufacturers were obliged to carry yearly, into the desert, two tons of 'coins' because the peasant distrusted paper money. The peasant demands exact payment, and, on principle, never carries any change, as he finds this an absolute necessity for bargaining in the Souks, where great commercial activity reigns at crop time. The peasants carry the roses in all kinds of packaging—wicker baskets, bags, djellabas (the Moroccan gown, of which they use the hood for carrying), old blankets etc, They use every means of transport available, the small donkeys typical of the area, mules and more recently, bicycles, though the great majority walk. Like processions of working ants, two files meet at the purchasing centres, one arriving laden with roses, the other going back, having sold their flowers; and, once again, counting their money, whilst hurrying to gather new roses. The flowers purchased at the factory are immediately processed, whilst lorries, trucks and jeeps travel along the rock-strewn desert tracks to bring in, as quickly as possible, the roses purchased at the outlying centres. Speed of transport is of first importance for the quality of product obtained, because conditions for preserving the flowers are important and the smaller purchase centres do not always have sufficient shaded areas for this purpose. The heaped up roses do not stand up to long preservation. The attar of rose obtained from these new installations and processes is a greenish-yellow in colour. Its extremely pure odour is very close to that of the Bulgarian attar of rose. The rose products of the Dades Valley are of fine quality and much is owed to the manufacturers who have made heavy financial sacrifices and braved the dusty and often ill-defined tracks and the torrid heat of the rocky desert, to create this flourishing industry more than three hundred miles from any industrial centre, and to add new resources to the Kingdom of Morocco by raising the standard of life of the peasant population of the Valley."

This fascinating story of the desert roses gives a remarkable picture of what goes on behind the scenes in the perfume industry. Apparently, when the Bulgarian attar was no longer available, even the roses of Provence, in Monsieur Chiris' own country, were not grown in sufficient quantities for present day needs. So these Moroccan fields became extremely valuable. We grow all the roses used in the Kazanlik fields, and some of those used in Morocco; so this article was of absorbing interest.

We love the tall, grey-leaved, R. *alba semi-plena*—a rose that is grown for hedges round the fields of Damask Roses in Bulgaria. Now, they are using also the crimson-purple Roseraie de l'Hay, a Rugosa, which has a rich scent and is very ornamental in the garden. We grow, also, the form of R. *gallica* used by the apothecaries in France and England for medicinal purposes, as well as in the manufacture of rose-water and conserves. The two Damasks, the Summer-flowering and the Autumn-flowering, complete our list of these useful, highly scented roses. It is a far cry from the days when the ancients steeped rose petals in liquid and oil, so that these could absorb the scent, and so made delicious perfumes. Ample rain or water are necessary for the blooms to produce oil of good quality: and this is available for the Roses of the Dades. They should be gathered early when the dew is still on them, for

> The rose looks fair, but fairer we it deem,
> For the sweet odour which doth in it live.

. . . the Rose is white,
The Rose it blooms in summer light.

Clare

THE IDEA OF A WHITE GARDEN DEVELOPED SLOWLY.
We felt a little prejudiced, against it, once, though we did use a few plants, judiciously placed, to highlight the colour in a blue perennial border. However, all our preconceived ideas were changed one evening when we saw the garden in the moonlight. The white flowers had become luminous and really lovely, whilst the blue ones had faded from sight.

At once, plans were made to convert one corner of our property into a spot where white flowers would hold pride of place. Fortunately, when we decided to establish this small garden-within-a-garden, there was a rectangular piece of land available in a sunken area; it could be seen from the house and lent itself admirably to such a scheme. Small trees and tall shrubs grew at either end; a high green trellis and netting bordered the tennis court along one side, the opposite side having a ten-foot grey stone wall along half its length. These gave the necessary shelter from prevailing winds, as well as a good background for the plants. The figure eight was used as a central motif, the elongated lower portion being a lawn surrounded by a very narrow paved path. The upper portion of this figure was completely paved, and here a small seat was placed, to make a focal point at the far end in front of a screen of trees and shrubs. The main access was by way of shallow steps and a wide paved path leading in to the bottom of the lawn. About halfway up the length of the garden, the symmetry was broken by a useful side path. This led on to a wider pathway running beneath the wall, and linking this white garden with other parts of the property.

Colour planning is one of the most delightful and absorbing aspects of gardening, and depends, to a large extent, on personal taste. One would not imagine that colour could come into the planning of a white garden; but in the flowers alone there are subtle and charming differences, some being greenish-white, some creamy-white, whilst others have petals of a cold, chalk-white—and these are the ones that stand out most vividly in the moonlight. Stamens can be white, green, yellow, blue, mauve, pink, red, or brown, and the reflected light from these can quite alter the tone of a white flower. All this adds interest and helps to prevent monotony. Contrasting foliage effects are valuable both in the daytime and at night; a pair of *Hoheria alba variegata* look particularly well in the moonlight, as do the many silver-leaved plants included in the scheme.

As in the garden proper, roses form the backbone of the planting in this small white garden. Though many of them are old roses and species, a certain number of valuable, perpetual-flowering modern varieties have been included. These in no way detract from the general effect, the old and the new appearing happily together. From the tiny modern Frosty Morn and the foot-high, early, Anna Marie de Montravel—both edging plants—the roses soar to a great height alongside the tennis court boundary. The Double White Banksia, R. *bracteata*, climbing Summer Snow, Boule de Neige, and Madame Plantier clothe this trellis fence completely, even cascading gracefully from the top. The side bordered by the grey stone wall—which is topped by a carport trellis—is now covered with a number of handsome evergreen climbers: stephanotis, mandevilla, rhynchospermum and clematis. The roses growing with them are the Moschata-Gallica hybrid, R. *dupontii* and R. *fortuneana*—a natural hybrid between R. *banksiae* and R. *laevigata*. This is a very charming rose indeed, practically evergreen, and flowering very early in the season, about the same time as its parents. R. *laevigata*, from which it inherits its habit of producing flowers singly from each leaf axil, grows not far away in a moist spot in front of a shorter length of green trellis. This continues the line down from the stone wall, leaving only an eight-foot gap through which runs a pathway linking up the white garden with a series of large rock pockets which lead along and up to the old rose and fuchsia garden.

The climbing roses are invaluable to us; but between them and the real dwarfs are a number of moderate-sized Hybrid Teas and Floribundas, all of which produce flowers over a very long period. Virgo, White Ensign, Iceberg, Irene of Denmark, Summer Snow, and White Bouquet, have already proved themselves and now we are trying out a new rose, Pascali. The taller shrub roses Prosperity, a Hybrid Musk; Karl Foerster, a Hybrid Spinosissima; Blanc de Vibert, a Portland; the single Rugosa and two doubles—Blanc double de Coubert and Souvenir de Philémon Cochet; and the bushy pruned plants of the Noisette, Madame Plantier all add greatly to the interest in this intimate garden, not only because of the diversity and attractiveness of their foliage, but because of their lovely and unusual flowers, some of which are delightfully scented. In our original plan two important points were decided upon at once. The first was to plant as many of the lovely old white roses as we could procure, and the second was to give pride of place where possible to scented flowers. Moths are particularly influenced by perfume; and certain plants such as the nicotianas rely on these night-flying insects for pollination; so scent in a moonlight garden is invaluable. The heady perfume of many of the old roses, to say nothing of the pinks, nicotianas, clematis, and jasmines, is the lure that draws hordes of silvery-winged moths to the garden. And a delightful and restful sight it is, at the end of a hot summer's day, to see them fluttering from flower to flower.

Of standard roses, there are only three. Mrs Herbert Stevens is planted on either side of the waist of the figure eight. A glance at the plan will show the importance of these key points. We have never regretted our choice of this hardy Tea Rose for these positions: the amount of bloom produced by the two standards of Mrs Herbert Stevens right through the year never fails to amaze us. Also, the nodding blooms on their thin, wiry stems are shown off to great advantage when grown in this manner, for the extra height suits them admirably. The only other standard in the garden is placed in the centre of a small rectangular area on the far side of the trellis that supports the Cherokee Rose, R. *laevigata*. For many years this hardy Rugosa, Blanc double de Coubert, has given us a wonderful display of flowers for months on end, the leaves colouring to a delightful shade of yellow as winter approaches.

As these were not all the white roses we grew, the overflow, including some very fine roses, was planted in a wide curving bed running along the front of a tall, dark green hedge. To support two vigorous climbers, Lamarque and Frau Karl Druschki, a high wire fence was placed just far enough out from the hedge to allow easy access to the back of the border. Though this long bed is primarily for white roses, two yellow ones, Harison's Yellow and Persian Yellow, were included here for convenience; this led us in the end to create a yellow and white border. This is a simple but effective colour scheme, with the addition of yellow and white bearded irises and foxgloves, white delphiniums, and clear yellow carnations. The roses in this border include, as well as the two climbers mentioned previously, the famous and very lovely Damask, Madame Hardy; another fine Damask, Botzaris; the Rugosa Hybrid, Schneezwerg; the Damask Moss, Blanc Mousseux; and the Alba, Jeanne d'Arc. Of these, only Lamarque, Frau Karl Druschki, Schneezwerg, and Blanc Mousseux flower continuously, the two climbers being outstanding in this respect. They often flower well into the winter.

A white rose garden need never be dull if one has so many types to choose from. It is often very beautiful, as well as restful and satisfying. Though the planting is not identical on either side of the garden, the balance is kept by growing roses and foliage plants in pairs—as, for example, the two standards of Mrs Herbert Stevens. Behind each of these roses is a bush of *Abutilon savitzii variegata*—which we do not allow to flower—and further back still is a pair of *Hoheria alba variegata*. Silver-leaved perennials are used in a like manner, to add emphasis and contrast where necessary. At the far end, where there is greater depth and heavier planting of shrubs, plain and variegated anthericums and some hostas add strength and character to the front of the border. This means that though roses hold pride of place in this small garden, monotony has been avoided by the inclusion of other plants. All the seasons have their special plants, especially with bulbs in early spring: it is only the roses and fuchsias that give us flowers throughout the year. Some of the roses bloom in mid-winter, others only in summer; but a great number flower continuously, their pale blooms lighting up the green background, which is so necessary a part of the planting in any white garden.

*Experience is a name everyone
gives to their mistakes*

Oscar Wilde

ROSES FORM THE BACKGROUND OF OUR GARDEN
planning and planting, and, in the main, these are old roses given to
us by friends, collected from roadsides and early settlements, or purchased
in New Zealand or in England. We were very fortunate in that our present
property had most of the essentials we hoped for: a secluded, sheltered
position with a gentle slope to the north, surrounded, but not encroached
upon, by trees; and a pleasant outlook. The soil was heavy, which was
rather astonishing as several hundred yards down the road lies the crater
of an extinct volcano, and much of the nearby land is light, porous, and
volcanic. Apparently, none of the lava flows had passed this way.

A tree-lined driveway ran down from the road, emerging in a very
useful position about halfway along one side of the property. This simplified the placing of the house and the general garden scheme. In order
to obtain the maximum benefit of views and sun, the house was placed in
the south-eastern corner of the section, with most of the garden lying to
the north and the west. It is now possible to get a good view of the different small gardens, with the garden proper, from the principal rooms in
the house, and from the long, sunny, paved terrace which links house and
garden.

Our architect kindly sited the formal garden, the tennis court, and the carport for us; but the detailed plans for the intimate gardens and all the planting were from our own designs—not completed all at once, but over a period of several years, during which time some of our original schemes were modified, simplified and, we hope, improved upon.

As we wished to create a feeling of space we practised perimeter planting so that all lawn spaces were left uncluttered. Our rainfall is very heavy in the winter and lawns and gardens, in Auckland, need attention through the year. Consequently, firm paved pathways were necessary; grass paths, though far more beautiful, are quite impractical in this climate, where there is so much winter garden work. All the lawns were edged with brick to allow mowers to operate with ease and to simplify the trimming of grass edges.

In any town garden, the composting and the disposal of garden rubbish are a problem. We overcame this difficulty by constructing grey stone compost pits and an incinerator in one unit. This is beyond the carport, out of sight from the house. Rock pockets above this unit catch the eye, and soften its severity.

What proved to be a useful and happy thought, a curving rock trough and wall, is described in the chapter "Small Roses for the Rock Garden". The white garden and the old-rose and fuchsia garden were designed a little later than the sunken garden nearer the house. The various parts were linked to one another either by small shrubberies, rock gardens, or curving pathways. At the bottom of the driveway a paved path runs alongside a six-foot-wide raised bank towards the rear of the house. At first, we were afraid this might prove an awkward problem; but instead, it has turned out to be a real boon, as it is here that we have found the right spot for many of our old roses. These are interspersed with fuchsias; and the edge of the three-foot-wall is well clothed with a variety of trailing plants. Both sides of this pathway, as it reaches the house, are lined with tall and short roses—so the long vista down to a brick wall at the far end is, at certain times of the year, most attractive.

As well as the garden proper, we have an additional area of borrowed land adjoining, but not in view of, the formal garden, the entrance being through a solid gateway in a high wall, clad with rose and creeper. There is no proper lay-out in this area—just a double series of long, narrow, raised beds linked by paths. We grow vegetables here and also have several beds for quarantining roses, striking rose cuttings, or planting roses that we wish to observe and photograph, until we can judge whether they are what we want in the main garden. The rear portion of the extra high wall that makes a background for the sunken garden is clothed entirely with rampant roses belonging to the Multiflora, Wichuriana, Moschata, Boursault and Noisette families—this height suiting them all admirably.

The plans will give some idea of the lay-out of each corner of the property, though roses also adorn walls, out-buildings, and the rear of the house, and a number of wild and semi-wild ones are in a narrowish border on the far side of the tennis court.

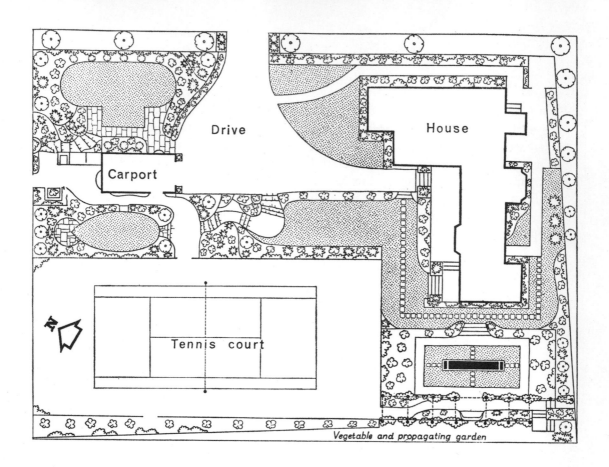

Drive

House

Carport

N

Tennis court

Vegetable and propagating garden

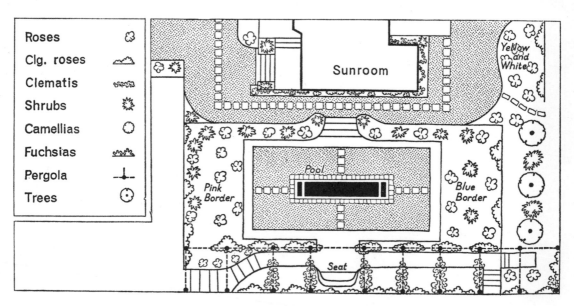

Roses

Clg. roses

Clematis

Shrubs

Camellias

Fuchsias

Pergola

Trees

Sunroom

Yellow and White

Pink Border

Pool

Blue Border

Seat

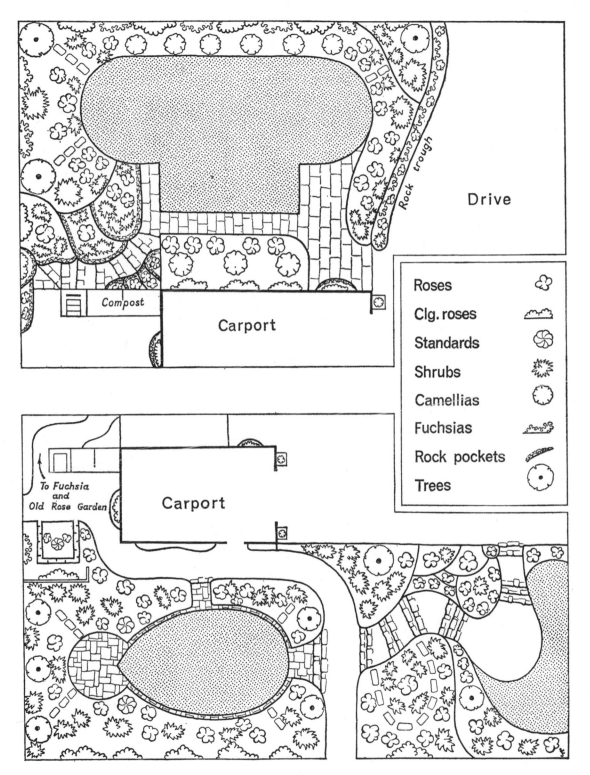

Drive

Rock trough

Compost

Carport

To Fuchsia
and
Old Rose Garden

Carport

Roses
Clg. roses
Standards
Shrubs
Camellias
Fuchsias
Rock pockets
Trees

INDEX

In both indexes, *Rosa,* and Roses, the roman numerals refer to text pages and the bold numerals to plate numbers.

INDEX ROSA

INDEX ROSES